Tax Incidence and Income Redistribution

An Introduction

Tax Incidence and Income Redistribution

An Introduction

Horst Claus Recktenwald
Professor of Economics
Friedrich-Alexander-Universität Erlangen-Nürnberg

translated by Martha V. Stolper

Wayne State University Press Detroit 1971

Published simultaneously in Canada
by The Copp Clark Publishing Company
517 Wellington Street, West
Toronto 2B, Canada.

Library of Congress Catalog Card Number: 72–85394
Standard Book Number: 8143–1421
The German edition, *Steuerüberwälzungslehre,* was published
by Duncker and Humblot, Berlin, in 1966.

Contents

Tables, Figures, Matrices

Tables

Preface

The theory of tax incidence is the core of the analysis of any tax effects. It holds in turn a central position in the theory of public finance. Why? If we do not know which individuals or which citizens ultimately *bear* rather than *pay* a tax, we cannot explain how a particular tax may influence the behavior of the taxed persons and how taxation may ultimately affect firms, households, market, and the domestic and foreign economy.

Tax and fiscal policy rests on weak foundations if the possible or probable or actual effects of a tax or a tax system are unknown. This statement is valid for fiscal policy with economic and social objectives as well as for purely fiscal taxation, for the government has to know the real tax bearer and hence the actual source of tax yields if tax receipts are to be maximized in the long-run. Furthermore, a fair distribution of taxes and subsidies on both the national and international levels is inseparably linked to incidence. Even the calculation of gross and net national product and national income is meaningful only if we know approximately who bears, for instance the 90 billion dollars of federal individual income taxes the American citizens paid in 1969–70.

Though economic and public finance theory have been dealing for some time with micro- and macro-economic tax effects including incidence, our understanding of the complex shifting mechanism is still unsatisfactory and our knowledge is frequently uncertain or unproved. For instance, the answer to the highly important question, whether a corporate income tax is fully shifted by the business firm to the consumers and to what degree and in what time range, remains most controversial. Opinions fluctuate from nothing (orthodox theory) via 100 per cent (Föhl) to 134 per cent (Musgrave-Krzyzaniak). If the thesis of full shifting is correct the existing tax system of most Western countries has to be drastically reformed.

The purpose of this study is to analyze all aspects of tax shifting and the resulting incidence. We will attempt to recognize and explain the causal and interdependent relations between taxation and the behavior and decisions of economic units as far as micro-economic (household, business firm, market) and macro-economic tax incidence are concerned.

We shall concentrate on three types of tax effects: (1) The *possible* or conceivable effects under alternative conditions in a comprehensive system, (2) the *probable* incidence, by testing the realistic contents of the often simplified assumptions about behavior and structure, and (3) the *actual* or effective incidence, by critically analyzing the methods, results and policy conclusions of empirical research published in recent years. Here we shall note which determinants of shifting theory have the strongest influence in specific empirical situations and in which direction the tax effects are moving. In addition, we shall develop six types of incidence, measuring the functional, personal, sociological, intersectoral, geographical (inter-regional and international), and inter-temporal distribution of income before and after taxation.

He who expects *one* generally valid and unique answer to the question of the actual tax bearer overestimates theorizing and underrates the limitations of the relevant methods and the real difficulties.

This American edition is a translation of the second German edition of *Steuerüberwälzungslehre* (Berlin, 1966), though the translation is considerably enlarged by new chapters and revision of many sections. It takes reasonably full advantage of recent thought and experience, and the factual and descriptive material has been brought up to date as far as possible. Critical suggestions in reviews and discussions have been taken into consideration, especially the comments of Richard Musgrave and Heinz Haller.

The macro-economic analysis now includes the incidence of the value-added tax. The revision of the section on the shifting of a general consumption tax reflects the renewed efforts of current theory. Sociological, intersectoral, and inter-temporal incidence are the subjects of new sections. I have enlarged the section on geographical incidence including inter-regional and international tax shifting, a field in which theoretical and empirical research is making remarkable progress.

In recent years the number of empirical analyses of effective and especially formal tax incidence has increased by leaps and bounds.

Hence I have arranged a new chapter separately treating the incidence of major taxes and the whole tax structure. The materials and most of the practical cases focus on the American economy.

For this American edition I have also developed two models, schematically presented, the one to illustrate tax incidence in the network of all tax effects, the other, taxation in a framework of fiscal policy.

I wish to thank all who have helped with stimulation and suggestions, especially critical ones. I feel indebted to Karl W. Roskamp who initiated and encouraged this American edition, to Martha V. Stolper who capably translated the often dry and technical text and to Wolfgang F. Stolper for his understanding and help.

Günter Eckstein, Horst Hanusch and Dietmar Dorn assisted in preparing the empirical and statistical materials. They have thoroughly revised the two indices and the bibliography. My thanks are also due Eva Pelikan for her care and patience in typing the manuscript.

H. C. R.

Abbreviations

AER	The American Economic Review
AJE	American Journal of Economics and Sociology
EcInt	Economia Internazionale
Econ	Economica
EJ	The Economic Journal
ESS	Encyclopaedia of Social Science
FA	Finanzarchiv
GE	Giornale degli Economisti
HdF	Handbuch der Finanzwissenschaft
HdSt	Handwörterbuch der Staatswissenschaften
HdS	Handwörterbuch der Sozialwissenschaften
IEJ	Indian Economic Journal
JbfN	Jahrbücher für Nationalökonomie und Statistik
JbfS	Jahrbuch für Sozialwissenschaft
JF	The Journal of Finance
JPE	The Journal of Political Economy
Ky	Kyklos
NF	Neue Folge
NS	New Series
NT	Nationaløkonomisk Tidsskrift
NTJ	National Tax Journal
P and P	Papers and Proceedings
PF	Public Finance
QJ	The Quarterly Journal of Economics
REP	Revue d'Économie Politique
REST	Review of Economics and Statistics
RSLF	Revue de Science et de Législation financières
Schmollers JB	Schmollers Jahrbuch für Gesetzgebung, Verwaltung und Volkswirtschaft
SchZ	Schweizerische Zeitschrift für Volkswirtschaft und Statistik
TLR	Tax Law Review
VfS	Verein für Socialpolitik
WdV	Wörterbuch der Volkswirtschaft
WWA	Weltwirtschaftliches Archiv
YR	Yale Review
ZfB	Zeitschrift für Betriebswirtschaft
ZfN	Zeitschrift für Nationalökonomie
ZgSt	Zeitschrift für die gesamte Staatswissenschaft

1
Introduction

I. *Significance and Necessity of a Theory of Tax Incidence*

Detailed research into all the processes of tax shifting and the resulting tax incidence is significant for the theory of public finance and necessary for fiscal policy. It is primarily determined by the twofold purpose of actual fiscal policy which

(1) attempts for fiscal reasons to adjust taxation as far as possible to the taxpayer's ability to pay and thereby also to produce in the long run substantial tax revenues and a maximum sustained tax yield; and which

(2) seeks for extra-fiscal reasons to affect by means of the specific tax structure the functional and personal income distribution, as well as the size, growth and composition of national income, social product and national wealth.

These two objectives of fiscal policy—both with respect to tax revenues and effect on income distribution and social product—are in the last analysis attainable only when the possibility, direction or preferably, extent of tax shifting are known, i.e., if it is known who ultimately bears the tax. The reasons for this are obvious:

(a) The more successfully the taxpayer is made into the actual taxbearer, according to his objective and subjective ability to pay, the more efficient is the tax source, and fewer friction losses arise in the national economy, since no unnecessary tax shifting arises in the economic process. Any tax shifting has detrimental fiscal and economic effects. For, each shift transfers in the clash of interests of the taxpayers the tax burden and pressure to another (intermediate) taxbearer with a different financial capacity and shifting ability. This stiffens tax resistance and tends to reduce the tax yield. To be sure, these "unburdening and burdening struggles" (Schäffle) between buyer and seller on the market are much less open than the parliamentary tax disputes between different interest groups and the fiscal authorities about the level, choice and form of taxation. Nevertheless, they have considerable importance, particularly during a recession or depression. In general, but especially when the tax burden is relatively high, real income low, and the tax morale indifferent, none of the economic groups or social classes will be willing, without struggle, to accept any additional tax, direct or indirect.

Hence, even when there is pressure for additional revenues, a rational fiscal policy cannot be satisfied to aim at immediate revenues and ruthlessly to impose taxes with the quickest and surest results. If the results of fiscal policy are to be desirable, the government must as much as possible take the economic effects into consideration, and must try to estimate to what extent the tax shifts reduce or activate puchasing power, and beyond this, to what extent they hinder or promote the whole process of adjustment in the market. Insofar as the process of shifting is successfully influenced by an appropriate tax structure, the later effects can be brought into line with the objectives of the fiscal authorities. This permits an approximation to a *maximum tax yield* without economic damage which, in the long run, would tend to reduce revenues.

This applies, all other things being equal, to tax reductions. Here too, knowledge of the actual, possible or surmised benefitting individuals or groups, and thus of the incidence, is fiscally important. An example is the tax provisions of the U.S. Revenue Act of 1964 which reduced the tax burden by $11.4 billion.[1]

(b) But even the objectives of taxation within the framework of a fiscal policy which *a priori* assumes certain tax effects, can be realized only if the possibility, direction and extent of shifting are known, because the changed expenditure pattern of the actual *taxbearer* determines in essence consumption, savings, investment and liquidity, that is, the very factors which taxation intends to affect. Thus, insight into tax shifting comes logically and practically before the knowledge of how to influence the formation and use of capital through taxation. This emphasizes the conditional effectiveness of fiscal measures for the solution of actual problems as long as public finance has not adequately clarified the problems of tax incidence. It follows also, that every correction of an income distribution, arrived at by the market by means of redistributive taxes, depends somehow on statements derived from the theory of tax incidence. Whether the redistribution of income is undertaken for ethical, social[2] or economic[3] reasons is irrelevant. Every tax policy intended to stimulate or dampen the business cycle must necessarily consider the probable incidence if it is to be effective. Thus it makes no sense to raise the income and corporation taxes sharply and progressively during a boom in order to limit the excessive tendency to invest by this means alone, since the recipients of the incomes will not fully bear the additional tax, but rather, the consumers will because the monetary expansion and the general price rise allow a substantial and easy shifting of the taxes.

(c) An *efficient* policy for economic growth, too, depends on an adequate understanding of long-run incidence. If we want to influence the determinants of economic development by means of taxes in order to ensure a continuing and balanced growth, we must know at least approximately how an individual tax or the tax system ultimately affects the continuous expansion of both capacity and demand, or the individual factors making for growth; how technical knowledge and its utilization, or the amount and training of labor as well as the infrastructure work in the final analysis. In other words, we must have a more thorough knowledge of dynamic incidence for purposes of economic policy, whether we are interested in the conditions of economic growth or in its course. This is equally true for industrially developed and less developed regions.

(d) Furthermore, to answer convincingly questions about tax pressure, multiplication of taxes[4] and fair distribution of the tax burdens on the national as well as the international level, we have to thoroughly study the principles of incidence if we are not content with a statistically calculated distribution of the tax burden (formal incidence).[5] For example, how can we judge a concrete tax system and make well substantiated statements about its economic, social and ethical value without knowing the *actual* tax incidence? Before we decide on the weight of the tax to be placed on income, profit, revenue, sales, expenditure or consumption, we must know whether the tax exerts its pressure where the tax burden is imposed. This knowledge is gained mainly through research into tax incidence. Judgements based only upon the text of the tax laws, tax rates and formal statistics, and neglecting the economic adjustments are, if at all, only of very limited use for practical purposes. Thus, for example, intentions of the legislators with respect to the taxbearer often prove impracticable, whether explicitly expressed in a law or not, because of erroneous assumptions about the real shifting abilities. It is evident that any economic judgement about particular taxes or a tax system must depend on who finally bears the tax and not, as happens in superficial statistical analyses, on the taxpayer or object on which the tax is initially levied. Legal and intended or expected incidence may often differ from actual incidence.

(e) If we substitute one tax for another, we have to know and measure the differential incidence in order to evaluate the tax policy:

FIGURE I–1
System of Fiscal Policy

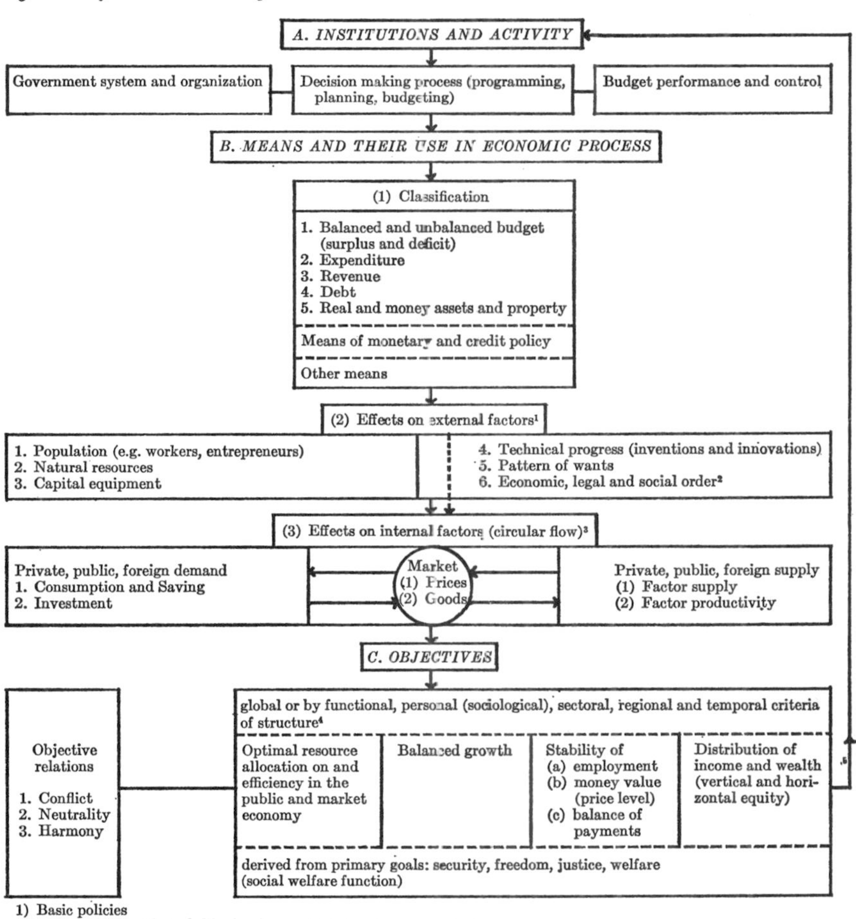

1) Basic policies
2) Order policy (with goals like freedom, private property, competition)
3) Process policy in short, middle, and long term
4) Comprehensive structure policy (concerning all objectives)
5) Reversal of the means-objective dichotomy. The question of how a change of the goal-variable does affect means, institutions, and activity is becoming a very important one for modern economic and fiscal policy.

Striking examples are expert proposals to substitute the American Corporation Income Tax for a value-added tax in order to profit from the benefits for economic growth and foreign trade.

(f) Like fiscal policy, the theory and practice of national accounting considers tax incidence an unsolved problem. Accepting the classification into direct and indirect taxes, shifting is only assumed in the last case. Such an assumption is as rough as its alteration is difficult, even today.

(g) A thorough study of certain tax effects is also necessary for other reasons. With the return to principles of the market economy on the one hand, and in view of the high taxation in all industrial countries on the other, the practical significance of tax shifting increases. If one third to one half of the national income passes through the public budgets,[6] the inpayments, holding, and outpayments of these substantial amounts cause firms, households and indeed the whole economy to adapt themselves to these changes in fundamental ways. The more competitive the market, the more important the thorough systematic analysis of these frequently structural adaptations. The more clearly we recognize these effects, the more we can contribute to keeping the market economy workable. Figure I–1 gives a systematic and general schema of fiscal policy.

II. *Conditional Nature and Limits of General Propositions—the Danger of an Agnostic Attitude*

The basic approach to the theory of incidence has been influenced mainly by difficulties in research which are generally acknowledged in theory and practice.[7] No doubt, "tax shifting is the most difficult but also the most important problem of tax theory" (Roscher) and in many respects of tax policy too. This opinion is to be found in older as well as more recent[8] literature all over the world. The Vienna meetings of the VfS[9] and the papers, expert opinions and discussions during the 54th, 58th, 65th and 72nd meetings of the American Economic Association[10] show quite clearly—and subsequent theoretical discussions have also made it evident—what special difficulties are involved in these problems and how conditional statements about incidence must be.

The obvious fact that the problems of tax incidence are complex and to be found on many levels of abstraction, has led to skeptical or negative attitudes toward the theory of incidence.[11] Thus, agnostics like Held and Bunzel maintain that it is utterly hopeless to make even approximate probability judgements, since one cannot make definite statements about a phenomenon which depends so much on economic power.[12] If we agreed with them, price and wage theory, for instance, would also lose its justification.[13] With all due reservations, I by no means share this extreme opinion. An agnostic point of view appears as uncalled for as the optimistic[14] and pessimistic[15] theories of tax diffusion seem in general indefensible. According to the pessimistic diffusion theory, the tax effects are eventually so diffused, that the whole burden comes to rest on the shoulders of the poorest, while according to the optimistic theory the tax burden is automatically diffused among the whole population. The representatives of these three theories simply and conveniently ignore the complex contexts of shifting. This is the danger of their theories: (Röpke points to it) it leads to nihilism in fiscal and tax policy, i.e. to an indifference toward problems of suitable and just taxation and it leaves unanswered the very basic questions concerning all important tax effects. Even if, because of the complexity of the subject, the abstract results of deductive theory and the results of empirical studies are often of limited usefulness for political purposes, it is by no means justifiable to be indifferent, considering the importance of the problems arising for fiscal policy. It is quite possible to recognize the *objective conditions of shiftability* in detail, and at least to make statements about the *probable incidence* in any particular real situation. Mann[16] rightly stressed, in reply to the vehement attacks of Bunzel on the achievements of the incidence theory, that the mere understanding that with few exceptions all taxes can be shifted in a market economy, is itself a positive result of theorizing.

In spite of all difficulties, economic and fiscal theory should continuously attempt to recognize and isolate these basic phenomena in the complicated economic process, in order to illuminate the manifold effects of taxation, until generally acceptable solutions are found.

III. *Recent Developments in Incidence Theory*

The mercantilists (Thomas Mun and William Petty) and the physiocrats (with the help of François Quesnay's Tableau Economique they prove that all taxes are borne by agriculture, the sole source of income) already called attention to the incidence problem and ever since the English classics the theory of tax incidence has formed an integral part of economics. Nearly every comprehensive textbook of economics and certainly every treatise on the theory of public finance deal with these various problems.

Because of the great significance of tax effects in economic life, it is not surprising that the number of theories has greatly increased in the course of time. Since the nature of tax shifting is closely connected with the price and distribution system, incidence theory necessarily depends on the current state of economic theory. Thus, the history of economic thought shows clearly, that the theories of incidence are frequently children (not to say stepchildren) of the price and distribution theories of each period. Even theories only loosely linked to the prevailing economic doctrine, which attempt to describe empirically the actual phenomena, depend in the final analysis on the theoretical insights into the economic process and its systematic interpretation.[17] While the macro-incidence is as old as the first concepts of a *Wirtschaftsordnung*, micro-economic considerations are much older.

The progress of the more recent as compared to most of the older theories, consists primarily in the exact formulation of the basic phenomena, a methodological refinement and the determination of simple regularities—under very restrictive conditions however. The prevailing pure theory, based on marginal analysis, has as its major assumption pure competition or pure monopoly; its view of incidence is mainly static and long run. Moreover, it considers profit maximization as the sole aim. The theoretical foundations were developed in the middle and toward the end of the 19th century by Cournot, Edgeworth, Marshall and Wicksell. The subsequent analyses and discussions led in all countries to mostly unimportant, at times exaggerated theoretical refinements, and a necessary systematizing and some fruitful beginnings. But on the whole they did not bring any decisive progress. The main cause of this lack of development seems to be, first, a hesitant application of recent pure theory to questions of tax incidence and second, a relative stagnation of the theory of market structure, which despite considerable progress in the thirties, lost somewhat its connection with reality.[18]

The latest endeavor to loosen the rigidity of the static market models in order to overcome their narrowness and thereby to alter the sterility of most incidence statements, is expressed with varying success in a few recent investigations. Inasmuch as the partial equilibrium analysis is retained,[19] the subject of research is extended by including public expenditures which directly influence the taxed market.[20] These studies (suggested by De Viti de Marco) did not lead to practical results. Nevertheless, they do modify past conclusions. Further studies have begun to analyze thoroughly the short run adjustments[21] or the duration of the shifting process[22] and to investigate tax incidence on markets where imperfect competition prevails.[23] This allows the thorough consideration of the different effects on tax shifting which emanate both from the *behavior* of the market and the aims of entrepreneurs and households (a shifting factor which has thus far been neglected). In addition, the influence of technical progress and the assumption of increasing capacity and demand should open the door to dynamic incidence on the micro-economic level.

The more recent development of macro-economic incidence looks rather different. Here we have experienced a renaissance in the fifties. Somewhat earlier R. Strigl, O. Englaender (applying the quantity theory of money), M. Kalecki, H. G. Brown, C. Welinder[24] had already taken up the macro-economic analysis which F. Quesnay, D. Ricardo, K. Wicksell and L. Walras[25] successfully used to explain the burden of taxation. Among the more recent studies of major importance are the works of E. R. Rolph, R. A. Musgrave, C. Föhl, H. Haller, A. C. Harberger, H. C. Recktenwald and more recently, D. Dosser.[26] These authors try to include incidence in a framework of a comprehensive economic theory similar to the modern theory of money. Here, on the one hand it becomes clear how important it is to consider the whole circular flow, especially the monetary changes and the close connection of the incidence with other economic effects of taxation; while on the other hand macro-incidence cannot consider and solve all shifting problems, because they simply cannot be handled in this broad framework.[27]

While empirical studies of formal incidence have been numerous in the last decade (leaving the shifting problem unsolved) the statistical investigations of actual or effective incidence are few as yet. We have the empirical attempts of Musgrave, Krzyzaniak and Roskamp. Musgrave's terminological contribution seems to be a step toward clarifying the concepts which are now more operational.

Insofar as economic theory has not built better tools to investigate tax incidence, research work should be continued in four directions:

(a) in considerably extending micro-economic (general equilibrium) analysis;
(b) in extensively refining macro-economic aggregates;
(c) in "dynamizing" the micro-and macro-economic models; and
(d) in intensifying the econometric and empirical studies, including the results of the theory of economic behavior.[28]

Notes

1. W. W. Heller, *New Dimensions of Political Economy* (Cambridge, Mass., 1966), p. 72.
2. See Adolph Wagner, *Lehrbuch der politischen Oekonomie,* 3d ed., Vol. V (Leipzig and Heidelberg, 1883).
3. See John M. Keynes, *The General Theory of Employment, Interest and Money* (London, 1936).
4. On the question of tax burden see Carsten Welinder, "Steuerdruck und Steuergerechtigkeit," *FA, NF,* VI (1938–1939), 564 f. On tax multiplication see Adolph Lampe, "Steuerwirkungslehre," *WdV,* 3rd ed. (Jena, 1911), III, 529, and Günter Schmölders, *Allgemeine Steuerlehre,* 4th ed. (Berlin, 1965).
5. Ursula K. Hicks, "The Terminology of Tax Analysis," *EJ,* LVI (1946), 49 ff.
6. Horst Claus Recktenwald, "Die Finanzwirtschaft der Bundesrepublik in der Mitte unseres Jahrhunderts. Wachstum und Strukturwandlungen," *JbfN,* 177, 2 and 3 (1965), 159 and 241.
7. A. Graziani, *Instituzioni di scienza delle finanze,* 2nd ed. (Torino, 1911), p. 329.
8. Myrdal even considers the theory of tax effects—as do later American authors—as the only possible subject of public finance. See Gunnar Myrdal, *Das politische Element in der nationalökonomischen Doktrinbildung* (Berlin, 1932), p. 280; English edition: *Political Elements in the Development of Economic Theory* (Cambridge, Massachusetts, 1953).
9. *Proceedings of the VfS,* Vol. 172 (München-Leipzig, 1926).
10. *AER, P and P,* XXXII (1942), 37; *P and P,* XXXVI (1946), 241; *P and P,* XLIII, 2 (1953), 504; and *P and P,* L (1960), 457.
11. See Lorenz von Stein, *Lehrbuch der Finanzwissenschaft,* 4th ed. (Leipzig, 1878), p. 493; Adolph Wagner, *loc. cit.,* p. 281; W. Lotz, *Proceedings of the VfS,* Vol. 172, pp. 336–340.
12. A. Held, "Zur Lehre von der Ueberwälzung der Steuern," *ZgSt* 1868, p. 422 and J. Bunzel, *Proceedings of the VfS,* Vol. 172, pp. 315–324.

13. See Wilhelm Krelle, *Preistheorie,* (Tübingen-Zürich, 1961), and Alfred Eugen Ott, *Preistheorie* (Köln-Berlin, 1965).
14. N. F. Canard, *Principes d'Economie politique* (Paris, 1801); M. A. Thiers, *De la Propriété* (Paris, 1848), and David A. Wells, *Theory and Practice of Taxation* (New York, 1900).
15. P. J. Proudhon, *Oeuvres complètes* (Paris, 1868), III, 166.
16. Mann, *Proceedings of the VfS, loc cit.* p. 351.
17. I will not discuss here the history of incidence doctrines but will mention only three fundamental works. To be sure, the two older works of G. v. Falck, *Kritische Rückblicke auf die Lehre von der Steuerüberwälzung seit Adam Smith* (Dorpat, 1882) and J. Kaizl, *Die Lehre von der Ueberwälzung der Steuern* (Wien, 1882) are neither as complete nor as thorough as the *Geschichte der Lehre von der Steuerinzidenz* by E. R. A. Seligman, which is written with acidity as well as a most thorough consideration of Continental-European and Anglo-American literature of fiscal theory. However, as a standard work the Seligman monograph (E. R. A. Seligman, *The Shifting and Incidence of Taxation* [New York, 1927]), seems overrated. Obviously a treatise of the history of doctrine from the standpoint of modern theory remains to be done. As a first attempt, W. Kitschler has recently published "Entwicklungslinien der neueren Steuerinzidenzlehre" (Diss. Mainz, 1965). Furthermore, R. A. Musgrave has included in his *Theory of Public Finance* a chapter (pp. 385–405) outlining some classical and neoclassical contributions to macro-incidence, limiting himself to Ricardo, Wicksell and Walras.
18. See Horst Claus Recktenwald, "Zur Lehre von den Marktformen," *WWA*, LXVII, 2 (1951), 298, reprinted in A. E. Ott, *Preistheorie,* pp. 62–84.
19. Bernard F. Haley, "Some Contemporary Tendencies in Economic Research," *AER, P and P,* XLIII, 2 (1953) 420; Haley refers to Harriss and Blough.
20. For example see M. Slade Kendrick, "The Incidence and Effects of Taxation," *AER,* XXVII (1937), 725–734, and John F. Due, *The Theory of Incidence of Sales Taxation* (New York, 1942).
21. See Elmar D. Fagan, "Tax Shifting in the Market Period," *AER, P and P,* XXXII (1942), 72–86, and H. G. Brown, *The Economics of Taxation* (New York, 1938).
22. Mario Fasiani, "Elementi per una Teoria della Duravata del Processe traslativa dell'Imposte in una Società statica," *GE* (1929) and Due, *op. cit.*
23. Joan Robinson, *The Economics of Imperfect Competition* (London, 1933), p. 76; Otto von Mering, *The Shifting and Incidence of Taxation* (Philadelphia, 1942); Fagan, *op. cit.;* Due, *op. cit.;* Carl S. Shoup,

Shifting and Incidence Theory; Taxes and Monopoly (New York, 1950); Musgrave, *op. cit.;* and others.

24. Richard Stigl, "Zur Lehre von der Steuerüberwälzung," *Die Wirtschaftstheorie der Gegenwart* (1928), IV, 188–204; Oskar Engländer, *Allgemeine Steuerlehre und Steuerüberwälzung* (Brünn-Prag-Leipzig-Wien, 1935). Critical to this, see Günter Schmölders, "Monetäre Theorie der Steuerüberwälzung," *FA, NF,* IV (1936), 280. Michael Kalecki, "The Theory of Commodity, Income and Capital Taxation," *EJ,* XLVII (Sept., 1937), 444–450; H. G. Brown, "The Incidence of a General Output or a General Sales Tax," *JPE,* XLVII, 2 (1939), 254–262; Carsten Welinder, "Grundzüge einer dynamischen Inzidenztheorie," *WWA,* LI (1940), 83–126.
25. François Quesnay, *Tableau Economique avec son explication, ou Extrait des économies royales de Sully* (Versailles, 1758); David Ricardo, *On the Principles of Political Economy and Taxation* (London, 1817); Knut Wicksell, *Finanztheoretische Untersuchungen und das Steuerwesen Schwedens* (Jena, 1896), pp. 21–75; Léon Walras, *Eléments d'économie politique pure* (Lausanne-Paris-Basel, 1874–1877); Recktenwald, *Lebensbilder, op. cit.*
26. E. R. Rolph, *The Theory of Fiscal Economics* (Berkeley, 1954); Musgrave, *Theory, op. cit.,* Carl Föhl, "Kritik der progressiven Einkommenbesteuerung," *FA, NF,* XIV, 1 (1953), 92, and "Das Steuerparadoxon," XVII (1956), 1–37; Heinz Haller, *Finanz-Politik. Grundlagen und Hauptprobleme,* 3d ed. (Tübingen-Zürich, 1965); Horst Claus Recktenwald, first edition of *Steuerinzidenzlehre* (Berlin, 1958); and Douglas Dosser, "Tax Incidence and Growth," *EJ,* LXXI (1961), 572–591; and the discussion by A. D. Bain, A. R. Prest, and D. Dosser, *EJ,* LXXIII (1963), 533–547.
27. See Duncan Black, *The Incidence of Income Taxes* (London, 1939). Although Black includes all effects of public expenditures, including the tax effect on the size of the population and its change, he uses partial analysis and comparative statics.
28. Recently, we have experienced a renaissance of empirical and statistical studies of incidence; for more details see Chapter 6.

2
Terminological Bases

I. *Introductory Remarks*

Since incidence is theoretically a distinct phenomenon which, however, is closely related to other tax effects, it is necessary to analyze it within a comprehensive framework of the effects caused by the collection of taxes. This, incidentally, points up very quickly the conditional character of many theoretical statements on incidence. A basic causal-genetic classification explains initially the micro- and macro-economic effects of the *withdrawal* of purchasing power due to the collection of taxes insofar as they can be empirically established. This will bring some order into the "maze of tax effects."[1] The system is based on distinctive economic criteria, which facilitates the use of theoretical tools and which can be related to other concepts.

II. *A System of Tax Effects*

1. Classification by Causal Criteria

Taxation has a direct impact on the economic activities of individual households or firms and on the circular flow of goods and money. It thus produces a variety of economic, social or political effects because of the general interdependence of economic and social spheres. Some of these effects are foreseeable, some cannot be traced; others may have narrow or wide effects or may offset each other.

In principle a change in taxation may take the following forms:

(a) the increase or reduction of an existing tax;

(b) the introduction of a new tax;

(c) the substitution of one tax for another, the yield of which may or may not be the same;

(d) cases (a) to (c), with either the same or changed public expenditures.

Unlike the situation with expenditures, governments usually fix only the tax base and the tax rates but not the amount of revenue.[2] This is often overlooked in theory but is significant for practical incidence and fiscal policy. Accordingly, different taxes and tax rates will have quite definite effects.

Furthermore, time plays a considerable role in two different respects. First, a tax may be limited in time;[3] secondly, the very announcement of a tax change may entail considerable consequences.[4] Finally, the manner in which taxes are levied and paid gives rise to a variety of reactions.

Let us now look more closely at the possible effects of a change in taxation. Since nowadays any tax is considered by the individual or firm to be an outside interference in his economic activities, this will lead to psychological reactions (either of defense or of stimulation) as well as to economic effects which, in turn, are reflected in a change of his economic behavior, and in the decisions and transactions of those households and firms whose economic plans are directly or indirectly affected. These micro-economic reactions in turn influence the process and the equilibrium of the individual market and—depending on the nature of the tax—they will all together affect the level, composition and growth of national income and wealth. Thus, the micro- and macro-economic effects are described in their entirety.

This analysis of effects requires a still further refinement. Already when a tax is announced, for instance during parliamentary discussion, the potential taxpayer may feel the "menace" of an (increased) tax load, provided he is conscious of the tax.[5] If he is not conscious of the tax, perhaps because it is negligible, or if he considers it justified—which is more likely with fees or assessments than with taxes proper—or if he has other purposes than the maximization of profits, the desire to defend himself against the tax or to react to it with a changed effort, may be absent.

If, however, the individual considers a tax a disturbing intervention in his plans, the following basic reactions are possible:

(1) He may evade the tax (immediately or eventually) by annihilating or reducing the bases of his tax liability (yield, profit, income, capital, property, turnover, expenditures, or consumption). Economi-

cally, we have here *direct substitution effects;* from the fiscal point of view we have attempts to avoid the tax. The tax has altered the conditions of alternative plans. This may result in new choices. In case of a general per capita lump-sum tax, for instance, the substitution effect is zero, if emigration does not appear reasonable.
(2) He may actually pay the tax, but then shift it or recoup it in the process of production. Since in a market economy[6] a tax is passed on through price changes,[7] these consequences of taxation are basically its *price effects.* These price effects should be distinguished from tax amortization[8] or capitalization. The value of all future taxes on a charged good is capitalized and imputed to its price when it is sold. The new owner continues to pay the tax but does not bear it, provided the tax has been amortized or discounted by deducting the capitalized amount from the price. The resemblance to shifting is evident. Both occur when the goods are exchanged, purchased or sold. They nevertheless differ since a shifted tax cannot be amortized.[9] Furthermore, tax amortization usually has other effects than tax shifting.
(3) Finally, the individual may bear the tax himself either directly, if he did not succeed in shifting or evading it or if he is not conscious of the tax or pays it voluntarily, or indirectly, through an increased price of goods or a reduced price of factor service as the tax is passed on (*indirect incidence*). This leads to a corresponding reduction of his income, with the result that he will modify his economic behavior and plans, which in turn may have considerable short and long-term effects on the result of his effort and in general of micro and macro-economic activity (production effects). We refer to these consequences as *incidence* or *income effects* of taxation. In fact, the tax diminishes the income or yield. This economic situation then causes a number of effects which we have also systematized in Figure II–1.

We will not discuss further any political or parliamentary feedback which a tax may have by way of its incidence.[10] An attempt will be made, however, to cover the other effects as exhaustively as possible. We will classify the incidence effects into effects on consumption, saving (including liquidity), investment, work effort, and technical progress. Furthermore, we will differentiate between psychological and economic effects, i.e. effects on the incentives to consume, save, invest (take risks) and to work, and on the size of these most important micro- and macro-economic factors.

Economic tax effects are thus classified into three groups: the *substitution,* the *price,* and the *income effects.* These groups are more or

FIGURE II-1
System of Micro and Macro-Economic Tax Effects

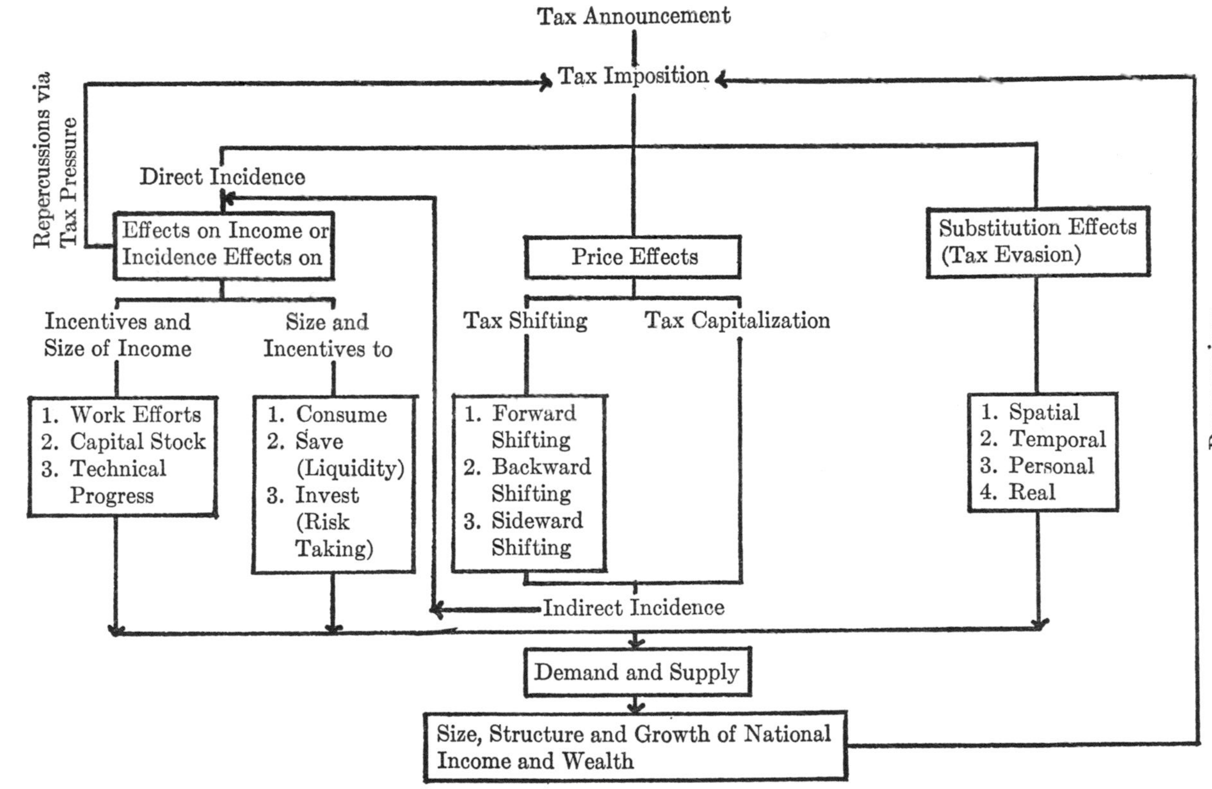

less closely interrelated, a point to be discussed later on. The effects may more or less permanently influence the level, composition and growth rate of national product and wealth, depending on the nature, form, and amount of the tax, and also on the neutral reinforcing or compensating effects of public expenditures and public revenues.

Those tax effects which we will not consider at length are illegal tax evasion[11] as well as any repercussions of a change in the distribution and amount of national product upon its very cause, namely the independent variable "taxation," that is, upon fiscal and tax policy itself.

To sum up I include a schema of micro and macro-economic tax effects. Of course, this schematic model can only be an auxiliary tool. It does not subdivide or combine groups of effects, though this could be done easily enough, but it enables us to see necessary and possible relations to conventional concepts.[12] Later when dealing with macro-economic questions of practical relevance, we will summarize adjustment effects in larger groups.

2. Definition and Types of Incidence

(a) *Narrow (Gross or Absolute) Incidence Concepts*

Our analysis of the possible forms of a change in taxation and its effects has revealed how, but not to what extent, incidence is directly and indirectly connected with all other effects of taxes. Our schema facilitates an isolated and thorough examination of the three groups of tax incidence without losing the important overall view.

A study of the literature reveals that even now the meaning of "incidence" and "tax shifting" remains controversial.[13] If there is to be any sense in a terminological discussion, we have to ask: Is the incidence concept appropriate to the objective of the study? In short, operational criteria must decide how narrowly or how broadly the concept is to be defined. In empirical analysis, the available data will also necessarily affect the concept. That a precise concept is nevertheless necessary also for empirical investigations, is shown by the Föhl controversy[14] on the shifting of the income tax, by the symposium at Wayne State University, and by Musgrave's[15] terminological efforts.

Let us retrace the normal process of taxation in order to elucidate the essence of incidence. Suppose the Federal Government introduces a tax on consumption amounting to 10 per cent of the selling price, according to which each manufacturer of television sets, say, has to pay the tax to the Treasury. The manufacturer will normally try to avoid a deterioration of his financial situation and will increase the price by the amount of the tax. While the manufacturer pays the tax, the buyer of the television set bears it in the form of a higher price. This happens to correspond to the intention of the government, though the shifted amount is not specifically stated. Only to the extent to which the supplier succeeds in getting a higher price independent of the intention of the Treasury is the tax shifted and the buyer "charged." The final "burden" on the buyers and sellers—the result of the shifting—is the incidence. The objective of the theory of incidence is to answer the basic questions: Is the tax shifted at all? To what degree? In which direction? And who ultimately has to bear it?

This is the meaning understood in the older literature by the terms "shifting" (German: *Steuerüberwälzung,* French: *tanslation,* Italian: *traslazione*) and "incidence of taxation" (*Steuerinzidenz, incidence, inzidenza*). Terminological problems arise only when we go further and try to distinguish them from the other qualitative and temporary effects of taxes.

For micro-economic theory, the initial direction of shifting is of special interest. Whoever is legally forced to pay taxes may try to shift them in different ways. If he succeeds in increasing his selling price, the tax is shifted forward; if he succeeds in lowering the purchase price, he shifts it backward. If one or several intermediate buyers or sellers are charged with an already shifted tax, one speaks of passing on.[16] Thus, a tax can be shifted forward, backward or passed on. Forward shifting is the type most often intended by the Treasury.

If a dealer offers several goods, he may shift the tax not via the charged article but via another one. It seems useful to regard this phenomenon also as a form of shifting, and to analyze it. Following Empoli, we call it sideward or cross shifting (*traslazione obliqua*).[17]

Finally, an entrepreneur may shift a tax to his factors of production. The manufacturer of television sets, for instance, shifts a consumption tax to his suppliers or workers by either reducing the prices for raw materials or lowering the wages. Here we have backward shifting under conditions which differ somewhat from those in the market for goods already described. As the shifting takes place within the enterprise, it is called internal shifting, contrary to the external backward shifting among consumer, dealer and manufacturer.[18]

FIGURE II–2

The Shifting Process

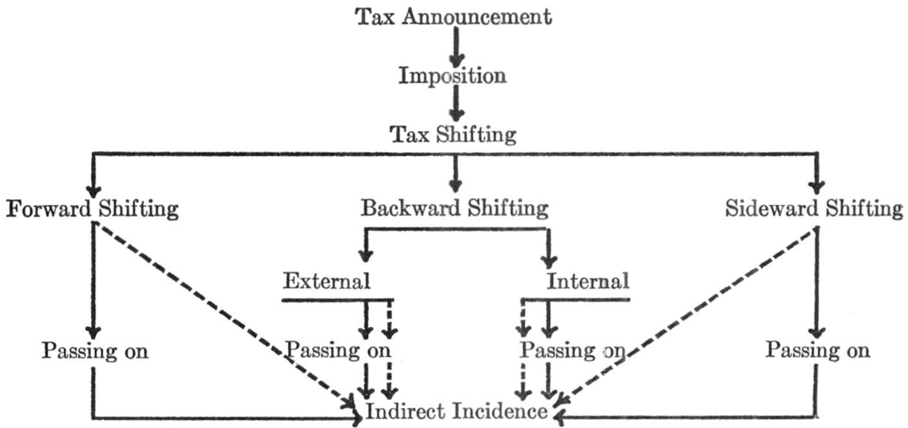

Thus the procedure of real taxation is sufficiently described. This process begins with the passing of the announced bill and the imposition of the tax. Because of the reactions of the taxpayers, it may take different roads and lead to indirect incidence via changes in prices and incomes. The direct incidence is less complicated since taxpayer and bearer coincide.

Thus, we can distinguish three forms of tax distribution:

(1) the *legal distribution* based on the tax payment according to law; whoever has to pay the tax is initially the bearer.

(2) the *incidence intended, desired,* or *expected* by the legislator; and

(3) the *actual* or *effective incidence.*

Contrary to Seligman it seems necessary to distinguish these concepts of tax distribution because they are real phenomena and help in explaining how the incidence of taxes is commonly understood.[19]

Indeed, there is a fundamental difference between the first two concepts and actual or effective incidence. We call both the legal and the intended incidence a *formal* one, because the very core of tax incidence, i.e. the real shifting process, is excluded. Most recent empirical studies in this field deal with formal incidence in our sense, *assuming* a certain degree of tax shifting and comparing the income distribution before and after taxation. These redistributional effects of a tax obviously differ sharply from actual or effective incidence though we measure both types of effects by income redistribution. Therefore we should keep in mind that any analysis of formal incidence assumes the unsolved problem of shifting and incidence.[20]

Our concept of formal incidence is evidently not identical with Hicks' well known expression, which seems analytically to be formulated less clearly. It should not be confused with our concept. But our actual incidence (case 3) corresponds substantially to Hicks' and Musgrave's effective incidence; and our direct or legal incidence (case 1), meaning the distribution of statutory tax liabilities, is equivalent to Musgrave's impact incidence.[21]

Whether shifting should be measured by the difference between the legal incidence and the final pattern of redistribution (actual incidence) or by the difference between the distribution desired by the Treasury (intended incidence) and the actual or effective incidence is ultimately a question of expediency.[22] The second definition measures the success or failure of tax or fiscal policy.

Summing up, we may define the concept of actual incidence as follows: direct and indirect incidence reflect the distribution of the tax among persons or groups. They are measured by income changes. With direct incidence the tax is paid by the taxpayer. With indirect incidence the tax is shifted through open or hidden price changes to the ultimate taxbearer. The price is changed indirectly when quantity or quality are reduced. It is useful to measure the withdrawal of real and monetary means by the income change of the persons who have to pay the tax. The income reduction of a person or a group is at least as great as the tax receipts of the Treasury.[23]

This does not exhaust, however, all the adjustments to the tax and the reduction of incomes. Thus, loss of interest due to delayed incidence may arise or price increases may reduce sales depending on the elasticity of demand. This means that the profit of the suppliers and/or the income of the factors of production decreases (for example by wage reduction or a fall in employment). Furthermore a welfare loss may result from a forced abstention or substitution of consumption (see Figure V–2). Undoubtedly, the process of shifting thus causes micro-economic losses closely related to incidence. This automatically raises the question whether this kind of income reduction should be terminologically distinguished from incidence. Schumpeter and Dalton,[24] among others, isolate these two aspects while, for instance Mann and von Mering hold quite opposite views. Von Mering wants to include only the loss of interest.[25] Mann, however, wishes to incorporate in the incidence concept not only the direct losses of money but also the indirect burden the taxpayer has to bear due to the decrease of demand.

Of course, in a classical model these losses are compensated by gains and in a statistical analysis it is nearly impossible to separate these redistributive effects of both price and output changes from incidence.

(*b*) *Broad (Relative or Net) Incidence Concepts*

We now return to the four forms of a tax change under different conditions discussed at the beginning of this chapter, and examine whether the effects of the government's use of the revenue should be considered in an analysis of tax incidence. Thus far we have dealt with the concept of gross incidence of a new tax, without considering the use of the tax yield. For a study of the incidence of a particular tax this concept seems useful provided the effects of the expenditure on the taxed market may be neglected. The principle of "non-affectation" on the revenue side of the budget commonly applied in modern times seems to make it unnecessary to allow for expenditure effects. But obviously the more the initial effects of taxation are offset by the way in which tax expenditures affect supply and demand, the more the primary incidence will be altered. This is the case in De Viti de Marco's[27] striking example of a fuel or gas tax, quoted by Kendrick and other American authors,[28] which is entirely spent on road construction and thus affects again the demand for and supply of fuel and gas.

If we widen our concept to include also the expenditure side of the budget, we are able to measure the relative or net incidence, leaving at first the resource transfer from the private to the public sector constant. Here, the possible use of the tax yield allows a further subdivision of tax incidence. The three forms of a tax change, i.e. imposition, reduction, and substitution, are to be compared with the revenue use for (1) a budget surplus (deficit), (2) the same purpose as before, (3) the purchase of goods and services, (4) transfer payments.

(1) In the preceding section we took the revenue use as given, holding constant the real public expenditure (including transfers) and any effect of the additional receipts of the new tax. In a macro-

economic analysis this simple assumption does not seem feasible. As a result of the new tax, public revenue rises and private income decreases. If government does not spend the surplus, the price level falls because private demand decreases. Furthermore, public expenditures must be cut if real purchases of goods are to remain constant. As a result, other tax yields fall, thus compounding the deflationary process. These classical deflation effects of a budget surplus may themselves alter the income distribution and are mingled with the incidence of the new tax.

Evidently, this concept of *gross, absolute* or *specific* incidence (Musgrave) becomes weak as soon as the budget surplus (or deficit) influences the general price level and production.[29]

(2) When we replace a tax by one or more other taxes while assuming the yield to be the same and the budget in real terms to be constant, the redistribution of real income measures the net incidence which Wicksell calls *differential tax incidence*. Musgrave has revived this concept using it extensively in his contributions.[30] He emphasizes that the equal yield of the two taxes must be expressed in real terms since different taxes may involve different transaction demands upon a constant money supply and thus cause price level changes.[31]

(3) In the third case the distributive effects of both tax and expenditure are combined. Here the government uses the tax yield to finance real expenditures of an equal amount. Unlike in the first two cases, we have a resource transfer from the private to the public sector. Musgrave refers to this concept as *balanced-budget incidence*. Since the budget is balanced in real terms, inflation and deflation effects are excluded. But here we are no longer considering tax incidence since it is impossible to separate the distribution effects of tax and expenditure.

If, however, we analyze the *formal budget incidence*, we measure separately the allocation of the costs and benefits of the public goods and services and we compare the distributive changes to get the net result of the budget on income redistribution on the assumption of a *given* degree of shifting or a *given* incidence.

(4) Suppose the government uses the tax yield to finance transfer payments, e.g. a social security program. In this case a formal resource transfer leaves the private sector ultimately unchanged, except for the administrative cost of transfer. Thus, we are dealing with a mixture of differential and balanced-budget incidence. If we compare the tax-induced redistribution of income with the financial transfer-

induced one, interpreting the social security payments as a negative tax, we formulate a type of *net or differential* tax incidence. The redistributive result tells us which persons or groups bear the net tax, i.e. the positive less the negative tax. This case may be of practical significance as it shows the cost allocation of a social security program.

Though the equality of tax receipts and transfer payments compensates losses and gains in the private sector, the changes of the gross and net pattern of income distribution may influence government revenue and private demand for money and goods even in a classical model, thus causing additional inflation and production effects. These were the effects with which Keynes thought to alter the propensity to consume as a means of anti-depression policy.

Our concept is akin to the balanced-budget incidence as the revenue and expenditure sides are equally enlarged, but there is no resource transfer into the public sector. This approach is ideal if we can separate the two distributive effects empirically. We call it the *tax-transfer incidence.*

(*c*) *Incidence and Production and Growth Effects*

Obviously in a macro-economic analysis, using broad concepts of incidence, the initial direction of shifting loses importance. If we understand incidence as the total distributive change in real income, this meaning covers (1) forward, backward, and cross shifting and (2) all losses and gains in sales and interest resulting from the shifting process. As we abstract from the production and growth effects of taxation, holding the total income unchanged, the additional charges of individual tax shifting are compensated by the corresponding advantages of other taxpayers.

If we modify our assumption that all tax effects on the level, structure, and growth of production (as well as the money effects) are excluded, then total losses are no longer balanced by total gains. In this case it remains an open question whether profits or losses are the direct consequences of shifting or whether they result from the tax-induced change in production. The results of these interdependent effects on distribution and production appear at the end of a process of adjustment and give the distribution of the changed real income (not of a given one, as initially assumed) as well as its altered amount.

There is yet another aspect. Any advantages of differential compared to specific incidence are lost as soon as we drop the classical assumptions: full employment, equality of planned saving and investment, and a balanced budget. In a compensatory system in which "changes in aggregate demand may originate from changes in the desire to spend available funds, and where such changes may give rise to changes in the level of employment as well as in prices,"[32] a tax substitution may influence effective demand and the level of employment regardless of whether the real or monetary tax yield is held constant. In this case, differential incidence includes changes in distribution which result from effects on employment and the price level. The concept of differential incidence becomes therefore questionable, not to say useless.

Following Musgrave's hint about the "necessity of looking at the problem in dynamic terms" (*Theory*, p. 210) and a suggestion by Shoup, Dosser[33] has recently tried to transform static into *dynamic* incidence. He analyzes the changes in distribution over time and measures the results of shifting by the rate of change in income. Since we will discuss Dosser's original contribution to the theory of dynamic incidence further on, we will omit here the explanation of his terminology which is oriented towards Musgrave's analytical definitions and distinctions.

Krzyzaniak had previously developed an interesting incidence concept for a growing economy in a neoclassical framework.[34] Starting from his empirical analysis of the shiftability of a general profits tax he attempts to link shifting and efficiency (production) and growth effects of a tax. He refers to Dalton's terminology, splitting the global tax burden into direct and indirect burden. The direct burden is the decrease in the nation's real net product induced by the tax. Like most recent studies, which consider both efficiency and distribution aspects of public goods, he combines the two types of tax effects (see Figure II–1) in order to measure the result of shifting in a more realistic way.[35]

The main weakness of this concept is the assumption that public expenditures are a complete waste. Krzyzaniak disregards in his *total* analysis the effects of government spending on the size and distribution of the tax burden and on all variables which determine the degree of shiftability. His argument that too little would be known about expenditure incidence (and, we might add, efficiency effects), is as true as it is weak. The progress towards a more "realistic" and operational concept gets lost if we neglect the fact that direct and indirect (e.g. increased productivity) benefits of government spending may influence the amount and distribution of the tax burden in a world of continuous economic growth.

3. Measurement of Incidence

Incidence can be measured by the change in the real or nominal income of a person or a group. The taxation of a household or a firm may affect both the origin and the use of the income. The combination of the two possible income changes allows the measurement of the *individual* or *micro*-incidence.[36]

If, however, we want to get hold of the *macro-economic* or *group-incidence,* the change in the *functional, personal, sectoral, regional, intertemporal,* or *sociological* income distribution before and after taxation is of major interest.

When discussing incidence the classical authors refer exclusively to functional income groups, i.e. the remunerations of the factors of production, wages, interest, rents, and profits. In more recent studies the personal income distribution is central without regard to functional income groups; group income is expressed either cumulatively by means of a Lorenz curve or absolutely by income classes. Nevertheless the other measures remain very important for fiscal and economic policy, e.g. the grouping by economic sectors (agriculture, industry, services). This is also true for the distribution of tax burdens according to sociological aspects (lower, middle, and upper classes, active and inactive population, labor and independent professions etc.) or according to regional differences in the level of development, i.e. the *geographical incidence.*

In principle, individual and group incidence are important even for the distribution of the tax burden over time, e.g. for the distribution of taxes or of the benefits from public installations among different generations. This is especially important in the discussion of the problem of timing in the theory of the public debt.[37]

The most important instrument for measuring personal incidence is the Lorenz curve which has been taken over from the theory of income distribution. In Figure II–3 the horizontal axis from O to A shows the cumulative percentage of income recipients in the economy of any relevant group. The ordinate states the cumulative percentage of the corresponding incomes. The diagonal OB represents an egali-

FIGURES II–3 AND 4

Measurement of Personal Incidence

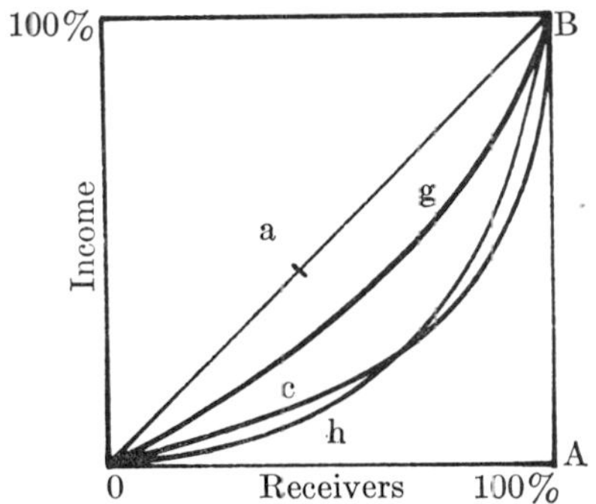

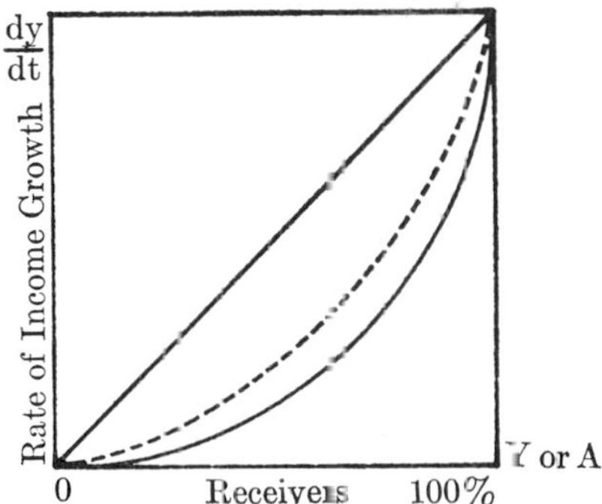

tarian distribution of income. At point a, for instance, 40 per cent of the income recipients also receive 40 per cent of total income.

Suppose the line OCB represents the original income distribution as generated by the market, and that after a change in tax policy income is distributed according to line OBG. The incidence is then measured by comparing the areas between the lines of distribution. If the ratio between area OGBA (new distribution) is greater than 1, the incidence is on the whole progressive, i.e. the income is more equally distributed. If however the ratio of the two areas is smaller than 1, the incidence is regressive, i.e. the new income distribution resulting from the modified tax policy is more unequal than the original one. If the area remains unchanged, the incidence is proportional or neutral. With the help of the Lorenz curve we can also examine the success or failure of a fiscal or economic measure and express it numerically. If OCBA shows the government's intended tax distribution (i.e. the expected incidence), and OGBA shows the actual incidence, then the difference between the two measures the success or failure of the policy.

Though the Lorenz curve is not without shortcomings, it can be easily adapted to measure incidence.[38] In this case the ordinate measures the cumulative increases in the available income resulting from a process of growth instead of the cumulative percentage of a constant real income.[39] When we mark the cumulative percentages of income on the abscissa (Figure II–3,4) we can tell whether the changed tax structure has at any one moment of time led to a yet higher or lower rate of growth. If, however, the abscissa indicates the cumulative percentage of the income earners, we can tell whether the change in taxation has led to a still faster or slower rate of growth in the incomes of the richer groups.[40]

4. Effects of Tax Incidence

We have explained in detail how closely the effects of incidence are linked to subsequent individual income reduction. These effects can initially be derived from the possible behavior of the final tax bearers. The households and enterprises may change their short or long term plans in response to their income reductions caused by the tax:

(1) They may try to increase their disposable income by increased productivity, borrowing, or reduced savings if they do not want to lower their production or their standard of living. Or
(2) they may reduce consumption
(3) save less than planned or hold less cash or
(4) they may invest less than intended.

The psychological incentives for activity, saving (liquidity), consumption, investment (risk-taking) as well as the immediate economic behavior of individuals and groups influence the volume and structure of effective supply and demand, and thus the total economic performance over time. The incidence effects therefore influence social product either by affecting the formation or the use of income. Though these effects of incidence are more or less closely connected in reality, an analytic separation appears useful (see Figure II–1).

In evaluating the incidence effects of a tax it must not be forgotten that, unfortunately, the initial tax may itself have been the uncertain result of a shifting process. Furthermore, the income effects may affect incidence *via* prices; and in addition the effects of public expenditures may more or less compensate for the effects of tax collections, when all the interdependencies in the economy are considered.

5. Excursus: Substitution Effects

In fiscal practice the substitution effects often appear as soon as the tax is announced. Households or firms may avoid the tax burden immediately or later: by offsetting, limiting or evading the taxable status and thus avoid the payment and burden. They may avoid the tax either by changing their dispositions over time, by changing their location, or by moving from taxed into untaxed objects. As long as these psychological and economic consequences express the endeavor to get advantages as far as possible before the tax law becomes effective, we speak of *announcement effects,* otherwise of the direct effects of substitution.

Temporal fiscal advantages can be achieved (1) by means of more (less) sales and purchases of goods and services to be taxed or to be relieved of a tax, or (2) by transferring, for instance, taxable profits to more favorable periods of assessment when the tax is temporarily limited (taxes on war profits) or when the rates and depreciation quotas vary or when the progression of the tax rate is great. For instance, one can manipulate investments (advertising costs) by delaying the realization of a speculative profit or another capital gain. Especially strongly progressive rates and the manner of assessment encourage this form of tax avoidance (fluctuating incomes through several periods are far more highly taxed than evenly distributed ones) though the technique of taxation limits these possibilities.[41]

Regional avoidance is of practical importance in countries with different fiscal units (Germany, U.S.A., Switzerland) and where tax rates vary considerably from one area to another.[42] The extent to which differences of taxation may influence the national and international location of enterprises depends on (1) the (mostly imperfect) mobility of the factors of production and on non-economic considerations and (2) the tax saving minus the cost of changing the location of the taxed property. Tax advantages for new enterprises influence their location to a high degree. Here periods of freedom from taxes or a generous interpretation of tax regulations may stimulate local avoidance. Today, the avoidance of taxed areas (highway tolls, a country levying transit fees) is less important than the building of plants and their branches in countries with high protective tariffs in order to avoid the tax or to protect the market.[43]

And finally a tax can lead to *real* evasion in many forms by households and firms. To mention but a few important examples of the many substitution effects: to avoid high marginal rates a (joint) income is formally distributed among several persons (family enterprise) or funds; or parts of the taxable income which are highly taxed may be converted into incomes which are less heavily taxed.[44]

Furthermore, the substitution effect may relate to the legal form of a company. When similar taxable situations are taxed differently according to the legal form of the enterprise, (joint-stock-company, limited liability company, partnership) tax saving may be an "invitation" to change the legal form.

The effects of a cumulative multiphase sales or turnover tax, (such as the former German *Umsatzsteuer*) which stimulates concentration are a further form of evasion.[45] Here the taxpayer tries to combine several stages of production or sales in order to save on taxes. The higher the rates the stronger is the incentive to merge previously independent enterprises (vertical integration).

6. Excursus: Illegal Tax Evasion

Illegal tax evasion (German: *Ausweichung*, Italian: *evasione*) is a reaction primarily of interest to the Treasury, because tax payment and tax burden, the two causes of economic effects, do not materialize. *Tax deception* (*Steuertäuschung*)[46] *tax concealment* and *tax fraud* as well as *the refusal to pay taxes* (a tax strike or flight) are forms of illegal evasion. Its fiscal importance grows with decreasing tax morale. It is closely linked to the amount and the (discriminating and cumulative) distribution of the total tax burden (tax pressure and multiplication or pyramiding) as well as to the height of the rates and the technique of taxation.[47] A growing burden increases the inclination for illegal evasion of taxes, because the financial "reward" for successful evasion also increases.

In Germany, no systematic study of the extent and composition of tax evasion exists. The amount varies from state to state and is probably overestimated.[48]

III. *Repercussions of Tax Incidence on Tax Imposition (Tax Policy)*

More or less powerful *reactions* to the *cause* of the manifold and far reaching tax effects, that is, to the change in taxes, can result from indirect as well as direct incidence. The more the incidence of taxes accumulates with individual taxpayers or groups, the more effective is the *pressure of the tax*. In other words, the more income is paid over in taxes and the more a particular income group is discriminated against compared to the rest of the taxpayers, and the greater the tax awareness, the more the burden is felt. Its reduction may often only be achieved by a change in tax legislation, which in turn presupposes political and parliamentary action.

While this kind of repercussion of the cumulated tax incidence has primarily a political content, other repercussions on fiscal policy have primarily economic or fiscal character. If the tax pressure caused by the cumulative incidence influences the economic activity to such an extent that the stimulating effects of public expenditures do not suffice to compensate for them, income and employment will decrease in the course of the multiplier process, which in turn will seriously affect tax revenues. It goes without saying that a reasonable fiscal policy will eventually be forced to draw certain consequences.[49]

Notes

1. Günter Schmölders' term in *Finanzpolitik,* 2nd ed. (Berlin-Göttingen-Heidelberg, 1965).
2. Exceptions are, for example, lump-sum or poll-taxes.
3. As an example I mention war profit taxes or capital levies
4. For example, the premature knowledge of expected reduction in customs tariffs may have the opposite effects from those intended by economic policy.
5. See R. Barlow, H. E. Brazer and J. N. Morgan, *Economic Behavior of the Affluent* (Washington, 1966).
6. In a centrally administered economy with fixed prices, open price effects of taxation are evidently impossible.
7. Any deterioration of quality as well as weight reductions must also be considered price changes, albeit hidden ones.
8. Tax amortization gained importance in the "Lastenausgleich" of postwar Germany.
9. The question whether tax amortization is a kind of shifting (Kaizl and Schäffle) or belongs to incidence (Pantaleoni and Mildschuh) is controversial.
10. Of course, the theory of public finance and particularly the theory of fiscal and tax policy must also give due consideration to those effects closely linked to tax pressure.
11. See section 6, Excursus: Illegal Tax Evasion.
12. For instance, our effects caused by a tax announcement are neither the same as Pigou's "announcement effects," nor are the direct substitution reactions of tax evasion identical with U. K. Hicks' substitution effects, since we define the economic and psychological consequences of an

announcement merely as a temporary behavior. The effects resulting from an announcement comprise all attempts to get economic advantages *before* the tax actually passes into law. Only when the tax has been passed do we distinguish our three basic effects.

Pigou's concept is much wider: "The announcement of a tax as a rule causes people to modify their conduct with a view, in some measure, to avoiding the pressure of the tax." He does not differentiate the announcement effects from either the substitution effects or from the incidence effects and he therefore distinguishes only roughly between announcement and distribution aspects of taxation. Depending on the problem to be solved, this may of course be reasonable and useful.

13. A list of the most important older works on tax shifting has been compiled by E. R. A. Seligman (*The Shifting and Incidence of Taxation, op. cit.*), further by W. Mildschuh (at the beginning of the article "Steuerwirkungen," *HdF*, I [1926], 94), by F. K. Mann ("Ueberwälzung der Steuern," *HdSt*, 4th ed., VIII, 361) and by Lampe ("Steuerwirkungslehre," *loc. cit.*, p. 567). Mildschuh deals briefly with the development of the terminological attempts to define the concept and forms of tax shifting and other effects of taxation. My bibliography includes the important newer works published in the last four decades.
14. Föhl (*FA, NF,* XIV), and in "Das Steuerparadoxon," (*FA, NF,* XVII). For the discussions mentioned see footnote 1, *ibid.*
15. R. A. Musgrave, "General Equilibrium Aspects of Incidence Theory," *AER,* XLIII (1953), 504–517, and *Theory, op. cit.*, pp. 205–231.
16. See C. von Hock, *Die Oeffentlichen Abgaben und Schulden* (Stuttgart, 1863).
17. Attilo da Empoli, *Teoria dell'inzidenza delle imposte,* I (Reggio, Calabria, 1926), 20.
18. Rolph and Stockfisch propose considering only the income formation, defining incidence as a change of factor earnings or a result of backward shifting. This narrowing of the incidence concept seems to be too restrictive. Rolph, *Theory of Fiscal Economics, op. cit.*, pp. 124–126, and J. A. Stockfisch, "On the Obsolescence of Incidence," *PF,* XIV (1959), 125 *passim.*
19. Seligman, *op cit.*, p. 2.
20. For this reason the title of this book separates (actual or effective) tax incidence from the (other) redistributional effects (formal incidence).
21. J. R. and U. K. Hicks (*The Incidence of Local Rates in Great Britain,* Occasional Papers VIII, National Institute of Economic and Social Research, [Cambridge, England, 1945]) understand by formal incidence, "the proportion of people's incomes which goes, not to provide the incomes of other people who furnish them with goods and services, but to form the revenue of a taxing body . . ." while R. A. Musgrave defines his impact incidence as follows: "the change that would result

if the income position of a new *tax-payer* [italics mine] were reduced by the amount of tax addition, while the position of all others remained unchanged . . ." (*Theory*, p. 230).

22. See below section 3, A Measure of Incidence.
23. See also the diagram, Figure, V-2, which makes these relations immediately obvious.
24. Josef A. Schumpeter, *Das Wesen und der Hauptinhalt der theoretischen Nationalökonomie* (Leipzig, 1908), p. 478, and Hugh Dalton, *Principles of Public Finance*, 4th ed. (London, 1954).
25. O. von Mering, *Die Steuerüberwälzung* (Jena, 1928), p. 1 *passim*. English edition: *The Shifting and Incidence of Taxation* (New York, 1942).
26. F. K. Mann, *Ueberwälzung der Steuern, op. cit.*
27. De Viti de Marco, *Grundlagen der Finanzwirtschaft*, German edition by Morgenstern (Tübingen, 1932). English edition: *First Principles of Public Finance* (London, 1950).
28. Kendrick (*AER*, XXVII), John F. Due, *Incidence of Sales Taxation, op. cit.*, and D. Black, *The Incidence of Income Taxes, op. cit.*
29. "Absolute incidence" does not at all mean that the tax is an absolute burden for the *group as a whole*, as is true when factors are transferred from the private to the public sector. Musgrave feels bound to point this out expressly (*On Incidence, op. cit.*, p. 306, footnote 2). In order to avoid any misunderstanding, the term "specific incidence" should be preferred.
30. Knut Wicksell, *Finanztheoretische Untersuchungen, op. cit.*, p 8, *passim*, and R. A. Musgrave, "On Incidence," *JPE*, XXXII (1953), 306, and *Theory*, p. 211, *passim.*
31. Musgrave, *Theory*, chapter 10.
32. Musgrave, *Theory*, p. 215.
33. D. Dosser, "Tax Incidence and Growth," *loc. cit.*, p. 572, *passim* and the discussion following between A. D. Bain, A. R. Prest and D. Dosser, *loc. cit.*, 533–552.
34. M. Krzyzaniak, "The Long-Run Burden of a General Tax on Profits in a Neoclassical World," *Public Finance*, XXII, 4 (1967), 472–495.
35. B. A. Weisbrod, "Income Redistribution Effects and Benefit-Cost Analysis," in Samuel B. Chase, Jr. (ed.), *Problems in Public Expenditure Analysis* (Washington, D.C., 1968), pp. 177–222; H. C. Recktenwald, "Unteilbare Güter, ihre Effizienz und Verteilung," in *International Institute of Public Finance, Efficiency in Government Spending* (The Hague, 1967), p. 61.
36. See in particular Musgrave, *Theory*, p. 217 *passim*. For the changes necessary to measure dynamic incidence, compare Dosser, "Tax Incidence and Growth," p. 575.
37. See H. C. Recktenwald, *Die Finanzwissenschaft unserer Zeit* (Stutt-

gart, 1965), p. 35; *idem, Finanztheorie und Finanzpolitik, op. cit.* chapter X.

38. As the curve OHB proves, the total distribution of incomes may remain neutral (equal areas) but considerable changes may nevertheless have taken place. This difficulty is easily resolved if instead of considering the income distribution of the entire population or the whole relevant group, specific subgroups are analyzed. We will omit the discussion of other shortcomings of the Lorenz curve as a measure of tax incidence.
39. See D. Dosser, "Tax Incidence and Growth," p. 570. In his paper "Incidence and Growth Further Considered," *EJ*, LXXIII (1963), 547, Dosser also points to the special aspects of the explicit and implicit measure of incidence.
40. D. Dosser, "Incidence and Growth Further Considered," p. 548.
41. See also C. C. Holt, "Averaging of Income for Tax Purposes," *NTJ* (December, 1949), II, 344–361.
42. For example: The tax preferences in Berlin or the founding of special German firms in Switzerland, Liechtenstein or Monaco to evade the higher German taxation, or foreign issues of shares or obligations.
43. Obviously, regional evasion may considerably affect the geographical or interregional incidence; see chapter 4.
44. See J. K. Butters, "Taxation, Incentives, and Financial Capacity," *AER, P and P* (1954), p. 504.
45. See D. Pohmer, "Betrieb und Unternehmung als Merkmalsträger von Konzentrationserscheinungen," *Festschrift für W. Rieger,* eds. I. Fettel and H. Linhardt (Stuttgart, 1963).
46. W. Gerloff, "Steuerwirtschaftslehre," *HdF,* 2nd ed., Vol. II (Tübingen, 1956).
47. G. Schmölders, *Steuerlehre, op. cit.*
48. P. Jostock, "Ueber den Umfang des der Besteuerung entgehenden Einkommens," *WWA*, LVII (1943), 27–78.
49. See Figure I-1 and Figure I-2.

3
Methods of Analyzing Incidence and Tax Effects

I. *Introductory Remarks*

Few areas of economic and fiscal theory face such manifold and far-reaching methodological problems as the theory of tax incidence. An understanding of these fundamental difficulties is important to recognize the limited[1] and conditional nature of all knowledge and statements, past, present and future. The discussions on the Föhl[2] and Musgrave-Krzyzaniak theories of incidence make this abundantly clear.

To begin with, anyone doing research on incidence must ask himself whether the deductive or the empirical method leads to more general and specific judgements on the possible, probable or actual distribution of a tax or subsidy. Is it meaningful and useful to apply the results of behavioral research and in particular of fiscal psychology and sociology, either exclusively or in combination with other theories or merely in an auxiliary fashion, in order to elucidate and explain real incidence? If we choose the deductive method, the basic question arises about correct choice of analytic tools: Should we consider and try to resolve incidence problems on a micro or macro-economic basis, from the point of view of a household or firm, or of a market or the economy as a whole? Furthermore, time raises some fundamental methodological problems: Is the comparative-statistical approach sufficient or should it be replaced by a dynamic one? In order to gain better insight into the relationships and practical results, should we investigate the long run adjustments to a tax change in a static or growing (evolutionary) economy, or should we pay more attention than we did so far to the short term changes also during the so-called *market period*? And finally, the theory of incidence shares with other areas of economic theory the methodological difficulties of marginalism.

In seeking answers to these many questions of procedure we should ask: Which method is most feasible, and should it be used exclusively or together with others?

II. *Partial or General Equilibrium Analysis?*

A short review of the history of tax incidence theory shows that both methods have been used almost equally and with almost equal success. Smith[3] and Ricardo[4] developed a theory of incidence which was primarily macro-economic. Later, micro-economic approaches moved more into the foreground, along with that development in economic theory. At the turn of the century, Wicksell once again analyzed incidence problems on the basis of general equilibrium theory. And recent contributions tend very strongly in the same direction.

What are the essential features of the two methods? The traditional partial analysis limits itself to a definite sector of the total economic process. The focus of the analysis is the household, the firm, or the market of the taxed good; we ask whether and how the tax is shifted to the actual taxbearer in the immediate economic process and who finally bears it. Under the *ceteris paribus* assumption, the effects of the shifting determinants included in supply and demand and thus the interactions of the taxed and the other markets as well as the rest of the private and the public sectors of the economy are more or less excluded.

General equilibrium analysis, by contrast, takes into account the general interdependence in the whole economy of all firms, households and the government. Although it considers only certain relationships in isolation, the parts are fundamentally different. Here, the direct relationships between taxpayer and bearer and the initial direction of shifting are not central, instead those global adjustments to a tax increase or decrease which are realized in a changed distribution of total income are the focus. We deal here with average results within individual income groups. The end result of these adjustments may not be identical with initial reactions and the final burden of any individual firm or household.

No doubt, both methods are valid. The choice of method depends primarily on the problem to be solved. Both partial and general equilibrium analysis have been applied with about equal and equally limited success. Both approaches have advantages and disadvantages. The strictly limited analysis of the individual firm or industry allows a much more detailed investigation of the process of adaptation and its direction. At the same time the partial equilibrium limitations may be so great as to falsify the results in their practical application.

Total analysis, on the other hand, has the great disadvantage that it neglects the problems of shifting incidence proper in favor of other tax or even expenditure effects.

Thus, at a time when he still was quite skeptical of general equilibrium theory, Musgrave criticized Welinder's and Kalecki's general theory as follows: "(They) start out with an *assumed* solution of the *initial* shifting problem, e.g. with a given change in income, wages, costs, profits, etc."[5] The dispute about diffusion theories through a whole century proves also that the general theory of the day is inadequate to solve satisfactorily the theoretical and practical problems of tax incidence.

Given the limits of each procedure, each is useful for a particular purpose. If the emphasis of an investigation is on the partial effects of a tax change, the partial equilibrium analysis is obviously adequate. This will be the case, for example, in the analysis of a tax which is small in relation to total tax receipts. General equilibrium analysis on the other hand is appropriate for the study of the effects and of the incidence of generally levied taxes or of receipts which are economically important. Moreover, it allows us to include the effects of expenditures and of the important money and credit relationships as well as the effects on employment which partial analysis does not permit at all or only with severe limitations.[6]

Finally, the proper degree of abstraction will also depend on the purpose of the investigation and, as Samuelson points out, "the fruitfulness of *any* theory will hinge upon the degree to which factors relevant to the particular investigation at hand are brought into *sharp* focus."[7] The more we want to draw policy conclusions, the less we can neglect related factors as well as empirical tests and the more we have to formulate our incidence concept in operational terms.

If we wish to develop a theory of incidence proper, our approach has to be limited to particular tax effects. But when we seek more practical conclusions, it seems desirable to extend the analysis and to lower the degree of abstraction.

III. *Deductive or Empirical Method?*

There is some dispute as to whether deductive or empirical-statistical methods are more fruitful in understanding the shifting process. Lotz thought, rather onesidedly, that only empirical research could bring considerable progress, though "with better tools."[8] Colm and Tarasow, on the contrary, thought that "even the most complete statistical material can never measure the incidence of taxation."[9] If we compare available studies we come to the following conclusions.

The empirical-statistical conclusions as to direction, degree and amount of shifting and incidence of certain taxes are completely inappropriate as the basis of generalization about who bears the taxes. First, the statistical proof about tax incidence succeeds only under very special circumstances. Secondly, there have been so few studies that we must reject any inductive generalization on this basis just as we would an intuitive generalization based on subjective experience (to which entrepreneurs and trade unions are rather naturally inclined).

The painstaking study of Laspeyres, covering data over 20 years, can even today be considered one of the most important in this field.[10] But even if he successfully proved *ex post* the shifting of the Prussian milling and slaughtering tax after carefully evaluating more than 1.5 million prices, we cannot generalize this single investigation. Further empirical analyses on incidence have been published in the last half century.[11] Based on historical price movements the Bureau of Internal Revenue of the U.S. Treasury Department discovered a shifting of the processing taxes but not the direction.[12] Coate's proposal, which appeared in Appendix XI of the Colwyn Report,[13] to find the shift by comparing the profit margins before and after taxation, remains as problematic as an inquiry into entrepreneurial opinion about incidence by Haig and Shoup.[14] The authors themselves considered data and conclusions unreliable. The testimony before the Colwyn-Commission in 1926/27 indicates how far practitioners and theorists differ in their opinions. Recently the number of empirical analyses has increased considerably, but the results are as controversial as ever. The Wayne State University Symposium may be the best example.

The fruits of purely deductive analysis are often "beautiful but inedible." Its premises are too general and partly unrealistic. Yet, this method has undoubtedly helped to extend our knowledge of the complicated process of tax effects.

Judging from practical results neither of these two methods is too fruitful. This is due mainly to the special difficulties of the subject. Incidence and other tax effects are so closely intertwined and the process of tax shifting is so far reaching and proceeds at so many different levels that any inductive research faces the difficult task of isolating the price and income changes caused by taxes from the manifold other factors which influence both variables simultaneously. Purely statistical analysis rarely succeeds in achieving this isolation, particularly as the quantitative importance of the individual factors frequently cannot even be approximately estimated. In order to recognize regularities in the extremely complicated adjustments of a market or an economy to taxation, we must be "prepared through the method of pure theory."[15] However, this "preparation of the phenomena"[16] must not separate closely related facts through a *ceteris paribus* assumption, as so often happens in pure theory, lest the chasm between it and reality become unbridgeable. How can we resolve this dilemma?

The more recent efforts to extend economic theory to the explanation of short and long run movements attempt a closer combination of empirical and theoretical approaches, of analytical thinking and exact observation.[17] Only this combination allows us to derive useful results which are, within limits, applicable.[18] The assumptions of pure theory are increasingly adapted to reality. The data themselves are critically examined and empirically founded assumptions are used or added to *a priori* premises. Thus, there is a greater chance to test certain results of incidence theory and theoretical conclusions may increasingly gain importance for policy. The econometric approach also becomes important in the field of tax incidence.[19]

Indeed, in an original and thorough study Musgrave and Krzyzaniak have estimated the incidence of the corporation income tax quantitatively with econometric methods. Their surprising results will be discussed later on. Even if one considers them with some skepticism, their procedure deserves thorough examination. Roskamp also used this approach in an empirical study. As statistical analysis alone cannot explain either the direction or the amount or the mechanism of shifting, all authors are forced to make certain hypotheses, some of a tentative character. Despite some reservations, this approach seems to be much more successful than the previous ones. In any case, it allows a better theoretical organization and interpretation of statistical data, and with it, of reality.

Here the big field of behavioral research is wide open for new work. Without knowing specifically the taxpayers' probable or actual individual and group reactions, the assumptions of the behavioral equations of any theoretical analysis hang in the air. Adjustments to tax changes in imperfect markets can also be largely explained by price and market-strategic behavior, e.g. "tax-induced collusion."[20] Finally, the somewhat onesided premise of profit maximization should be supplemented by the added consideration of other economic goals.

IV. *The Neglected Time Dimension*

1. Comparative Statics or Dynamics?

Partial as well as total equilibrium analysis uses comparative statics for incidence studies. The starting point is the equilibrium on the market of the taxed good or of the economy as a whole. A tax change is then assumed and the new equilibrium is compared with the old in order to deduce the adaptations caused by the tax in the theoretical model. Depending on the kind of tax effects under investigation the different directions of the adaptations are isolated and their extent measured, among others, by means of price and income changes.

This kind of static analysis largely neglects the actual process of adjustment over time, since it only compares two equilibria. Occasionally the analysis is supplemented by a concurrent reference to empirical data.

But if sequence or period analysis[21] is introduced, in order to trace the time sequence of the adaptation from the introduction of the tax change to the final equilibrium, we have to pay all the more attention to all the essential factors which influence incidence. This method therefore logically requires, first, that we define the concept of incidence very widely and, secondly, that we change for a long term analysis from a stationary to an evolutionary economy.[22]

In recent studies on dynamic incidence, Hinrichs analyzed the dynamic regressivity[23] of the American income tax; Dosser dealt with some "dynamically structured" taxes,[24] and Prest, following Dosser, analyzed the economic policy aspects of dynamic incidence.[25] The last two authors concentrate on (a) the importance of redistribution in a statistical sense and on the difficulties of introducing dynamic considerations, (b) on whether and how a progressive income tax should be used as a "built-in redistributor," and (c) on how unequal rates of growth could be corrected by other taxes.

2. Short or Long Run Analyses?

The last methodological problem concerns the time period relevant for the investigation of the adjustment process. Most theories of incidence start with the assumption that when a tax is levied "all other things" remain equal until *all* economic forces have had time enough "to work out their full effect,"[26] i.e. until the productive capacity of the individual firms, industries and the whole economy have adjusted themselves to the new situation. The mobility of the factors of production, their movement to untaxed markets is therefore logically the center of analysis.[27] For Graziani this mobility is the only criterion of shiftability.[28] As factors of production are relatively immobile and indivisible and taxes often general, the relevance of this kind of long-term analysis is restricted. The convenient fact that "friction" which might disturb the process of adaptation is assumed away simplifies the model, but increases its remoteness from reality. Obviously, the "other things" that are assumed to remain equal will in fact change substantially in the long run: public expenditures, real income and the supply of money. But this means that the price level and employment will also change which strongly modifies, if it does not totally change, the process of shifting and the incidence of the tax. As a rule, the process of adaptation is different in an underemployed or depressed economy from that in a fully employed or growing one.

Undoubtedly the insights which comparative statics allows are useful. However, we need to supplement the analyses of long term adjustments with the evolutionary analyses of short term adjustments by introducing the concept of dynamic incidence.[29] In any case the rough and simplifying assumptions that incomes, the value of money, public expenditures, etc. remain equal, are more appropriate for the short run and market periods.[30]

V. *Limited Applicability of Marginal Analysis*

In common with other parts of economic theory, incidence analysis faces the methodological difficulties related to marginalism. From the voluminous critical literature we merely extract a few points. An analysis of price policy, for example, may conclude (a) that strict profit maximization by entrepreneurs or utility maximization by households is frequently modified by a desire for long run stability and security; (b) that present-day competition takes different forms and may even have changed its character; (c) that marginalism is *ex hypothesi* inconsistent with an aggregative model; and (d) that a cost-plus calculation, including profits taxes, rather than marginal cost or marginal revenue caculations are the rule in reality.

This no more implies a radical rejection of marginal analysis than the application to practical tax problems of theorems derived from marginal analysis requires that one neglect these more recent insights into price policy. The theories of imperfect competition and of market strategy will modify all those generally accepted results of incidence theory which have been derived from the assumption of perfect competition.

VI. *Summary*

All the analytic and empirical methods which we have discussed contribute individually and collectively to the gradual satisfactory solution of the problem of incidence. The multiplicity of the available methods is an advantage and the discussion about their usefulness or uselessness irrelevant as long as the limits of each method are understood and complementary methods are simultaneously applied. Within these limits any *Methodenstreit* is meaningless. On the contrary, the demand for the exclusive use of this or that method would lead to onesidedness, stagnation and even retrogression in research and theory.

Notes

1. See G. Holden, "Incidence of Taxation as an Analytical Concept," *AER*, XXX (1940), 774–786; B. Higgins, "The Incidence of Sales Taxes—A Note on Methodology," *QJ*, XXXV (1940), 665, *passim;* E. E. Oakes, "The Incidence of a General Income Tax," *AER*, XXXII (1942), 76–82; H. C. Recktenwald, "Methodologische Probleme der Steuerinzidenztheorie," *PF*, VI (1951), 221, *passim;* P. Tabatoni, "Concept et Méthode dans la Théorie de l'incidence," *RSLF*, Number 4 (1952), p. 24 *passim;* and Musgrave, *Theory, op. cit.*, and *Aspects, op. cit.*, pp.

504–517. More recently also J. M. Buchanan, "La Metodologia della Teoria dell'incidenza: Una Rassegna Critica di Recenti Contributi Americani," *Studi Economici* (1955), 377–399; C. Goedhart, "Some Reflections on the Scope and Methods of a Macro-Economic Theory of Tax-Shifting," *PF,* XIII (1958), 7–12; and M. E. Fieser and J. G. Ranlett, "In-Lieu Taxation: A Methodological Comment," *NTJ,* XVIII (1965), 97–103. See also Adolph Wagner, *Lehrbuch* (I.2), *op. cit.,* pp. 332–369, who devotes much attention to this question.

2. Föhl, "Kritik," *loc. cit.,* and "Steuerparadoxon," *loc. cit.,* The contributions to the discussion are mentioned there, footnote 1.
3. Adam Smith, *An Inquiry into the Nature and Causes of the Wealth of Nations,* Cannan edition (Oxford, 1904).
4. David Ricardo, *On the Principles of Political Economy and Taxation,* 3rd (Sraffa) edition (Cambridge, 1951).
5. R. A. Musgrave, "Discussion," *AER, P and P* (1942), 106–108.
6. See C. Goedhart, *loc. cit.,* p. 7 *passim.*
7. P. A.. Samuelson, *Foundations of Economic Analysis* (Cambridge, Mass., 1947), p. 9.
8. Lotz, *VfS,* Discussion Report, *op. cit.,* p. 336.
9. G. Colm and H. Tarasow, *Who Pays Taxes?,* TNEC-Monograph No. 3, 76th Congress, 3rd Session (Washington, 1941), p. 2.
10. E. Laspeyres, "Statistiche Untersuchungen zur Frage der Steuerüberwälzung, geführt an der Geschichte der preussischen Mahl und Schlachtsteuer," *FA* (1901), pp. 46–242.
11. See the bibliography.
12. Bureau of Internal Revenue of the U.S. Treasury Department, *An Analysis of the Effects of the Processing Taxes Levied Under the Agricultural Adjustment Act* (Washington, 1937).
13. *Report of the Committee on National Debt and Taxation* (London, 1927).
14. R. M. Haig and C. S. Shoup, *The Sales Tax in the American States* New York, 1939).
15. A. Spiethoff, "Anschauliche und reine Theorie und ihr Verhältnis zueinander," *Synopsis. Festgabe für Alfred Weber* (Heidelberg, 1948), p. 573.
16. *Ibid.*
17. W. Eucken, *Die Grundlagen der Nationalökonomie,* 5th ed., improved (Godesberg, 1942), p. 45. English edition: *The Foundations of Economics: History and Theory in the Analysis of Economic Reality* (London, 1950).
18. See Wagner, *op. cit.,* p. 341
19. See Elmar D. Fagan, "Tax Shifting and the Laws of Cost," *QJ,* XLVII (1933), 680–710.
20. E. R. Rolph, "Discussion," *AER, P and P,* XLIII (1953), 540. See also

the empirical work of G. Schmölders, *Finanzpsychologie* in *FA, NF* 13.1 (1953) p. 26, and of the Harvard Graduate School of Business Administration. Also H. Laufenburger, "Aspects psychologiques des Finances Publique" in *Beiträge zur Geld- und Finanztheorie, op. cit.;* P. L. Reynaud, "La Psychologie du Contribuable devant l'impôt," *RSLF* 1947 No. 4; R. Giraudoux, La Psychologie du Contribuable Français," *PF* 5 (1950).

21. D. H. Robertson, *Essays in Monetary Theory* (London, 1940), p. 114 *passim.*
22. For terminological explanations see Ragnar Frisch, "On the Notion of Equilibrium and Disequilibrium," *RESt,* Vol. III (1935/36) and E. Schneider, "Statik und Dynamik," *HdS,* X, 23–29.
23. H. Hinrichs, "Dynamic-Regressive Effects of the Treatment of Capital Gains in the American Tax System During 1957–59," *PF,* XIX (1964), 73 *passim.*
24. D. Dosser, "Allocating the Burden of International Aid for Underdeveloped Countries," *RESt,* XLV (1963), 207.
25. D. Dosser, "Tax Incidence and Growth," *loc. cit.,* and A. R. Prest, "Observations on Dynamic Incidence," *EJ,* LXXIII (1963), 541 *passim.*
26. A. Marshall, *Principles of Political Economy,* 5th ed. (London, 1940), pp. 342 and 347.
27. The problem of factor movement from private to public sector should be strictly separated from incidence. It requires a separate analysis.
28. Graziani, *Istituzioni, op. cit.*
29. See Dosser, "Tax Incidence and Growth," p. 572. If economic growth is introduced, the "incidence" has to be changed in order to reach a given aim. But if the aim is changed then some taxes tend to automatically adapt themselves while others do not. "This difference in taxes, in respect of the distributive function of the budget in a growing economy, is obscured by the standard theory of incidence" (p. 591).
30. For the definition of these concepts, see Marshall, *op. cit.,* p. 360.

4
Macro-Economic Analysis of Incidence

In the section on measuring incidence we have suggested a classification of actual and formal incidence summarized in Table IV–1. This short survey helps us to arrange the fourth chapter. We will start with functional and personal incidence, the subject of most approaches. We will continue by dealing with sociological and sectoral incidence followed by an examination of interregional and international tax distribution, two aspects of recent interest. At the end we will consider inter-temporal incidence, a new branch in the study of distributive tax effects.

TABLE IV–1

Types of Formal and Effective Incidence

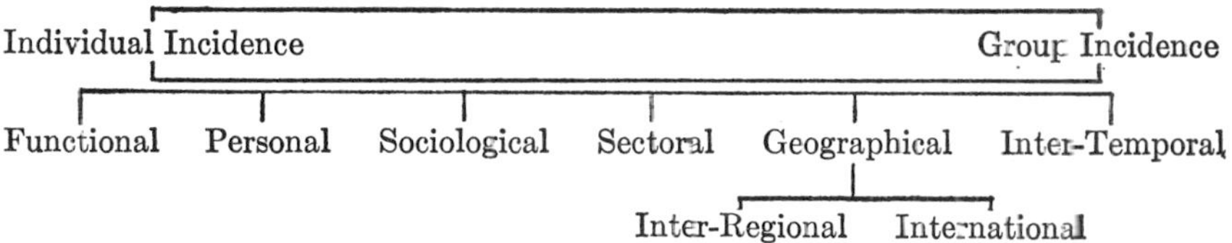

I. Functional and Personal Incidence

In order to recognize the interactions in the economic shifting process and the incidence resulting from taxation, we will start from a simple model of the circular flow that we will later alter step by step. As we measure incidence in principle by the changed distribution of a given real income, let us take an economy which has the following characteristics:

(a) the production of goods and services remains the same and is consumed in each period, i.e. net investment is zero (stationary economy);
(b) factors of production are fully employed;
(c) there is no liquidity preference;
(d) the budget is balanced;
(e) there is no foreign trade (closed economy);
(f) pure competition prevails, i.e. each market is cleared at a uniform price.

Goods and services are exchanged among the following sectors: private firms of all branches and levels in which factors of production are combined (P), private households (H), households of entrepreneurs (H_e), wealth or capital formation (Pr), and the government (G), which receives income only through taxation (T) and not via public enterprises or via property sales or the printing of money and issuing of credit.

Let us first look at the following simple relations in a so-called square matrix of interlocking accounts, a circular flow matrix in which the separate sectors are included in such a way that each entry in a column represents a debit due to a purchase or a service received and each entry in a row represents a credit due to a sale or a delivery.[1] One single entry credits therefore the sector at the beginning of the row and simultaneously debits the sector appearing at the head of the column. The column sum and the row sum of each sector are the same.

1. Incidence in a Pure Consumption Economy

In a pure consumption economy the value of the produced goods in each period, the social product (Y) equals the earnings of the factors of production, more precisely productive services (E), and also the value of the consumer goods flowing to the households (C):

$$Y = E = C$$

Let us further assume that the value of total production is DM 200 (figures represent billions). This was about the social product of the Bundesrepublik in 1956.

We shall now introduce government into the circular flow. It claims

10 per cent of the total product (=20) which it obtains by means of taxation (a) of the factor incomes (b) of business ("cost") and (c) of profits. We want to know what changes taxation causes in the direction and volume of the production and money streams.[2] We shall compare the situation before and after taxation, then analyze the course of adaptation and measure the incidence by the changed real income distribution by size classes. Since the treatment of taxes and subsidies differs in the theory of national accounting, the state should indeed, as is customary, be viewed as a sector producing public services.[3] However, we sometimes also consider taxes as pure transfer payments, i.e. as income transfers to households, which eliminates the factor-transfer between private and public sector, which is to be distinguished from incidence.

If government claims 10 per cent of the national product for its own purposes, i.e. seen from the expenditure side, half of it from private households in the form of services and half of it from production firms in the form of consumer goods, and if furthermore it pays for these goods and services by taxing the incomes of both household groups, the following changes occur as seen in Matrix 1. We shall assume that the entrepreneurs' payments are roughly 8 out of their income of 40 and the private household payments are 12 out of their income of 160.

The enterprises deliver output of 148 units to the households of the employees, 32 units to the entrepreneurs and 10 units to the government. They receive 150 and 40 units respectively from the two household groups. The government "sells" public services in the amount of 12 and 8 units respectively to the two household sectors, (their amount is equal to the tax and is autonomously determined by

MATRIX IV–1

Unshifted Income Tax with Factor Transfer

output (sells) \ *input (buys)*	*P*	*H*	H_e	*G*	
P		148	32	10	190
H	150			10	160
H_e	40				40
G		12	8		20
	190	160	40	20	

the government, not by means of a market price). The government buys goods and services from H and H_e, amounting to 10 units from each. In other words it pays its employees and defrays its expenditures for consumer goods. Apart from the decreased production in P as a consequence of the transfer of labor to the civil service, the income of H and H_e which was available for consumption purposes decreases in the amount of the tax. This measures the direct incidence. The indirect incidence is zero because relative prices remain constant.

To eliminate the transfer of production factors (here of labor only) from the private to the public sector, we shall assume that the government claims 10 per cent of the national product in the form of consumer goods (hence not from household services) in order to direct them via income transfer to the private households. For this purpose government taxes the income of both household sectors; as above, the entrepreneurs pay 8, the other group 12, together, therefore, 20 out of their incomes directly to the government. The two figures show the circular flow before and after taxation.

Only the disposable income of business households is reduced by 8 units in this case. Since the price level remains unchanged due to the constant volume of total monetary demand $(168 + 32 = 200)$, the income reduction reflects the direct incidence. Taxpayer and taxbearer are the same; we can easily measure the incidence by income groups by means of tax assessment and the Lorenz curve. This is pure tax incidence, since the expenditure effect on incomes of H_e is zero.

FIGURES IV–1 AND 2

Circular Flow and Real Transfer

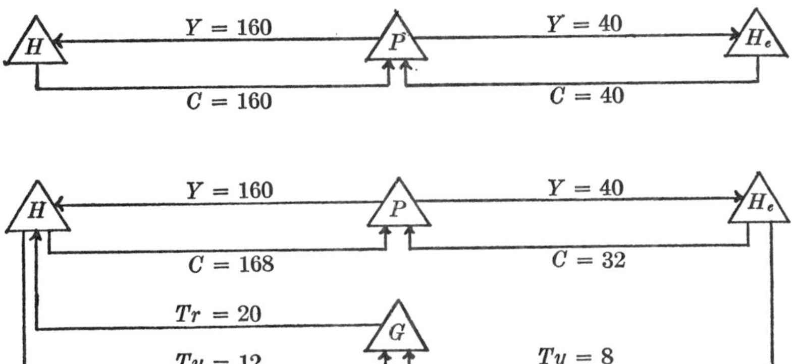

In sector H, however, the redistributive effects of the governmental transfer payments (expenditures) overcompensate for the effects of tax collection; a comparison of income distribution by size classes before and after taxes within this sector gives us the budget incidence. However, in the unrealistic case of a proportional income tax (without exemptions) and proportional expenditures (transfers) all non-entrepreneurial households have an advantage of 8 units ($Tr - Ty = 20 - 12 = 8$) which are distributed in the same percentage among all taxpayers.

Assuming that government finances the same expenditures by taxing production or consumption instead of incomes, and keeping to the second example, we can see the following relations in the circular flow: P is obliged by government to pay 20 units (or 10 per cent) of the goods offered for sale as a tax. H and H_e have the same incomes from P as before. Since we have assumed the real production conditions and the production volume to be constant, P can only pay the tax, (a) by a 10 per cent increase of the sales price and (b) if the monetary demand in the period increases as much as the nominal value of the unchanged production of goods due to the increased price. Figure IV–3 shows this simple case of a completely successful shifting of a general consumption tax.

The total income, increased by 20 units (Tr) ($160 + 20 + 40 = 220$), has led to an effective demand for consumer goods, so that the supply, nominally increased by 10 per cent, could be sold. Since prices for all consumer goods have risen by 10 per cent, the real income of all households decreases correspondingly so that the direct tax incidence is zero in all sectors. The indirect incidence is measured by the decrease of real incomes. It is proportionally distributed among all households, but is overcompensated in sector H by government expenditures in the form of an income transfer (Tr). A comparison of the real income of H before and after taxes shows the budget incidence of the consumption tax. The non-entrepreneurs are better off at the end than at the beginning of the tax adjustment due to the (assumed) purely redistributive effects of public expenditures (162:160).

This extreme case of a completely shifted general consumption tax (and of all indirect taxes) underlies the existing systems of national accounting. It appears, however, in a different form. It is implied in the assumption that government produces public services, that therefore its services are not confined to transfer payments. Let us look at

FIGURE IV–3

Circular Flow and Taxes on Costs

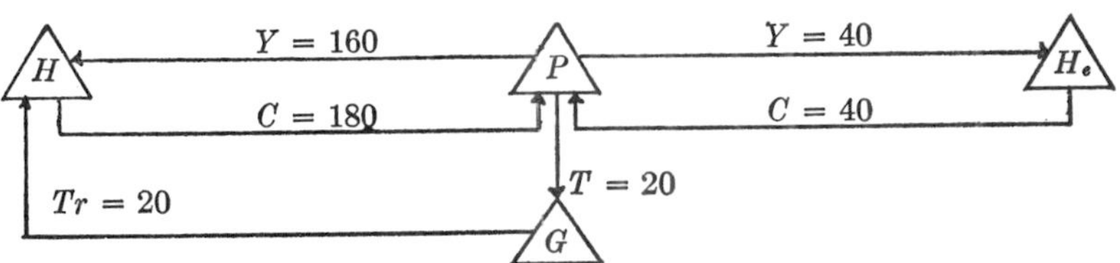

these relations of incidence. Matrix IV–1 serves as a starting point. Let government tax consumption additionally; it obliges the production firms to pay a tax of 12. It spends this amount only for goods from the production sector and not for services (labor) from H. The firms try in return to make up for the tax payment through price increases, in which they succeed because of a corresponding increase of demand. The adjustments are shown in Matrix IV–2.[4]

The nominal value of the unchanged production (the national product at factor costs) has increased by the tax amount (12) to 212; this is the national product at market prices. Now government receives 32, 10 as before in the form of services from H and 22 instead of 10 in the form of consumer goods from P. The additional total tax payment is paid exclusively by the production sector. Its proceeds have grown at the same rate due to the price increase and the higher effective total demand. The nominal incomes of the two household sectors remain unchanged, total real incomes, however, decrease exactly by the additional goods claimed by the government. The distribution of the

MATRIX IV–2

Forward Shifting of a General Consumption Tax

output (sells) \ *input (buys)*	*P*	*H*	H_e	*G*	
P		148	32	22	202
H	150			10	160
H_e	40				40
G	12	12	8		32
	202	160	40	32	

nominal income between H and H_e remains unchanged as does the income distribution by size classes within each sector. The difference in the real incomes before and after taxation measures the absolute incidence of a balanced budget. Thus the general consumption tax has been shifted entirely; the consumers bear the tax proportionately to their incomes which are equal to the consumption expenditures ($E = C$). The relative income positions remain unchanged. As far as government buys consumer goods with its revenues, its actual share of the consumable national product is reduced. The real burden of private consumers is a little less than 12.[5]

The shiftability in the indicated direction depends decisively on the elasticity of the money supply. But the proportionality of incidence depends primarily on the composition of demand. Qualitatively, demand remains unchanged (a) when households do not alter their consumption pattern in spite of increasing prices or decreasing income, and (b) when government or the favored households which receive transfer payments buy those consumption goods for which the demand of the taxbearers has diminished. The second condition makes a reallocation of factors unnecessary. It is reasonable to expect such a compensation when there is no great difference in consumption between the income groups bearing the taxes and the income groups receiving the public funds. However present day policies tend to diminish income differences by means of public expenditures. On the whole, however, some branches of the economy will register a decrease in demand and others an increase, so that partial price adjustments upwards or downwards are necessary. In some branches the market price will rise by more than the tax, thus creating additional profits; in other branches the market price will rise by less, so that profits will fall and the tax cannot or only partially be shifted. But on the average—and this is decisive for our total analysis—profits and losses balance out and micro-economic disequilibria neutralize each other. Another aspect is remarkable for its effect on incidence. The change in the individuals' economic position is as a rule more or less the same in all income size classes, so that the distribution by income groups within each sector is not much affected.

Let us reconsider the first assumption concerning the elasticity of monetary supply. In our pure-consumption economy we can, (for the moment), eliminate liquidity preference and consider purely quantity-theoretical relationships. No doubt, the social product whose nominal value has increased by the tax can only be sold without trouble if either the quantity and (or) the velocity of circulation of money increase *pari passu.* Since in our stationary economy current income is exclusively spent for consumption purposes, the payment velocity in the public sector may be also assumed to be constant. Hence the money supply must be so elastic that either the government or the producing firms can finance the expected revenues by means of credit at the proper time. If this process is to move without friction, the creation of money, tax payment and public expenditure have to be dovetailed precisely in time and amount. We return to this point in our discussion of dynamic incidence.

Without prefinanced additional demand of the government the general consumption tax cannot be shifted forward to the consumer. In our example on transfer payments, the following incidence occurs.

As in the previous case, the firms pay the tax (T = 20) to the Treasury. Since the forward-shifting via increased prices is not successful because of lack of additional demand, the profits of the entrepreneurs must be cut by 20 units to enable them to pay the tax. Having explicitly assumed a constant production, the so-called indirect taxation has the same incidence effect as a profits tax. The following possibility, however, is more realistic: the production units try to lower the factor payments at least partially, i.e. incomes of sector H instead of the residual incomes of the entrepreneur households. In our model this attempt is successful because the transfer payments compensate for the lowered income of H. But in reality it will fail because of the downward rigidity of nominal wages, especially in a fully employed economy which we have assumed. We shall discuss this in greater detail later on.

Let us now consider these relations more closely in Matrix IV–3. The following picture emerges when we assume that with a constant

FIGURE IV–4

Circular Flow and General Excise Tax

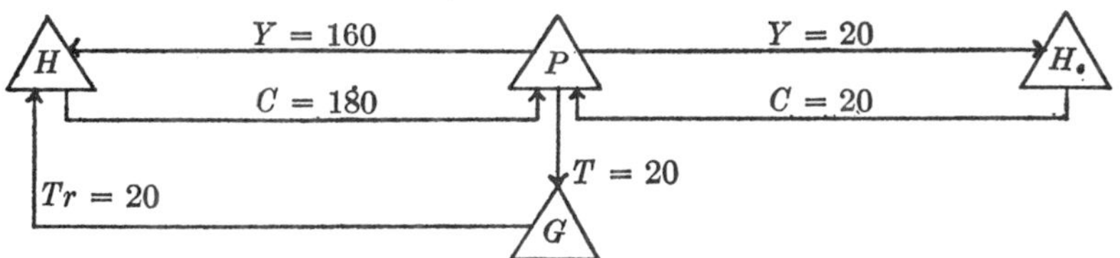

MATRIX IV–3

Unsuccessful Forward Shifting of a General Consumption Tax

output (sells) \ input (buys)	P	H	H_e	G	
P		146	22	22	190
H	148			10	158
H_e	30				30
G	12	12	8		32
	190	158	30	32	

social product the business units succeed in reducing H's factor income by 2 and H_e's income by 10.

We can disregard the incidence of a profits tax in a stationary model, because this problem is closely linked to changes in wealth and capital formation, and consideration in a dynamic setting is advisable. Besides, the elementary relations have already been shown in Matrix IV–3.

2. Incidence in a Capital-Formation Model

We can now approximate our model of circular flow step by step to reality by changing the basic assumption (1) so that the whole income is not consumed but is partly saved and invested. The production of goods and use of income extends to consumption goods (C) and investment goods (I) and savings (S) respectively, which are currently invested.

We replace $\quad Y = E = C$

by $\quad Y = C + I$ and

$E = C + S$

(*a*) *Incidence of a General Consumption Tax*

Let us now introduce government activity. Government levies for its purposes a uniform tax on all consumption goods. This is the basis of nearly all modern macro-economic analyses of tax incidence. We start from the situation shown in Matrix IV–1. The expenditures of the entrepreneurs' households are divided into 22 units for consumption and 10 for savings which P invests. The savings of H are at first zero. What happens when an additional 12 units have to be paid to the government by all firms, and who ultimately pays the tax?

Forward Shifting through Price Increases of the Taxed Goods. We have already described the two extreme adjustments in two directions and their results, namely a reduction of real income for all households, shown in Matrices 2 and 3 under the simplest and in Matrix 4 under changed assumptions. We now reconsider the first case allowing specifically for the fact that time must elapse. If the production units increase the price on all consumption goods by the same percentage, they can maintain their sales only if total demand increases *pari passu.* Since under conditions of perfect competition the suppliers are quantity adapters and since the individual cannot influence the price directly because of his small market share, the incentive for price rises must come from the demand. For our analysis this means that either government or entrepreneurs prefinance the tax through credit or that the private households develop an additional demand which corresponds to the tax. The latter behavior is for the time being eliminated from our consideration as being too unrealistic.[6] Since the households are not yet directly affected by the tax, neither consumer credit nor dissaving (or less liquidity) seem necessary to maintain the standard of living in the short run. The government's behavior conforms much more to reality. In industrialized countries with a developed money and credit system and a developed governmental apparatus, the cash-holding policy of the government is generally sufficiently elastic that an increased demand can be continuously satisfied to the limits of public indebtedness and

MATRIX IV–4

Forward Shifting of a General Consumption Tax

output (sells) \ *input (buys)*	*P*	*H*	H_e	*Pr*	*G*	
P		148	22	10	22	202
H	150				10	160
H_e	40					40
Pr			10			10
G	12	12	8			32
	202	160	40	10	32	

that the corresponding amounts can be spent. In order to allow a smooth shifting, the Treasury must create additional demand at the beginning of a tax-paying period financed with credit or reduced liquidity (which can only be temporarily maintained without trouble). If the entrepreneurs pay monthly a tax of 12 units to the Treasury, as in the case of the French production tax, it is sufficient if the government borrows 1 unit which does not have to be repaid at the end of the year in order to have rising prices, to secure the existing sales and to increase the receipts of P by the amount of the tax payment.

But the entrepreneurs themselves can help to bring about the shiftability if they finance their monthly tax payments by means of a credit. Experience has taught us that credits caused by tax payments are taken up by the Treasury as well as the entrepreneurs. The evidence of short and long term indebtedness of the government and of the tightening of the money and capital market at the times when major tax payments are due suggests that expected tax revenues or tax payments are financed by credits to a considerable degree in some though by no means in all periods. The theoretical problem of incidence lies here in the fact, that the interest payments may raise the cost of the private but not of the public borrower significantly. Our assumption of constant investment and production becomes therefore inconsistent.

The process is reversed in reality insofar as the suppliers will try to raise prices due to various kinds of imperfect competition and their ability to influence the market price. Success finally depends on the timely and adequate financing of the additional demand. In this case, consumer credit also plays a (modest) role.

The taxed enterprises and the government as well as an elastic money supply must coincide if price shifting is to succeed and all households and the government are to bear the consumption tax wholly or partially (provided its consumption goods bought from P are not taxfree). They bear the tax proportional to the consumption expenditures of each period.

The statements of "classical" incidence theory are by contrast more definite. According to this theory an indirect tax always leads to price increases, though under entirely different adjustments of the market and the total economy. Let us look at the reasoning more closely before we discuss in greater detail the interrelations among consumption, savings and investment within the context of incidence.

The Traditional Incidence Theory of a General Consumption Tax. Conventional theory maintains that a general consumption tax is fully or partially shifted forward onto the consumers who bear it. Based on partial equilibrium theory and generalizing the effects of a tax on an individual good, it is usually argued that a consumption tax will increase the marginal cost of the taxed good of each supplier and thus reduce his profits. As the enterprises, under conditions of perfect competition, adapt the quantity to the price they will reduce their production with a given demand and in an attempt to recoup their position; this will raise the price.[7] In the long-run, marginal producers are eliminated from the market until a new equilibrium is established. The question is usually not asked, nor can it be answered under the limiting micro-economic assumptions, into which industries the taxed firms or factors should move if all goods are taxed equally and hence there exists no untaxed or less taxed industry in which profits or factor payments would be higher. Whether the price will rise by the amount of the tax or by more or less will depend on the shape of the marginal or average cost curve and on the manner in which it is calculated (e.g. cost plus, etc.). Apart from minor modifications a general indirect tax will reduce supply and lead to a price rise and will thus be shifted to the consumer. A possible alteration or increase of monetary demand is not taken into account. In combination with the empirical observation that a larger part of lower than of higher incomes is spent on consumption, the effect of consumption taxes appears as strongly regressive.[8]

We have already suggested that the partial method is too limited to explain the incidence of such a tax satisfactorily. If, for example, a supplier of production factors or of consumer goods cannot avoid the taxation because tax free or tax favored sectors simply do not exist, the resulting incidence changes fundamentally. We shall discuss this later on. Right now we want to examine critically Due's explanation of, incidence which also amounts to forward shifting.

Due's Shifting Theorem. Due's view of incidence can be considered typical for all those incidence theories which on principle see the decisive factor for the possible or actual price increase (and thereby for the forward shifting of a general consumption or production levy onto the consumer) in the rising total monetary demand.[9] His argument, however, differs essentially in one point from the others. If we have understood Due correctly, his analysis is as follows: because of imperfections of the market, the sellers are able to raise the market price by the tax amount after first having felt out the market. The consumers are not in a position to raise their available income. Consumer credits remain implicitly excluded. With their constant money income consumers buy, therefore, the goods made more expensive by the tax but receive fewer than before. The sales shrink. This leads to under-employment. Government now intervenes into this regressive development, an idea which is peculiar to Due's theorem. Public expenditures increase to an extent which is sufficient to re-employ the factors which have been set free. Such an anti-depressive measure is only possible if monetary policy keeps the money supply so elastic that as the result of the credit expansion the market can be cleared even at the higher prices. Due's "trick" concerning business cycle policy excuses him from explaining why the government increases its indebtedness if it expects increased revenues, and above all, why it maintains the indebtedness. Further, an elastic monetary policy with decreasing sales, in spite of previous inflationary price increases, appears thus more understandable. According to Due the incidence of a general consumption tax falls entirely or, after modifications partially, on the consumer.

In his recent article "Sales Taxation and the Consumer,"[10] Due critically analyzes the studies of Buchanan, Musgrave, Rolph and Break on the shifting of a consumption tax.[11] He changes his own view on an important point, stating:

> Most analyses of (this) question (about the use of tax incidence and fiscal-monetary policy), including previous ones by the author, have failed to distinguish clearly between the pattern of burden distribution of various *types* of taxes and the consequences of deflation or inflation to which the tax may give rise if the *level* of the tax does not accomplish the desired economic result of offsetting the increase in factor demand caused by repeal of another tax or increased government spending. These are two distinct questions. Richard Musgrave recognized the problem but does not deal clearly with it.[12]

Musgrave's basic position is well known: the incidence of the sales tax compared to that of a proportional income tax depends upon the relative change in factor and commodity prices, rather than on the direction or the absolute change in prices. Thus the incidence is the same (under certain highly simplifying assumptions) whether consumption-goods prices rise relative to factor incomes or factor incomes fall relative to consumption-goods prices.[13]

To Buchanan's, Rolph's, and Break's basic question: Can increases in the general price level be attributed to taxes, Due replies: "Obviously the general price level cannot increase in response to a tax or anything else unless monetary adjustments take place."[14] This appears quite correct in an analytical sense but Delphic for practical purposes. Indeed, the hen-or-egg question causes the most trouble in empirical work.[15]

Backward Shifting to Factor Incomes. Let us now analyze the second extreme manner in which taxes may be shifted in a competitive economy. We refer to Matrix IV–3 where we concluded that lack of additional demand forces production enterprises to reduce factor remunerations rather than raise prices of goods. Which are the conditions for successful backward shifting?

Since we assume the national product to be constant, the entrepreneurs can neither lower their demand for factors nor reduce the price for these services under conditions of perfect competition in the supply markets. They therefore have the choice of either reducing the share of profits of the entrepreneurial income or raising the price of goods, while maintaining production.[16] Under conditions of perfect competition the latter possibility is excluded. Brown, Rolph,[17] and Musgrave[18] bypass the employment problem by assuming a perfectly inelastic supply of factors of production. Thus labor cannot reduce its supply with falling wages, because it now prefers more leisure. By means of this assumption the three authors succeed in maintaining the level of production despite reduced factor remunerations.

Let us investigate the possibility of (1) a falling profit, (2) a reduction of all factor prices and (3) a price increase under conditions of imperfect competition and constant aggregate supply. In Matrix IV–3 the income of the entrepreneurial households is reduced by 8. This reduction affects the entrepreneurial wages and interest as much as the residual risk premium, if the supply of entrepreneurship and of the factors of production is fixed. On the expenditure side, H_e may reduce either consumption or savings or both. The ultimate reduction depends to a large extent on the income (profit) elasticity of consumption and savings, if investor and saver are identical (as in a private company). It depends also on the propensity to invest which is sensitive to risk. Since all profits are cut in the same proportion, the *desire* to save need not be immediately affected. The more the tax-financed public expenditures take the place of the reduced entrepreneurial demand, both as to amount and composition, the smoother the adjustment which *ceteris paribus* is the same as in the case of a direct profits tax which cannot be shifted. The case of a consumption tax burdening profits becomes practically important if wages and interest for the savings of non-entrepreneurial households cannot be reduced and the prices of the taxed goods cannot be raised.

If the supply of labor and savings is completely inelastic, backward shifting of the revenue-reducing general consumption tax to the factors is successful. Theoretically, wages and interest would be reduced in the same proportion as in the case of a proportional income tax, leaving the relative position of both groups unaltered. In practice, enterprises will, in such a case, try to shift the largest part of the tax to wages. Let us assume that the factor yields are now divided into wages and interest on savings, that H and H_e receive incomes from these two sources and that the supply of savings and labor have different elasticities. In this case the relative position of those interest and/or wage and salary recipients improves whose supply of savings and/or labor is more elastic. This however means that the enterprises lower even further the remunerations of the factors of production whose supply is completely inelastic.[19]

But if the firms raise prices immediately because they have a monopolistic influence on the market, sales decline, depending on the price elasticity of demand and stocks increase as long as the money supply is constant. The government's tax-financed demand which sets in at the end of the first month is then not sufficient to get rid of stocks and current production at the higher price. The firms are therefore forced either to further curtail their liquidity or to borrow or to lower production. Only to the extent to which they finance the monthly tax additionally do they create the requirements for a final tax shifting. If the initial fall in sales discourages the firms so much that even the later demand of government has no effect, they will reduce their stocks immediately and below their normal level, and will reduce their production. Total output decreases until effective monetary demand can take up the supply at higher prices. Apart from the negative effects on employment and production, the consumers in this case bear the tax in proportion to their consumption expenditure, but only insofar as their consumption is reduced by the price increase. The fall of incomes as a consequence of shrinking production has nothing to do with shifting and incidence.

How realistic are these assumed reactions and the possible course of shifting? Can the proceeds of the factors of production be curtailed so easily and is this the actual direction of tax shifting, as Brown and Rolph maintain without qualification?

The Brown-Rolph Theorem. Brown and Rolph's analysis of the incidence of a general as well as a specific consumption tax completely contradicts traditional doctrine.[20] Both hold the obviously extreme view, that these taxes would be shifted from the tax paying enterprises to the factor owners, but not at all to the consumers; that they are not inflationary but on the contrary deflationary or anti-inflationary. Brown proves his thesis by starting from the assumption that with actual production conditions, demand structure of the private and public sectors and distribution of the financial means among the income groups, any general and uniform production and consumption tax initially would curtail the revenue of the enterprises by the reduced unit profit. Like the traditional theorists Brown furthermore assumes that the reduced profits would cause firms to make an adjustment by lowering production. According to Brown the firms do not move to less taxed branches of the economy, but reduce their demand for factors of production. Their planned demand for factor services depends on the marginal value product of each factor which in turn depends on the sales price of the goods produced. The tax is injected between marginal and average cost on one side and the market price on the other.[21] It lowers the unit profit. Because demand has decreased, the factor owners can only obtain a lower price on the goods market, which again results in a fall of the remuneration for their productive services. Since it has been explicitly assumed that the supply of factors is fixed, the price effects on the supply of labor, that is, the substitution of leisure for work is excluded. The incidence, therefore, is borne by the factors. According to this theory, the general consumption tax is shifted backward. It changes absolutely or relatively neither the price of commodities nor the structure of supply. The incidence of this tax is therefore similar to that of a proportional income tax.

Rolph has supplemented Brown's thesis by saying that under conditions of perfect competition, the suppliers could not just set the price tentatively higher because suddenly everybody was legally obliged to pay taxes. This argument deserves unqualified agreement but it cannot be used against traditional incidence theory because the traditional theory assumes as a rule an adjustment of quantity to price. He has also tried to strengthen the Brown theory of an anti-inflationary effect of any general consumption tax system with a model of the

Robertson type. We shall reproduce it here in order to discuss it critically.

Rolph starts from a deficit budget "since this state of affairs is typical of the times" (which in our opinion is not always correct)[22] to counter the view, that a tax theory is forced to start from a balanced budget. In turn a general system of a uniform consumption tax is introduced with the following monetary effects:[23]

TABLE IV–2

Monetary Effects of a General Excise Tax under Inflationary Conditions

	PERIOD 0		
Consumption expenditures	125	Private money income before tax	200
Private investment	25	Government income*	40
Government expenditures	50	Private money income after tax	160
Net value product	200	Total income	200
	PERIOD I		
Consumption expenditures	134	Private money income before tax	210
Private investment	26	Government income	50
Government expenditures	50	Private money income after tax	160
Net value product	210	Total income	210
	PERIOD II		
Consumption expenditures	134	Private money income before tax	210
Private investment	26	Government income	50
Government expenditures	50	Private money income after tax	160
Net value product	210	Total income	210

* Government income is a net conception, government transfer payments to private groups being thought of as deducted from tax revenue.

The budget in Period 0 with a net production of 200 has a deficit of 10. As full employment is assumed, every additional expenditure leads to a price rise. This occurs in Period 1 because private expenditures increase from 150 to 160 due to the budget deficit in the previous period. The uniform tax, introduced in Period 1 on all currently produced goods is anti-inflationary at the earliest in Period 2. In that period private consumption and investment expenditures no longer increase; without the taxation in Period 1 this would probably have happened as a consequence of the budgetary deficit policy. The tax has stopped the inflationary trend. Increasing the rates of a proportional income tax with the same tax yield would have the same result. ". . . excise taxes operate as deflationary influences for the same reasons as do income taxes; both act as negative influences on private demands for products as compared with less taxation."[24]

The deflationary effect can also be proved, according to Rolph, by a model with a balanced budget. If the budget in Period 0 is balanced, and if in Period 1 the tax is introduced then the private total demand in Period 2 will fall because the tax has lowered the private money income below that of Period 0. In this case "the paradox that excise taxes lower rather than raise prices would be illustrated."[25] But, unlike the first case, Rolph does not consider the compensating effects of public expenditures with regard to prices. Keeping to his model, we see the following interconnections:

PERIOD 0

Consumption expenditures	135	Private money income before tax	200
Private investment	25	Government income*	40
Government expenditures	40	Private money income after tax	160
Net value product	200	Total income	200

PERIOD I

Consumption expenditures	126	Private money income before tax	200
Private investment	24	Government income	50
Government expenditures	50	Private money income after tax	150
Net value product	200	Total income	200

PERIOD II

Same as Period I

In Period 1 private incomes are cut by 10 and public revenue increases correspondingly. As a result, private consumption decreases by 9 and private investment by 1 in favor of (unspecified) public expenditures of +10. Rolph sees exclusively the effects of decreased private total demand as compared to Period 1 but not the effect of public expenditures which have increased by the same amount. If there is no important lag between tax payment and expenditure and if the fall of private and rise of public expenditures are qualitatively identical—an assumption peculiar to all general incidence theories—the deflationary and inflationary price effects cancel out and there are no production effects. Here it must be stressed that since private investment decreased by 1 the potential supply of goods will fall at least for the next period unless public investment in the same amount does not compensate for the negative *growth effect*, which is improbable.

Far more important for our analysis of the course of backward shifting is to know why the factor remunerations are cut. Independent of the controversy about whether taxes should be treated as costs at all, we can state that the general consumption tax initially lowers the firms' revenues. According to the Brown-Rolph theory and based on the theory of marginal productivity the value of the marginal products of each factor falls. The firms tend to limit production and therefore proportionally reduce their demand for the productive services of the factors. This leads to a price reduction. The factor remunerations can, however, be decreased only if we assume a fixed supply or monopsony of the firms in the market. Only then is it possible to buy the same quantity of factor services at lower prices and so to maintain production and shift the tax completely to the factors. If the demanding enterprises have considerable influence on the factor markets or if the supply is completely fixed, the question arises why they have not taken advantage of their market power before in order to influence price earlier. If the number of firms is large however, it is *possible* that a tax which affects all demanders equally may induce them to come to an open or secret agreement and to act accordingly. In this case it is questionable whether, when faced with a consumption tax, they prefer a reduction of factor remunerations to an increase in consumer goods prices. In practice the most important factor market, the labor market, is hardly suitable for backward shifting. There are indeed professional groups who value the advantage of leisure resulting from a wage and salary decrease more than the income effect and therefore limit their labor supply. On the other hand there are also people who react inversely and work longer if their wage rate falls. But assuming full employment on the labor market, the union members are so strong that a wage reduction would be difficult to attain in practice. More likely is a dismissal of workers with unchanged wages. However, this makes the assumption of constant production untenable. Rolph offers the decrease of factor remunerations as the only solution, with the heroic assumption that factor supply is fixed. But in reality things are not so simple. The assumption of an inelastic factor supply in the long run seems untenable in the case of a partial consumption tax because the factors can move to untaxed areas.

In conclusion, a general consumption tax can only be shifted backward to the owners of factors of production if their supply is entirely fixed and the majority of the taxed enterprises chooses and attempts this direction of shifting. But if the factor supply is more or less elastic the prices and hence the factor incomes cannot be reduced as desired.

A cut in production is unavoidable. With different elasticities the relative marginal revenues will change in favor of the elastic factors and the income distribution will be altered. The production structure and in the long run also the growth of the social product will be affected.

While, therefore, the backward shifting of a general consumption tax depends mainly on the structure of the factor markets and the (mutual) behavior of supply and demand, the forward shifting presumes, aside from similar reactions of the taxable firms as to price increase and borrowing, a specific behavior of government as well as an elastic money supply if the shifting to the consumers is to be successful. The reduction of factor remunerations is actually a greater burden than the price shifting. And the affected groups are not identical. Finally, a shrinking of production and employment is possible. In this case, the smaller tax yield with smaller real social product rests either on the factor remunerations or on the consumers. Since forward and backward shifting require a more or less similar behavior of the taxed enterprises, the probable answer to the incidence of a general consumption tax depends less on the mixture of the two extreme directions of the shifting process than on the effect of forward or backward shifting on the reduction of production. To be sure, the final incidence can be measured independently of the initial price movement by the change of the income distribution by groups. Musgrave, in his criticism of the Brown-Rolph theorem emphasizes this, but since the adjustment takes time, the first step is nevertheless significant.

The Employment Effects and Incidence. Break thoroughly investigates the employment effects of a sales tax, especially the restoration of the pre-tax level of employment, which apparently can take place in three different ways: the unemployed workers may be hired (1) by government, (2) by investment-goods industries or (3) by consumer-goods industries.

The first possibility is ruled out for our purposes because it takes us away from tax incidence *per se*.

> Investment goods industries are subject to opposing influences as a result of the decline in the production and sales of consumer goods induced by the retail sales tax. On the one hand, the pretax level of private capital formation may appear less profitable now since it will continue to add to the economy's consumption-producing capacity, but on the other, the presence of unemployed resources will push wage rates and other costs downward, making an expansion in the output of investment goods more attractive. Private capital formation, then, may or may not rise as a result of the sales tax, but if it does, consumers in effect will have given up consumer goods and ser-

vices now in return for the prospect of a higher level of consumption in later years. Some people will undoubtedly be pleased with this tax-induced increase in the rate of economic growth, but others may be equally displeased. Whether on balance a net consumer benefit or a net consumer burden will have resulted cannot readily be determined. Needless to say, the occurrence of a net benefit would be a disconcerting outcome to confirmed advocates of the consumer-burden theory of sales tax incidence.[26]

The third possibility results in all unemployed resources being reabsorbed into the consumer goods sector. This will happen when factor incomes are reduced sufficiently to permit restoration of the pre-tax price level. The sales tax, in other words, first raises consumer goods prices by 10 per cent; this price rise then brings about unemployment and reduced output levels (given that consumer spending remains constant in money terms) and the owners of underemployed resources then gradually bid down wage rates and other cost prices until pre-tax prices and output levels are restored. All this may take place without altering the composition of consumption output, in which case the consumption tax simply lowers factor incomes but imposes no consumer burdens.

Non-Marginal Behavior. Most analyses of sales tax shifting are based on marginal behavior of the producers and consumers. In reality other attitudes seem to dominate. I have emphasized at the beginning of this chapter and again in chapter nine that short and long-run profit and benefit maximization is not the general rule in practice. Business men strive either after a satisfactory profit, or maximization of gross receipts subject to profit constraint or viability, or to enlarge their market share, or to apply the full cost principle. Somers has analyzed the shifting of a general sales tax under the assumption that the sellers aim at the highest turnover instead of maximum profit, being content with a constrained profit. He first deduces incidence on the assumption of sales maximization.

> The aim is presumably to keep sales receipts as large as possible net of the sales tax. We assume that the demand curve (based on total amount paid per unit) is the same as it was before and that the sales tax is a certain percentage of gross sales. Some price led to maximum gross sales before the tax was imposed. If the consumer continues to pay this amount per unit, the total amount received from him will continue to be the greatest. This conclusion is unchanged if a certain fixed percentage is taken from the gross amount received and designated "sales tax." Thus the gross receipts (either before or after tax) will continue to be maximized if the seller cuts the base price per unit by the full amount of the tax, i.e. absorbs the tax completely himself. In other words, if the business man were simply interested in max-

imizing gross sales (whether gross or net of tax) he would absorb the tax completely.[27]

What effects will the profit constraint have? This behavior might sharply cut into profits or might cause losses.

> If the seller was previously operating well within the profit constraint the conclusion just reached would not be upset: no new gross price (base price plus tax) would have to be charged and the seller would continue to bear the full burden of the tax. If the seller had been operating at or near the limits of the profit constraint he would have to give up somewhat the objective of maximizing gross sales. The result would be to absorb some of the tax and shift some of it to the consumer. Only in the most unusual circumstances would he shift all of it to the consumer. The general conclusion we derive is that the seller will absorb some or all of the sales tax under conditions of gross sales maximization subject to a profit constraint. The introduction of the assumption of maximization of gross sales has the effect of increasing the number of situations in which the seller will absorb the sales tax.[28]

The Result: Different Results. If we compare the different analyses, we see that the answer to the basic question apparently depends on the assumptions. Indeed, the imposition of a sales tax may result in an increased, unchanged, or even decreased price. The consumer may bear all, some, or none of the tax burden. Under certain conditions backward (and cross) shifting may be successful in charging the productive factors. And finally the change of the price (and output) level depends in general on the monetary policy the government pursues.

The more realistic the conditions assumed the more useful is the result. It seems that from this point of view a general sales tax is shifted in the initial phase at least partly to the buyer.

(b) *Who Bears the Value-Added Tax?*

Nature of the Tax. The base of a value-added tax is defined as the money value of goods and services produced within the business enterprise minus the money value of specified goods and services used up by the firm. The firm is the legal taxpayer. The tax is imposed on the value added by each business unit to a product as it passes through the successive stages of production from raw material to the final consumer.

The tax differs from a turnover tax by allowing a deduction for all purchases from businesses which were themselves subject to the value-added tax. It differs from a business income tax in that it includes in the tax base not only net income but all costs as well, except those consisting of payments for material, services, and capital equipment which have already been subject to the value-added tax.[29]

Forms of the Tax. The main problem in establishing a reasonable tax base arises in the treatment of capital equipment purchased from others and hence already subject to the value-added tax. As Smith correctly pointed out:

> to maintain tax neutrality between the use of direct labor and the use of machinery and other capital equipment, the tax included in purchases of machinery must be allowed as an offset against the tax on the output of the machinery, just as is the tax included in purchases of raw material or semi-finished goods. The question is whether to allow the deduction of the tax immediately or to require it to be amortized over the life of the capital equipment.[30]

As a consequence there are two types of value-added tax: the consumption type and the income type. Shoup describes both forms as follows:

> Under the (first) type of value-added concept the business firm subtracts from sales the cost of all capital equipment bought from other firms in the year of purchase. Under the (second) type of value-added concept the firm instead deducts depreciation year by year as the equipment is used up.
>
> Ultimately, the same total is subtracted from sales, but in the former case (deduction in year of purchase) value added is much smaller in the year of acquisition of the equipment and somewhat more in each of the subsequent years.[31]

Effects of the Tax. Opinions differ strongly on the effects of the variants of the value-added tax. While Due[32] suggests that both the consumption and income forms of the value-added tax should be regarded as sales taxes, since they produce the same general price effects as retail sales taxes, raising the prices of consumption goods relative to income received by factors, Eldridge[33] holds that the income variant of the value-added tax conceptually has results similar to a general, flat rate income tax, the consumption variant, effects similar to a general tax on all consumption items.

Under simplified conditions Eldridge's opinion seems to be right. As Due points out: "this approach is a consequence of similarity to the total bases under the two forms of value-added tax with a sales tax and an income tax, respectively. The total base of the consumption form is equal to that of a retail sales tax confined to consumption goods. The total base of the income form of value-added tax is equal to the sum of factor incomes."[34] In an all-consumption economy it makes no difference whether the value-added tax is the sales or income type. A proportional tax on factor income and a retail sales tax on all final products are equivalent, if we ignore institutional rigidities.

> In the actual economy, however, with savings, with a portion of output consisting of capital goods, and with significant rigidities in prices and noncompetitive markets, sales and income taxes are not identical, the price effects and influences on work incentives and on savings consumption incentives may be very different. Under such circumstances, a value-added tax may be appropriately classified as a sales tax or an income tax only on the basis of the price effects to which it gives rise. For this classification *an analysis of shifting of the tax is necessary.*[35]

The Shifting of the Tax. The value-added tax, like a general ad valorem tax on sales, is conventionally assumed to be shifted forward to the ultimate consumer via a rise in the prices of consumption goods. In the form of a retail tax it is the equivalent of a proportional spending tax collected directly from individuals on the basis of their consumption outlays.

The orthodox shifting process runs as follows:

> Under a purely competitive economic system, the tax will raise the marginal costs of private concerns, making some production unprofitable at current prices. To restore profits the entrepreneur reduces output, thus freeing resources for government use. Given the employment of these resources by the government and, therefore, probably the same aggregate demand for consumers' goods despite a smaller output, the average price level of consumers' goods will rise by the amount of the tax.
>
> Given pure competition and the condition that the consumers' goods industry is neither labor intensive nor capital intensive [Rolph, Stockfisch and Musgrave] largely substantiate the conventional position that the incidence is on the ultimate consumer.[36]

If we change the classical premises these results must be modified. Since we have examined the shiftability of a general consumption tax at length we will only deal with the particularities of this tax using Due's simple numerical example which applies to our three assumptions: (1) monetary policy permits the upward adjustment in the price level; (2) fiscal-monetary policy insures that aggregate real factor demand remains unchanged; and (3) competitive conditions and pricing policies are such as to permit direct adjustment in prices.

Due maintains, as do many other authors, that the value-added tax of the consumption type will increase commodity prices more or less, in the same fashion as a retail sales tax.

A retailer buys an item for $70 and sells it for $100, before tax. A 5 per cent value-added tax is introduced. The supplier now charges the retailer $70 plus $3.50 tax, separately invoiced. The retailer applies the 5 per cent tax rate to his $100 selling price and charges his customer $105. The retailer himself pays the government the $1.50 tax on the basis of this transaction, and has already had the $3.50 transmitted forward to him.

If the tax were applied to a calculated figure of value-added in each instance and were not separately invoiced, the retailer would pay $73.50 for the item (assuming a 5 per cent tax rate); he would apply a 5 per cent tax rate to his margin ($30), and add the $1.50 tax to the $73.50, thus charging his customer $105. But absorption of the tax element in the price might lessen uniformity in policy among competing firms. There is also the danger that the retailer would apply his markup to $73.50 instead of to $70, and thus charge the customer $106.50—provided competitors followed similar policies.[37]

Due investigates the shifting effects of a specific example of this tax type, as often suggested in the U.S. and used in France.

The vendor is authorized to deduct taxes paid on capital equipment and other items in addition to materials and goods sold. Thus the retailer does not owe to the government the amount calculated by applying the tax rate to the figure of taxable sales, less tax on these goods which has passed forward, but somewhat less to the extent of the total tax paid on purchases of capital equipment. In fact, were capital equipment purchases sufficiently great, the vendor might owe no tax at all.[38]

Thus the shiftability becomes more complicated especially when competing firms have differing ratios of purchases of capital equipment to taxable sales in a period.

It must be recognized, of course, that the firm is not receiving any sort of bonus because tax on capital equipment is deductible; tax is paid on the purchases of the equipment, and then is rebated by the deduction against the provisional tax due on sales. Thus there is not outright subsidy for investment at all; simply the tax penalty on investment which would occur if the deduction were not granted is avoided. But it is by no means obvious what the effect of this system on prices and burden distribution will be. If the firm regards the credit for this tax as merely a refund of tax paid on the purchases of capital equipment, the credit will have no influence at all. But if the vendor treats the tax on the purchase of capital goods as a portion of the purchase price of the capital goods and charges the entire sum to capital account, and then considers the tax on his sales to be reduced by the credit on capital goods purchases, he may reduce the amount of tax collected on his sales. Since the ratio of tax credit on capital goods purchases to sales of taxable goods will vary widely among individual firms, some firms may find it impossible to shift their entire tax liability if others adjust tax supplements downward because of the tax credit. With a retail sales tax with capital goods exempt, this phenomenon does not arise, since there is no tax credit which may be handled differently by various firms.[39]

Furthermore, Due examines the case where the tax is determined by applying the rate to the calculated figure of value added. How does the non-taxability of capital equipment purchases alter the incidence?

> The purchases, including the tax element, will be deducted from the figure of taxable sales to ascertain value added, on which tax is to be paid. Relatively large capital equipment purchases will, of course, reduce the tax due and the ratio of tax paid to taxable sales. If the firm considers the net tax rate, thus determined, as the figure to add to the selling price, the tax increases will be less for the rapidly expanding firms than for others, and shifting will be restricted. Thus, using the same example, the retailer buys the item for $70 plus $3.50 tax. He sells the item for $103.50 plus tax; if he applies the tax rate to the $30 value added, he will shift the exact amount of tax. But suppose that his total purchases of capital goods equal his total margin—to take an extreme example. He will owe no tax. Logically he should collect tax from his customers to reimburse himself for the tax shifted to him on his purchases of the capital goods. But, again, he may not do so; he may consider that he has no tax liability and thus adds nothing to prices, but charges the tax element in the purchase prices of capital goods to capital account. Thus, depreciation charges will be higher, and presumably prices will be higher in the future. It is impossible to predict whether this will occur or not; but the possibility must be noted.[40]

We turn now to the income type of a value-added tax.

Shoup,[41] Eldridge, and Musgrave[42] argue that this tax form causes the same effects as the proportional income tax. Since we will analyze the basic effects of income taxation in the next sections we discuss here primarily the assumptions of the following argument.

> Under the income form of value-added tax, a firm's investment costs are not deductible as incurred. They are written off in determining the annual tax base, as the investment is consumed in the process of production. The difference between receipts and payments to other firms (except for net investment) reflects all the costs of factor payments, including implicit costs of firm-owned factors and profits. The tax burden will tend to be spread evenly over all incomes derived from private production, in a manner similar to a flat-rate income tax on individuals. Since the tax has to be covered by firm receipts, prices of factors will be lowered relative to the prices of products. With uniform tax shifting, the relative reduction will be proportional for all income sources. All product prices, including capital goods, are affected proportionately, and there will be no change in alternatives available on the income uses side for individuals or households. For the whole private economy, the accounting for value added equals current value of total net product or total factor payments, or a tax base equivalent to total income after capital consumption allowances.[43]

The three assumptions of Eldridge's deduction are of dubious realism. We need to refer only to our basic critique on the extreme theorem of backward shifting. It is possible but not very realistic to assume that (1) the monetary policy will hinder an adjusting rise in the general price level and (2) factor (and commodity) prices are not rigid. As observations in all countries confirm, the decrease or a slower rise of wages (and other factor prices) is seldom if ever possible. (3) The same objection applies to the hypothesis that the interest costs of additional capital due to taxation are borne by the savers instead of the consumers. At least both backward *and* forward shifting of the extra costs may occur simultaneously, and after all we should not forget the third possibility, i.e. the failure of both reactions or direct incidence.

Most recently Oakland has published the results of his study on the incidence of a value-added tax.[44] He concludes that under any reasonable set of assumptions about shifting behavior, wages will fall and profits will rise in the short and long-run. The substitution of a value-added tax for a profits tax will have a regressive effect by increasing the degree of income inequality in both the short and the long run.

(*c*) *Incidence of a Net Receipt or Profits Tax*

As mentioned several times already the incidence of a profits tax may be similar to the unsuccessful forward shifting of the general consumption tax. Starting from Martrix IV–1 and enlarging the economic sectors by the capital-formation sector we get the following Matrix IV–5 which illustrates the incidence of a profits tax:

MATRIX IV–5

Incidence of a Profits Tax

output (sells) \ *input (buys)*	*P*	*H*	H_e	*Pr*	*G*	
P		148	16	4 + 6	16	190
H	150				10	160
H_e	40					40
Pr			4		6	10
G		12	20			32
	190	160	40	10	32	

The entrepreneurs pay the profit tax of 12 out of their incomes of 40. They curtail their demand for consumer goods (22) and their savings available for investments (10) each by 6. Government demand takes the place of demand of the entrepreneurs, by increasing its consumption and its saving (investment), also by 6 each. Since we disregard changes in the structure of demand, and since incomes and the demand of the private households remain at the same level, prices and sales are not affected. The incidence of a profits tax and its expenditure is measured by the decrease of the reduction in the nominal profits, which equal the reduction in real profits since all income groups have been proportionately cut. This behavior of the entrepreneurs is only one of several possible reactions:

If they are not willing to accept the fiscal burden of their profits they have different methods of shifting the tax. If they borrow or reduce their liquidity in order to maintain, at least in the short run, their standards of living and their investments, they thereby create, if unintentionally, the essential monetary precondition to pay the tax, namely additional purchasing power. The price shifting is on the average successful even under conditions of perfect competition, i.e. even when they have no direct influence on price. Aside from the same kind of behavior with regard to financing of the tax payments, the essential condition is full employment, when each increase of effective demand causes prices to rise. When monopolistic or oligopolistic competition prevails and the suppliers act similarly and jointly, by adding the profits tax to the price, the complete forward shifting succeeds only if the necessary credit expansion either of the government, the consumers, or the suppliers themselves occurs. If price shifting succeeds, their nominal profit is not affected. The real profit will be diminished and to this extent the suppliers bear a part of the tax. For the incidence of the spent profit tax rests with the higher prices on all consumers proportional to their expenditures. Government also bears the tax to this extent (namely with regard to its consumption in the amount of 6). Matrix IV–6 illustrates the complete forward shifting of the tax without a fall in production, which depends on a number of conditions which are not *automatically* given simultaneously. As to the propensities to consume and to save, saving by H_e (and H) becomes obviously more attractive in the case of a forward shifted profits tax. But this is only one side of the coin. Without money illusion households on the contrary will raise their consumption expenditures to maintain their standard of living. In

MATRIX IV–6

Forward Shifting of a Profits Tax

output (sells) \ *input (buys)*	*P*	*H*	H_e	*Pr*	*G*	
P		148	22	10 + 6	16	202
H	150				10	160
H_e	52					52
Pr			10		6	16
G		12	20			32
	202	160	52	16	32	

case of non-shifting, any change between savings and consumption depends on their profit (income) elasticity.

Shifting of a Proportional Income Tax. The shifting process can be explained easily by the results of our previous analyses based on a proportional 10 per cent income tax. We assume the government taxes the income by 20, of which H pays 16 and H_e pays 4. In order to exclude the factor transfer from the private to the public sector, which is of no interest for incidence and which has to be clearly separated from it (see Matrix IV–1) we assume that the government buys for 15 units consumption goods from P with its revenues and that it saves 5 which P invests; that before H_e has saved 8 and H 4 units from the available income and given to P for investment purposes. They have consumed the rest.

If H and H_e do not try to shift, the following changes have oc-

MATRIX IV–7

Proportional Income Tax before Taxation

output (sells) \ *input (buys)*	*P*	*H*	H_e	*Pr*	*G*	
P		156	32	12		200
H	160					160
H_e	40					40
Pr		4	8			12
G						
	200	160	40	12		

cured in the exchange between the sectors: All incomes of H and H_e are lower by 10 per cent (=20) and public revenue has risen by the same amount. While the consumption of H has fallen by 14 and the savings by 2 because of the lower net incomes, (income minus tax) the entrepreneurial households have cut their savings by 3 and their consumption only by 1. Since the use of public revenue is identical with what private households would have done with the income which they lost, changes in the structure of supply and in absolute and relative prices need not be considered. The income-expenditure incidence is distributed among all incomes proportionally.

If we examine the assumed and still possible behavior for its realism, we can state that generally, non-entrepreneurs are less able to shift the tax than entrepreneurs.

If the non-entrepreneurs borrow for consumption purposes or if they dissave because they do not wish to lower their living standards, they raise the effective total demand with the result that (a) prices and with them the profits of the entrepreneurs rise, favoring their shifting intentions and even promoting their own additional burden, or that (b) they set off an expansion in the case of an underemployed economy. In the latter case shifting is also not successful. To be sure, aggregate income increases because of increased employment but taxes also increase in proportion. If the individual taxpayer gets his available income up to where it was before taxation through more or more efficient activity, then we cannot talk *any longer* about a *shifting effect*.[45] He fully bears the tax in the original and the additional amount. Even an unconscious or unintentional financing of the wage tax by means of a credit is certainly not the rule. The behavior

MATRIX IV–8

Proportional Income Tax after Taxation

output (sells) \ *input (buys)*	*P*	*H*	*H_e*	*Pr*	*G*	
P		142	31	12	15	200
H	160					160
H_e	40					40
Pr		2	5		5	12
G		16	4			20
	200	160	40	12	20	

of the unionized workers, on the other hand, is more realistic: they will react to a noticeable tax which is felt to be unjust with wage demands, particularly when there is full employment. Such a reaction is even more to be expected, the sooner and the more spontaneously the entrepreneurs try to offset the tax by a price increase. Only if an energetic restrictive credit policy prevents all price increases or at least keeps them lower than the wage increases will the tax be shifted to H_e completely, or with relatively slight price increases, partially. Those persons whose incomes remain unchanged or lag behind (pensioners, civil servants) continue to bear the tax and in the case of price increases even bear the tax of other groups. The change of the real income distribution and thereby the incidence depends in this case essentially on the functioning of what we might call "the monetary shifting brake."

The possible strategies of the entrepreneurs in response to a profits tax have been discussed in the previous section.

3. The Shifting Process in an Underemployed Economy

If we alter model (b), namely, full employment of factors of production, the production effects of taxation which we have mentioned casually before have to be systematically included in the analysis of incidence. What is the shifting like under these realistic conditions of a more or less elastic aggregate supply in the short run when total income increases because of the forward shifting attempts? We start from Matrix IV–1 and observe the adjustments which take place between the beginning and the end of the process in order to indicate the incidence. If entrepreneurs finance their profit tax of 8 by credits and if they fully maintain their expenditures, the additional demand in the case of expanding employment and production leaves prices entirely or largely untouched, and it increases profits only relative to better performance by entrepreneurs. Under these conditions the shifting effect is nil and the production effect is 8. It is distributed among the groups engaged in the production according to their productive contribution.[46]

First, it takes time before the demand created by the credit-financed tax payments works itself out completely on the distribution, amount and growth of income and production. Secondly, in reality an expansion will lead to price rises when the economy is close to full employment and growth is unbalanced. This will be all the more so since taxation under conditions of imperfect competition induces frequently similar and common action with respect to prices (tax-induced collusion). If real social product increases, with rising prices —a process which is typical for the "normal" cyclical upswing—so that incidence and production effects are mixed, it is not easy to isolate the two groups of tax effects, particularly if we complicate matters by varying the assumptions.

The time sequences can be explained by means of multiplier analysis. Since in our example the entrepreneurs set off the multiplier process by borrowing and tax payments, the sequence is based on a *tax multiplier*, the so-called "instantaneous multiplier" so far assumed to be 1. That is, we compared the initial and final situations of the process which is indeed decisive for incidence. In a study of pure tax incidence obviously only this one is of interest and not the expenditure multiplier; although in our case of equal tax revenue and public expenditures ($T=G=T_r$), the multiplier of public expenditures has the same effect on the amount and distribution of real and aggregate income.[47] Even if the practical use of the multiplier principle in the fiscal field[48] has so far not been very fruitful and results discouraging, we shall include it in our analysis and not assume, as we did before, an instantaneous multiplier of 1.[49] We assume (Matrix IV–1) that the aggregate demand, which is now increased by 8, leads to a corresponding rise in income, i.e. by 6 for H, while the profits of the entrepreneurs increase by 2. The entrepreneurs pay a tax of 2 for the first payment period of 3 months which raises the national product and national income by the same amount, i.e. the profit by $\frac{2}{8}$ and the factor remunerations by $\frac{6}{8}$. If the entrepreneurs continue to finance the profits tax in the successive payment and income periods to the extent to which additional profits are not sufficient, then the increases in gross income of H and H_e as well as the taxes and credits will, over time, be a converging geometric series which approaches the following amounts as time approaches infinity.

$$\nabla He = 8 \qquad \nabla Y = 32$$
$$\nabla H = 24 \qquad \nabla K = 0$$
$$\nabla T_{He} = 8$$

The aggregate amounts with initial profit will approach the following levels:

$H_e = 48$ $T_H = 12$ (unchanged)
$H = 184$ $X = 232$

The following matrix illustrates results:

MATRIX IV–9

Production Effects of an Income Tax

output (sells) \ *input (buys)*	*P*	*H*	H_e	*G*	
P		172	40	10	222
H	174			10	184
H_e	48				48
G		12	8		20
	222	184	48	20	

If entrepreneurs are to pay the tax due in each period entirely with the additional profits and without credits—which is theoretically possible after infinite income and tax payment periods—income must increase to such an extent that the share of profit in the additional income equals the tax to be paid. If the taxes to be paid periodically are multiplied with the tax multiplier which, as the reciprocal of the share of profits in the additional income $(1 : \frac{2}{8})$ is 4, we get the final additional aggregate income of each period. If the expansion is 32, the entrepreneurs can pay a tax of 2 every 3 months or 8 per year, without lowering their initial profit.

It should be re-emphasized that these are pure production effects and not shifting and incidence. In addition, this analysis of the multiplier process neglects the taxing practice of calculating and assessing profits not by a fixed amount of the initial profit, but by a tax rate of current profits, here for the average of each period. Hence the additional profits are also taxed. In our example this means that a further increase in income and with it a change in the value of the multiplier k becomes necessary if net profits (gross profits less tax) are to remain unchanged. If, for example, profits are taxed progressively[50] because, say, increased profits are taxed with an excess profits tax of 50 per cent, the multiplier $k = 1 : \frac{2}{8}$ is replaced by $k = 1 : (\frac{2}{8} \times 1 - \frac{1}{2})$ $= 1 : (\frac{1}{4} \times \frac{1}{2})$.

4. Dynamic Incidence in a Growing Economy

As in other fields of fiscal theory, modern authors begin to combine tax effects with a view towards two or more policy objectives. In recent approaches (see chapters 6 and 8) we find a tendency to widen the scope of tax incidence analysis by including the production or efficiency effects of a tax in order to measure the total tax burden including the indirect burden as well as the tax burden of the non-taxed groups.

The tax impact on production and on growth factors is also considered, and instead of traditionally measuring the tax shifting by changes in *absolute* income, new indicators are introduced.

Krzyzaniak and Musgrave measure these types of tax effects by

(1) The rate of return on capital $Y_{x,T}$

(2) The gross share of capital $F_{x,T}$ and

(3) The net (after tax) share of capital in the value-added for private use $H_{x,T}$.

Other empirical concepts of relative income as shifting measures are: (1) the marginal product of capital in U.S. manufacturing industries (Hall); (2) relative factor prices and income distribution (Harberger, in analogy to the theory of international trade), (3) productivity (in a model of markup pricing behavior) as an input thus obtaining consistent tax shifting coefficients relative both to the corporate rate of return and the income share (Gordon), (4) the gross (before tax) rates of return in the U.S. of all manufacturing industries in the twenties and the early fifties (Lerner and Hendriksen) and (5) the changes in the share of U.S. capital in value-added over time (Adelman).

Musgrave and Krzyzaniak define their incidence indicators as follows:

$$Y_{x,T} = \frac{\pi_{x,T}}{K_{x,T}}, \; F_{x,T} = \frac{\pi_{x,T}}{Q_{x,T}}, \text{ and } H_{x,T} = \frac{\pi_{x,T} - R_{x,T}}{Q_{x,T} - R_{x,T}}$$

Then they define measures of tax effects on such variables by analogy to the proper measures of shifting $S_{\pi,T}$ and $S^{*}_{\pi,T}$, namely:

$$S_{Y,T} = \frac{Y_{x,T} - Y_{o,T}}{xY_{x,T}} \qquad S^{*}_{Y,T} = \frac{Y_{n,x,T} - (1 - x)Y_{o,T}}{xY_{o,T}}$$

$$S_{F,T} = \frac{F_{x,T} - F_{o,T}}{xF_{x\,T}} \text{ and } S^{*}_{H,T} = \frac{H_{x,T} - (1 - x)H_{o,T}}{xH_{o\,T}}$$

There is a valid interest in these measures per se.

Krzyzaniak shows in the following model that the approaches using factor shares as an indicator contain little or no information on shifting, while the rate of return gives this information but only for the long-run and only indirectly. In his model[51] Krzyzaniak uses the Cobb-Douglas production function and assumes: constancy of the propensities to save, investments equal the available funds ($S = I$); exogenous growth of the labor force; neutral technological progress and full employment. Propensities to save by businesses differ from those of other incomes. He then builds into the model a general tax on profits, the proceeds of which are invested in projects of no benefit to the people or the economy as a whole.

His model yields in the short-run the "neoclassical" solution. In the long-run, however, the tax affects new capital formation which in turn changes the after-tax incomes of the various groups. Thus for the long-run the incidence of a profits tax is reflected in tax-induced changes of real income variables.

The model reveals such changes. It is represented by the following four equations:

(1) $Q_{x,t} = e^{gt} K_{x,t}{}^{a} L_t{}^{b}$	production function
(2) $L_t = L_o e^{ht}$	growth of labor force
(3) $I_{x,t} = \dfrac{d K_{x,t}}{dt} = s_x Q_{x,t}$	available funds investment theory
(4) $s_x = bs_i + as_p(1 - x) + as_i(1 - s_p)(1 - x)$ (wages) (retained profits) (withdrawals)	average saving rate

As $a + b = 1$ the last equation may be rewritten

$$s_x = s_i + as_p(1 - s_i) - ax(s_p + s_i - s_p s_i)$$

Thus

$$s_o = s_i + a\, s_p(1 - s_i) \text{ and } s_x = s_o - a\, x(s_p + s_i - s_p s_i)$$

Krzyzaniak sees two ways of making his model more general. First, a different production function, for example of the CES-type could be used, but the results do not differ substantially. Second, the return to new investment could be considered as a determinant of investment. This should not affect the results substantially either. If the tax on profits is not shifted, both aggregate savings and the incentives to invest will decrease. Consequently on either count aggregate investment has to decline. Thus, despite two quite specific assumptions ($\sigma = 1$ and $I_{x,T} = s_x Q_{x,t}$) the results of his model are quite general.

To find the solution of his model Krzyzaniak considers $N_{x,t}$ the average product of capital

$$N_{x,t} = \frac{Q_{x,t}}{K_{x,t}} = e^{gt}\left(\frac{K_{x,t}}{L_t}\right)^{-b}$$

By integration and rearrangements he gets

$$N_{x,T} = (G_x)^{-1}N_{o,T},\ Q_{x,T} = (G_x)^{a/b}\,Q_{o,T,\pi x,T} = a(G_x)^{a/b}\,Q_{o,T},\ \text{and}\ K_{x,T} = (G_x)^{1/b}K_{o,T}$$

Table IV–3 contains the values of stationary variables at impact ($T = O$) and in the long run, the measures of long-run shifting and of tax effects on relative income variables and the ratios of the tax burdens.

Krzyzaniak illustrates the measures and relative tax burdens numerically with "realistic" values of the parameters. The results are somewhat surprising. The real income position of capital owners has deteriorated. They not only pay the tax at impact and in the short-run; they additionally suffer another 51 cents loss for each dollar paid to the Treasury. Thus the resulting value of the shifting measure is no longer zero but turns negative.

Another surprise is the result that the global tax burden is approximately 2.7 times the tax revenue (direct burden). Unexpectedly the tax does not strongly curtail new capital formation or lower future incomes. Nearly 44 per cent of the tax burden falls on wage earners (i.e. on the rest of the population) who suffer a decrease in real wage rates compared with the pre-tax rates. Though the tax has been imposed on capital owners, it becomes widely diffused in the economy, falling heavily on other groups in the society as well.

II. *Tax Distribution by Social Groups: Sociological Incidence*

When discussing the measurement of incidence (chapter 2) as well as in our System of Fiscal Policy, we distinguish six types of individual and group incidence. Having dealt, in the preceding section, with functional and personal incidence, we turn to specific problems of sociological tax distribution followed by sectoral, geographical, and inter-temporal incidence.

Since in reality no social groups correspond to functional income

TABLE IV–3

Long Run Shifting and Relative Burden of a Profits Tax

Variables in the Long-Run

Effective saving rate on total income		Average product of capital		Gross rate of return on capital		Gross share of capital		Net share of capital		
in absence of tax	*with tax*	*in period zero*	*long-run, with tax*	*in period zero*	*long-run, with tax*	*in period zero*	*long-run, with tax*	*long-run, in absence of tax*	*in period zero*	*long-run, with tax*
s_0	s_x	$N_{0,T} = N_{x,0}$	$N_{x,T}$	$Y_{0,T} = Y_{x,0}$	$Y_{x,T}$	$F_{0,T} = F_{x,0}$	$F_{x,T}$	$H_{0,T}$	$H_{x,0}$	$H_{x,T}$
$s_i + as_p(1 - s_i)$	$s_0 - ax[s_p + s_i - s_p s_i]$	$\frac{[(g/b) + h]}{s_0}$	$\frac{[(g/b) + h]}{s_x}$	aN_{x0}	$aN_{x,T}$	a	a	a	$\frac{a(1 - x)}{1 - ax}$	$\frac{a(1 - x)}{1 - ax}$

Long-Run Measures[1] *of Shifting and of Tax Effects on Relative Income Variables*

$S_{\pi,T}$	$S_{Y,T}$	$S_{F,T}$	$S^*_{\pi,T}$	$S^*_{Y,T}$	$S^*_{H,T}$
$\frac{1}{x}[1 - (G_x^{-a/b})]$	$\frac{1}{x}[1 - G_x]$	0	$\frac{1-x}{x}[(G_x)^{a/b} \sim 1]$	$\frac{1-x}{x}[G_x^{-1} - 1]$	$\frac{a(1 - x)}{1 - ax}$

[1] These measures collapse to the short-run by setting $G_x = 1$.

The Relative Tax Burdens

On investors	On recipients of wages	On the whole population	On investors	On recipients of wages
relative to the direct tax burden			*relative to the global tax burden*	
$\frac{B_{c,x,T}}{R_{x,T}} = \frac{[1 - (1 - x)G_x^{a/b}]}{xG_x^{a/b}}$	$\frac{B_{w,x,T}}{R_{x,T}} = \frac{b[1 - G_x^{a/b}]}{axG_x^{a/b}}$	$\frac{B_{x,T}}{R_{x,T}} = \frac{[1 - (1 - ax)G_x^{a/b}]}{axG_x^{a/b}}$	$\frac{B_{c,x,T}}{B_{x,T}} = \frac{a[1 - (1 - x)G_x^{a/b}]}{[1 - (1 - ax)G_x^{a/b}]}$	$\frac{B_{w,x,T}}{B_{x,T}} = \frac{b[1 - G_x^{a/b}]}{[1 - (1 - ax)G_x^{a/b}]}$

distribution, wage, rent, interest, and profit, the distribution by sociological criteria is of specific interest for policy. Besides his wage a worker may earn interest, rent, and even profit, and a pensioner may receive more interest and dividends than pension (transfer payments), i.e. functional and sociological income distributions differ.

Obviously there are numerous criteria according to which we may reasonably characterize and form social groups, for instance, the distribution pattern of income by males and females, active and inactive population, rural and urban population, households of workers and of employees, lower, middle and upper classes, labor and independent professions, married and unmarried persons, or race or religion. However, it is often difficult to find relevant data for empirical studies on sociological tax incidence.

While theorizing on the actual tax incidence of such social groups is insufficient, our insight and knowledge of formal (intended) incidence is much better. Three German studies on the sociological incidence of the national tax structure are available.[52] Though their procedures differ, their results are rather similar.

Table IV–4 indicates the intended (formal) distribution of taxes among four social groups on the rough assumption that direct taxes, including social insurance taxes, are borne by the taxpayers and all indirect taxes are fully shifted. The pensioners pay only 5 per cent of the direct taxes but contribute 19.5 per cent of the indirect taxes to the public budget. Altogether, their share in the tax yields is 11.7 per cent, one third of the workers' contribution. If we compare the payments to social insurance (positive tax) with the disbursements (negative tax) we measure the formal *tax-transfer incidence* leaving the resource transfer from the private to the public sector constant. This concept of net redistribution indicates, for the pensioners group, 67.7 minus 6.5, while the net result for the wage earners is 20.2 minus 51.1, i.e., a negative effect. Column five which shows the social security transfer indicates a sharp progression in favor of the pensioners.

III. *Intersectoral Shifting and Incidence*

A tax budget policy which is directed only towards *one* economic sector, will nevertheless affect the other sectors of an interdependent system directly and indirectly. The relative positions of most, and if

TABLE IV–4

Percentage of Taxes, Contributions to Social Insurance and Social Services Paid by Social Groups, Federal Republic of Germany, 1960

Social Group	*Direct Taxes*	*Contributions to Social Insurance*	*Indirect Taxes*	*Government Revenue (total)*	*Expenditure for Social Insurance*
I. Households headed by wage earners	21.2	51.1	32.0	36.4	20.2
II. Households headed by salary earners (including civil servants)	22.0	34.4	24.1	27.3	7.4
Total I. and II.	43.2	85.6	56.2	63.7	27.6
III. Households headed by self-employed	51.8	7.9	24.3	24.6	4.7
Total I.–III.	95.0	93.5	80.5	88.3	32.3
IV. Households headed by pensioners	5.0	6.5	19.5	11.7	67.7
Total I.–IV. in %	100	100	100	100	100

the tax is important, of all sectors of the economy will change via price adjustments.

Specific incidence is irrelevant for sectoral shifting in the real world. If income and production of one sector are changed, economic policy is primarily interested in the case in which a tax is imposed on the output of one industry and the proceeds are used to subsidize the output of another industry. An ideal example is the German tax policy which discriminates against the oil and fuel industry in favor of the coal mines. Though subsidies to certain branches formally increase public expenditures, we can consider this a special case of differential tax incidence because we have to deal only with transfer payments, while leaving the factors of production of the subsidized sector untouched. Just as in the case of a tax substitution, the tax payers of one industry lose what others gain.[53] Subject to this limitation sectoral incidence has a place in this book. It differs from the result of cross shifting or inter-market incidence.

In considering the global effects of the budget on the economy we evidently disregard the indirect effects caused by the specific structure of the economic system. "These indirect effects can be very important; if we extend our attention to them, the budget composition, other than the budget level, becomes relevant for economic policy decisions. We can find that, in order to attain the same objective of economic policy, the budget level *and* its composition may be very different from the budget level required when considering only the aggregate direct effects."[54]

In order to get more precise results than those obtained by the aggregate approach to the problems of fiscal policy, we can use a static multi-sector model of the Leontief type.[55] This basic system permits us to analyze all direct and indirect effects (i.e. the results of fully or partly successful forward, backward or cross shifting) by comparing the final intersectoral distribution with the initial or intended distribution.

For the sake of brevity we will use Pedone's simple multisector model:

> Let (a) be the matrix of input-coefficients, whose element a_{ij} is equal to x_{ij}/X_j, where x_{ij} is the amount of commodity i used in the total production of commodity j, $X_j \cdot X$ is the column vector of production levels, whose element X_i represents the periodic rate of total output of industry i. Y is the column vector of final demands, whose element Y_i represents the amount of product i made available for "external demand" or final use; I is, as usual, the identity matrix and P the price vector.
>
> Let us indicate the technical input matrix by $(I - a) = \Delta$, and the recip-

rocal matrix by $(I-a)^{-1}=R$. L is the total amount of labor available in the economy, is the vector of labor coefficients, and w is the wage rate. We assume that $(I-a)$ is a Leontief matrix, i.e. $\sum_j a_{ij} \leqq 1$ and $a_{ij} \geqq 0$, and that (a) possesses the Mosak-Metzler properties, i.e. $a_{ii} > 0$, $a_{ij} \leqq 0$, and $Y_i > 0$.

The equilibrium production relations of the model then are $X = RY$, and the equilibrium price relations are $P = Pa + lw$. If we assume that labor is the only primary input of the system, and if we put $w = l$, then we can express the price relations in terms of labor, $P = RL$.[56]

If we tax one sector in favor of others, the effect depends largely upon two factors:[57] (1) the importance of the taxed and subsidized goods in the production of other goods and of the latter commodities in the production of the taxed and subsidized commodities, (2) the ability of producers and consumers to change the proportions in which they purchase various goods in response to the changing structure of prices. One of the assumptions evidently limits the results of the model, namely, that relative price changes do not immediately alter the proportions of inputs required to produce a certain good nor affect the composition of consumption.[58] Even under this and the other highly simplified assumptions,[59] it is difficult to find out how prices in the model will be affected by a combined tax- and-subsidy program. In a competitive system budget policy will alter the price of each commodity to the extent that the new price will be equal to the average cost of production plus the tax or less the subsidy in the involved sectors. But we should consider this *prima facie* result skeptically and cautiously, because the combined effects of all these interdependent price movements are often quite complex. Metzler, for example, considers the effect of the tax-and-subsidy upon the price of the *taxed* commodity:

> In the new position of equilibrium, after all prices have been adjusted to the tax-and-subsidy, the price of the taxed commodity must of course exceed cost of production by the amount of the tax per unit, and this suggests superficially that the tax-and-subsidy will increase the price of the taxed good. Suppose, however, that the taxed commodity is one which requires a substantial amount of the subsidized commodity in its output. If the price of the subsidized commodity falls as a result of the new fiscal arrangements, the cost of production of the taxed commodity will thereby be reduced, and the question arises as to whether this secondary effect upon the price of the taxed article may not be more important than the primary effect of the tax itself.[60]

From this we obtain an unexpected result: The price of the taxed good may fall because the secondary decrease of its cost of production exceeds the amount of the tax itself.

The price of the *subsidized* good and service, too, will be subject to primary and secondary effects. Though a subsidy[61] initially will reduce the price of the commodity, "a secondary rise in cost of production could exceed the amount of the subsidy and, as the consequence, the combined effect of the tax-and-subsidy might be a rise in the price of the article subsidized."[62] The main effects could be easily shown in the model:

If a tax (of unit amount τ) on commodity h and a subsidy (of an equal unit amount σ) on commodity m are introduced, and the whole tax subsidy operation is indicated by T, the variation in the price of any commodity i ($i = 1, 2, ..n$) will be equal to: $\frac{dP_i}{dT} = R_{hi} - R_{mi}$. Extending this result to the case of taxes and subsidies on many goods, and of a tax rate τ different from the subsidies rate σ, we get the variation in the price of any commodity i from the following formula (where the subscript h indicates the taxed goods, and the subscript m indicates the subsidized goods):

$$\frac{dP_i}{dT} = \sum_h R_{hi}\tau_h - \sum_m R_{mi}\sigma_m.$$

It can be easily seen that—since R_{ji} is the element in the *j-th* row and in the *i-th* column of the inverse matrix of $(I\text{-}a)$, and it represents the total amount of commodity j used, directly or indirectly, in sector i—the effect on the price variation of commodity i of an equal tax (or subsidy) rate will be different according to the value of R_{hi} (or R_{mi}). If, in the equation that gives us the price variation of any commodity i, the value of some R_{hi} (or R_{mi}) is equal to zero, it means that the commodity h (or m) does not enter (directly and indirectly) in the process of production or commodity i. Consequently, a tax levied on sector h (or a subsidy paid to sector m) will have no influence on the price of commodity i.[63]

The effects of the budget policy will depend, as we have pointed out, largely upon the importance of the tax-and-subsidy program and upon the degree of the interdependence among the productive sectors.[64]

In these specific relations the classification into basic and non-basic commodities is most important. Non-basic products such as most public expenditures will not influence the price relation of the other goods. If, e.g., an invention halves the amount of productive factors needed to produce a commodity, the price of the good tends to fall, but without further consequences. In the case of a basic good, all other prices and the rate of profit would be affected.

The distinction is most important if we trace the sectoral effects of the budget in a growing economy. Such multi-sector growth models are production-maximizing growth models.[65]

Pedone concludes that taxes and expenditures influence the growth rate in four ways:[66]

(1) If the tax or budget policy changes the sectoral distribution, the effects on the growth rate depend upon the initial situation of the basic system. Only if the basic system has not yet attained the maximum equilibrium growth, will the fiscal measures increase the rate of growth;[67] otherwise the budget will cause a decrease in the growth rate.

(2) When the budget causes a shift of resources from the basic to the dependent sub-systems, it will necessarily cause a decrease in the growth rate if the basic system had originally reached maximum equilibrium growth. On the contrary, the decrease in the growth rate cannot occur if the basic system had not originally reached its maximum equilibrium growth, because in this case the withdrawal of resources from the basic system could be such as to leave the remaining resources in the proportions required by the technology prevailing in the basic system.

(3) When, on the other hand, the budget is used to move resources from the dependent sub-systems to the basic system, this will not cause any change in the growth rate if the basic system was originally in an equilibrium situation. On the contrary, the shift of resources carried out through the budget may have a positive influence on the total amount of surplus obtained in the basic system, if this shift makes possible an increase in the level at which productive processes are conducted in the basic system.

(4) Finally, when the budget influences the distribution among the different sub-systems (or among the sectors of one sub-system) the growth rate of the economic system will remain the same; the only consequence of the budgetary action will be the changes of prices, of intensities and of the expansion rate of the sectors directly affected by the budgetary action (and of those other sectors tied to them by productive relations).

IV. *Geographical Tax Incidence*

In the last decade tax incidence on both the regional and international level has become the favorite object of many theoretical and empirical studies. International tax shifting, for a long time a neglected step-child of both fiscal and international trade theory, has become the center of interest in many intellectual contributions in the field of European, African, and Latin American economic integration.[68] In attempts to create the framework of a comprehensive theory of fiscal and tax harmonization, national and international tax shifting is of great importance. Can taxes be exported at all? If they can, how are international trade and regional or national production and income distribution affected?

1. Interregional Aspects

In the growing literature on fiscal federalism the shifting of state and local taxes from residents to non-residents of the taxing region has received increasing attention.[69]

In principle we have to deal with two cases: (1) The effects of a uniform taxation upon industrial location. Without knowledge of the local tax incidence assessment of this influence is impossible. (2) The regional tax shifting in a federal system in which governmental units independently tax their residents and have their own revenue sources.

Albers examines differential incidence substituting a proportional and progressive income tax for a general consumption tax and a tax on productive factors respectively.[70] He compares the effects on the economic location in the taxing state concluding that there is no neutrality of tax and fiscal policy with regard to the allocation of economic activities and industries.

McLure recently has published the most comprehensive study of the second type of regional incidence. His method to estimate the interstate exporting of state and local taxes is derived from the procedure used by Musgrave and others in their investigations of incidence.

> It consists in using insights gained from theoretical analysis of tax incidence in open economies to allocate each tax to the consumer and producer groups likely to bear it and then imputing the part falling on each group to the states of residence of the members of the group. The portion of the tax not borne by residents of the taxing state may be said to be exported.

He illustrates this method by a brief consideration of the incidence of a tax levied upon the production of a given article in one state.

> If firms located in the taxing state face competition from untaxed firms located in other states, they have no alternative, at least in the short run, but to absorb the tax in the form of reduced factor earnings, most likely from

the earnings of capital. But this information is not enough; the state of residence of the owners of the factors whose incomes are reduced must also be known, so that the tax can be allocated between residents and non-residents of the taxing state.

On the other hand, if the tax were reflected in higher prices of products and therefore borne by consumers, it would be essential to know the state of residence of purchasers of the taxed item. Finally, for those parts of taxes ultimately borne by satutory taxpayers or by business firms, allowance must be made for the fact that most state and local taxes may be deducted by individuals in computing their liability under the federal personal income tax and that all expenses, including taxes, may be deducted by business firms in computing their income tax liabilities. To the extent of these offsets against the federal income taxes, state and local taxes are exported to the federal government.[71]

McLure defines tax exporting as the loss in real income suffered by non-residents of the taxing state; the incidence of state and local taxes is the change in the interstate distribution of income available for private use as a result of these taxes. He restricted his study to the immediate tax effects upon real incomes via changes in the prices of factors and products most directly affected by the tax, i.e. backward and forward shifting.

In order to measure or estimate tax exporting two concepts have been developed. According to one view, called the Michigan approach

the taxes of all other states are assumed to be of no consequence, or at least of no more consequence than any other condition beyond the control of the taxing state. In employing this approach the analyst ignores completely all taxes except those of the state under consideration. In this analysis the possibility of competition in product and factor markets from firms located outside the state and therefore not subject to the tax becomes crucial. The geographic extent of the product market, the taxing state's position in that market, and the interstate mobility of factors are important determinants of incidence.

The other view is called the Wisconsin approach. To estimate the export of any one state's taxes, the taxes of all states are taken into account, since the incidence of taxes levied in one state is not independent of the pattern of taxation in other states.

Because taxes in all states are considered together, the analysis resembles much more closely the analysis for a closed economy, except that differentials above the level of taxation common to all states are treated in a manner similar to the Michigan approach's treatment of the entire tax. This means that the interstate competition and factor mobility that are crucial in the Michigan approach are only secondary in this approach. Moreover many taxes are likely to be assumed shifted forward under this approach, while under the Michigan approach capitalization is likely to be thought an important phenomenon.[72]

If states levy their taxes while considering more or less what other states do, the Wisconsin approach is useful. If on the other hand each state determines its tax policy independently the Michigan approach seems more appropriate.

Without criticizing McLure's assumptions and his method of analysis we can add the results of the estimates based on the Michigan approach and summarized in Table IV–5. It indicates the export rates of the most important taxes in the short-run (S.R.) and in the long-run (L.R.).[73] (Delaware is the largest and Vermont the smallest of tax exporters).

2. International Problems

Incidence in the Controversy over the Destination versus Origin Principle: General Aspects. Specific tax structures affect international trade by distorting national price systems, thus disturbing optimization of international trade. The destination principle attempts to compensate for these distortions by specific methods of tax adjustment.[74] GATT has sanctioned it in 1947, limiting tax policy to indirect taxation. Both the Tinbergen Report[75] and the Neumark Report[76] support the traditional arguments in favor of the destination principle.

If we accept the results of classical shifting theory, the arguments of the destination principle seem to be obvious. Indirect taxes are shifted; direct ones are not; *ergo,* a country with a comparatively high quota of indirect taxes is disadvantaged in the competition on the world market. Its high indirect taxes "inflate" its prices. If we accept, however, other degrees of tax shifting and other directions, the arguments in favor of the destination principle become weak. Bombach, for instance, argues, using a model based on Kaldor's distribution theory, that the type of tax has no influence on the shifting process.[77] Thus the origin principle, though not ideal, is to be preferred because its distortion effect is zero. Indeed, the validity of both principles depends mainly on the tax incidence.

In recent years two studies have been made to find out the factors which determine incidence in open economies. Parks intends to prove that domestic tax shifting is influenced by the prices of foreign competitors.[78] His method is similar to the theory of comparative costs since tax incidence cannot be divorced from international costs and prices. He examines the effects of business and consumption taxes as well as those of personal and property taxes. Besides differences in tariffs and quotas, national tax structures and other obstacles to free

TABLE IV–5

Estimated Export Rates, by States and Type of Tax, 1962
(percent)

State	General Retail Sales and Gross Receipts Taxes S.R. (a)	General Retail Sales and Gross Receipts Taxes L.R. (b)	Selective Sales, Miscellaneous and License Taxes S.R. (c)	Selective Sales, Miscellaneous and License Taxes L.R. (d)	Corporation Income and Franchise Taxes S.R. (e)	Corporation Income and Franchise Taxes L.R. (f)	Total All Taxes S.R. (g)	Total All Taxes L.R. (h)
Alabama	22.5	20.2	17.9	16.8	78.4	45.9	23.4	19.4
Alaska	22.7	20.9	14.6	14.0	72.3	48.7	21.2	18.8
Arizona	25.7	24.8	20.6	18.1	68.8	49.2	27.6	24.5
Arkansas	23.0	20.6	19.3	17.7	76.7	45.4	24.1	20.2
California	27.2	24.9	17.6	17.1	70.0	46.1	23.5	19.7
Colorado	23.0	21.4	18.9	18.4	69.3	48.0	22.4	19.0
Connecticut	24.5	22.8	21.8	19.7	87.6	52.6	26.0	20.4
Delaware	—	—	24.0	22.5	91.0	81.9	37.9	34.6
District of Columbia	31.6	30.5	19.2	18.1	—	—	18.0	17.3
Florida	27.4	25.9	20.6	19.1	—	—	20.2	13.8
Georgia	23.6	21.3	16.8	15.8	72.4	48.3	23.8	19.0
Hawaii	27.3	23.0	26.8	23.7	69.8	50.0	25.4	22.0
Idaho	—	—	17.1	15.8	75.6	47.5	24.0	19.8
Illinois	28.0	25.0	20.7	18.6	—	—	25.3	20.7
Indiana	14.9	11.0	17.2	16.3	—	—	23.3	17.2
Iowa	23.3	20.6	19.2	17.8	73.7	45.4	21.1	17.1
Kansas	22.6	20.8	16.8	16.4	77.8	45.9	23.0	19.3
Kentucky	24.5	21.2	16.1	14.8	79.6	45.2	25.1	19.9
Louisiana	23.9	21.7	15.1	13.7	77.3	47.0	31.7	26.6
Maine	24.7	20.0	20.1	18.2	—	—	19.6	15.1
Maryland	24.3	21.7	16.2	14.4	75.2	46.4	23.7	20.6
Massachusetts	—	—	20.4	20.4	72.9	45.9	22.1	17.1
Michigan	23.9	21.7	20.0	19.5	76.9	44.7	29.4	21.4
Minnesota	—	—	17.7	15.7	73.6	47.7	24.3	19.3
Mississippi	22.6	20.8	19.0	17.7	76.0	45.7	24.5	20.3
Missouri	22.6	20.1	17.1	15.3	74.4	49.5	20.5	17.7
Montana	—	—	17.0	15.3	71.8	48.1	24.5	22.0
Nebraska	—	—	17.5	17.5	—	—	18.6	17.3
Nevada	33.4	31.2	44.7	44.1	—	—	36.3	34.9
New Hampshire	—	—	22.9	21.5	—	—	18.3	15.8
New Jersey	—	—	21.2	19.4	87.0	52.0	24.4	18.6
New Mexico	21.2	20.3	18.2	17.2	64.8	50.7	23.6	21.0

TABLE IV–5 (*Cont.*)

State	*General Retail Sales and Gross Receipts Taxes* S.R. (a)	L.R. (b)	*Selective Sales, Miscellaneous and License Taxes* S.R. (c)	L.R. (d)	*Corporation Income and Franchise Taxes* S.R. (e)	L.R. (f)	*Total All Taxes* S.R. (g)	L.R. (h)
New York	28.9	25.0	20.6	19.1	76.0	54.3	23.8	20.0
North Carolina	22.7	20.8	21.9	19.1	89.2	50.6	27.8	21.4
North Dakota	20.0	18.4	15.7	14.2	60.7	51.2	20.0	18.5
Ohio	22.7	21.0	22.7	19.8	77.6	44.9	25.3	19.5
Oklahoma	21.9	21.1	21.0	19.6	60.7	46.4	24.9	22.4
Oregon	—	—	21.6	19.9	71.5	47.6	23.8	19.3
Pennsylvania	22.2	20.7	17.1	15.7	71.7	45.0	23.9	19.3
Rhode Island	25.4	21.7	14.3	17.7	87.4	53.4	25.7	19.4
South Carolina	21.4	19.4	15.4	13.4	80.1	44.4	26.8	19.4
South Dakota	19.3	18.6	18.8	18.2	—	—	17.0	16.3
Tennessee	23.7	21.4	20.8	18.2	76.5	45.0	24.9	20.2
Texas	24.9	22.4	19.1	16.6	73.7	47.0	34.1	28.5
Utah	21.7	20.0	18.8	17.9	72.5	47.4	23.9	20.5
Vermont	—	—	17.8	16.2	76.2	44.2	18.4	15.2
Virginia	—	—	14.3	12.2	74.8	47.0	19.8	16.4
Washington	22.2	18.5	16.2	13.8	—	—	20.1	16.4
West Virginia	25.6	20.6	17.4	16.6	—	—	24.3	20.1
Wisconsin	22.0	20.1	16.9	14.6	77.1	44.8	24.7	17.7
Wyoming	20.1	19.3	22.6	21.0	—	—	25.8	23.3

trade also bear directly on the degree of competition, and accordingly, on tax incidence.

The purpose of McLure's analysis is more ambitious.[79] He measures tax exporting by the allocation of income loss between regions or countries resulting from retail sales and production taxes. He restricts himself to a partial equilibrium analysis such as is dealt with in chapter 5. While traditional theory focused primarily upon the effect of taxes on expenditure or price he is concerned with their influence on income sources or factor incomes, since they are no longer neutral when geographical incidence is examined.

In principle, tax shifting ultimately depends upon the elasticities of supply and demand on the factor and product markets. The limitations of the approach are evident: Monopolistic elements are omitted and the essential inter-dependence between consumers and producers in the markets of the two countries or regions cannot appropriately be examined in a partial equilibrium analysis.

Tax Shifting among Economic Unions. We will first consider incidence problems in a combined customs and tax union. In the long-run how will the adoption of a tax union influence the allocation of productive resources? A general indirect tax will not distort this allocation whether a group of countries adopts the ideal form of the destination principle or the restricted principle of origin with a common external tax. Shibata examines the shifting problem in this connection. One

> objection to long-run consequences of the origin principle is based on the possibility of an international shifting of tax incidence as a result of origin principle taxation. This objection would be correct if this argument referred to the real-income transfer that takes place when there is no common external tax rate. But it is only partially correct if, instead, it simply means that under the origin principle consumers of one country (A), who buy goods imported from the other (B) will pay the taxes of the exporting country (B), which were included in the price of the goods, and that these payments would not occur under the destination principle. Even under the destination principle, if the tax in the exporting country (B) is a partial tax and depresses output of goods exported to the other (A), thereby increasing world prices of the goods, B's tax will, in fact, be partly shifted to A. We should also not lose sight of the fact that at the same time, under the origin principle, consumers of the partner (B) are now buying the commodities of A, the prices of which now include A's taxes; moreover, as we have seen, if the argument deals with universal application of the origin principle, the differences in tax rates between A and B are (in the long run) exactly compensated for by the difference in the values of A's and B's currencies, assuming the taxes of both countries are general taxes. Strangely enough, those who oppose the origin principle on the basis of international shifting rarely have raised the question of income taxes on wages, embodied, so to speak, in the goods exported or imported (assuming the supply of labor is not perfectly inelastic). They are not opposed to charging a higher price, corresponding to costs paid for additional services necessary to produce a good; it does not seem unreasonable to assert that taxes paid in connection with production, in the form of sales taxes on producers, represent, not penalties, but costs, corresponding to the values added to the products in question in the form of government services rendered, directly or indirectly. In short, insofar as commodity trade is balanced in the long run, a general single-stage sales tax levied at the same state of production in all countries cannot change any country's real terms of trade between its exports and imports, regardless of what rate and which principles the country employs for this sales tax. Therefore, in this case there will be no possibility of international shifting of tax incidence.[80]

If we combine a free trade area with a tax union, the international shifting of internal taxes beween member countries in a free trade area is a serious economic problem. As in the combination mentioned above the consumers of any country in a customs union bear a part of their country's tax imposed on products up to a rate corresponding to the common compensatory import tax. If the common external tax and the internal tax differ, the difference will be absorbed or obtained by the producers of the country until changes in the domestic price levels eliminate the advantage or disadvantage of the producers among the members. "In any case the burden of a domestic tax falls on either consumers or producers in the taxing country, and there is no possibility of international shifting of internal general indirect taxes."[81]

In free trade areas the relation between world market prices and intra-area prices is often cut by product discrimination caused by the principle of origin. Shibata concludes that "there is a wide range of possibility for international shifting of the incidence of taxes imposed by low-tariff member countries to high-tariff member countries within a free trade area."[82]

Taxation in Economic Unions—Harmonization of Indirect Taxes. Possible distorting effects of indirect taxes are closely linked with the problems of tax harmonization. Although the Neumark Report states that full harmonization could never be attained because national tax and expenditure policies in the European Economic Community[83] differ, it strongly suggests that all members should adopt a value-added tax with a uniform-rate carried through all stages of production up to the final one of retail trade.[84]

In a recent article Friedländer[85] supports this recommendation of the Neumark Report which analyzes the retail sales tax, the wholesale tax, the manufacturer's sales tax, the value-added tax, and the turnover tax in order to examine their neutrality in the sense that they do not influence relative prices. The report concludes that a value-added tax is the best form of indirect taxation which does not distort the trading patterns.

Substitution of a Value-Added Tax for a Corporate Profit Tax. Such a tax substitution is of great importance for the world market and for the United States' competitive position expressed in the balance of payments. There is considerable discussion of whether export rebates and compensating import taxes may affect the international trade of the European Common Market with the rest of the world. Have the

Common Market countries a competitive advantage with regard to the United States where the direct taxation is a high percentage of GNP and total government revenue as Table IV–6 indicates?

The substitution of a value-added tax for a corporate profits tax has at least two aspects: (1) the distorting effects of national tax systems on international trade including capital flows; (2) the effects of tax structure on the balance of payments. We will deal first with the narrow view.

(1) Salant attempts to answer the question of how substitution for part or all of the corporate profits tax by a value-added tax at an equivalent rate, which is rebated fully for exports and which applies to imports, would affect the United States balance of payments. It is evident that the conclusion of any analysis depends largely on the answer to the question: does the substitution leave domestic prices unchanged and lower export prices or, vice versa, does substitution raise domestic prices leaving export prices untouched?

Salant argues as follows:

> How prices would be affected at first appears to depend on whether the tax is shifted forward or is borne by corporate profits. This is not quite the issue, however. The basic debate about the incidence of the corporate profits tax concerns its effect on the real return to profits which, at given total output, depends on how it affects the relation between money profits and other money incomes, rather than on how it affects the money value of profits and the level of money prices. Alternative effects on relative shares are compatible with the same effect (or lack of effect) on absolute prices. Thus, the issue of incidence is not concerned with the effects of the tax on absolute prices, which are what counts for a country's international competitive position (given absolute prices abroad).[87]

If we assume that the corporation tax is *not shifted* in the short run, a substitution would not lower export prices and would have no direct effect on merchandise imports. Prices of domestic goods and services and of imported goods would rise relative to disposable income as a result of imposing the value-added tax thus reducing consumption. Furthermore, Salant states that the reduced tax rates would affect the flow of capital, attracting capital from abroad and retaining capital in domestic industry.

Under the "reasonable" assumption that the corporate profits tax is *shifted*, export prices may tend to decline on balance, increasing the value of exports and reducing a balance of payments deficit as in the United States. On the other hand the substitution may be expected to raise the price of imports protecting domestic industry.

TABLE IV–6

Comparison of Tax Structure in Various Countries[86]

<table>
<tr><th rowspan="2">Countries</th><th rowspan="2">Direct Personal and Corporate Income as a percentage of total tax collections of central government only (1960)</th><th colspan="6">Direct Taxes, including only employee contributions to Social Security, as a percentage of GNP and as a percentage of total government revenue, all levels of government (1961)</th></tr>
<tr><th>Total Taxes on Persons</th><th>Direct Taxes on Corporations</th><th>Employees contributions to Social Security</th><th>Total Direct Taxes</th><th>Total Direct Taxes as Per Cent of GNP</th></tr>
<tr><td></td><td></td><td colspan="4">as per cent of total taxes</td><td></td></tr>
<tr><td>France</td><td>33</td><td>11</td><td>7</td><td>9</td><td>27</td><td>9</td></tr>
<tr><td>Germany</td><td>43</td><td>22</td><td>9</td><td>13</td><td>44</td><td>15</td></tr>
<tr><td>Italy</td><td>19</td><td colspan="2">21</td><td>6</td><td>27</td><td>8</td></tr>
<tr><td>United Kingdom</td><td>51</td><td>29</td><td>11</td><td>6</td><td>46</td><td>13</td></tr>
<tr><td>United States</td><td>80</td><td>36</td><td>15</td><td>7</td><td>57</td><td>16</td></tr>
</table>

Salant judges all initial effects on exports and imports on net balance very pessimistically and concludes, furthermore, that there would be no favorable effect on the competitive position, and in the case of the United States even some unfavorable effect.[88]

Musgrave and Richman on the contrary hold that in the case of non-shifting the effects of a substitution on the balance of payments are clearly favorable via the influence on the international capital flow.[89] If domestic prices rise, a more realistic assumption, short-run trade effects on the balance of payments will be "neutral." If domestic prices do not rise in the long run, a shift of domestic capital into the export industry will add a favorable structural effect to the short-run price effect on exports. In case of shifting the short run trade effects on the balance of payments are much less pronounced and longer-run domestic capital allocation and international capital movements will be little affected.

(2) We turn now to the second point of view concerning the influence of tax substitution on international trade and capital flows. In a most stimulating paper Musgrave and Richman examine the international consequences of taxation. They investigate the differential incidence of the corporate profits tax and value-added tax. They assume that a profits tax (PT) and a value-added tax (VT) are applied in one country only, thus simplifying matters, because the absolute and differential rates are equal.

The crucial problem here as in all formal incidence analyses is the result of profits tax shifting, i.e., its effective or actual incidence is a most controversial matter. The authors assume "(1) that the profits tax is not shifted in the short run sense; and (2) that it is thus shifted, i.e., that the rate of return is maintained. . . ." In the case of forward shifting onto the product, shifting is assumed to occur only with regard to domestic sales of products, the prices of which are not dominated by import competition. "Shifting of a tax differential is assumed to be impossible with regard to export sales. Also, short-run shifting that resulted from imposition of a profits tax is assumed to be reversed when the tax is removed."[90]

How do the two types of taxes distort both commodity and factor flows from the point of view of efficiency? According to the conclusions of the analysis:

> . . . a profits tax by origin of capital, though not affecting factor flows, nevertheless may give rise to changes in demand patterns, which in turn may

> have repercussions on commodity flows. But such repercussions are merely responses to changes in effective preferences, and are not to be considered distortions. If the profit tax is by country of activity, the distorting effects on factor flows will again react on commodity flows, such reaction now emanating from both the supply and the demand side. The former are part and parcel of the distorting effects on factor flows, the adjustment to which involves responses in commodity flows; and the latter again reflect changes in demand patterns. In all, it appears that income taxes whether by country of residence or of activity have not direct distorting effects on commodity flows, even though they may in many ways affect the volume and direction of commodity trade.[91]

The combination of a value-added tax of the income type that is rebated on exported goods with a compensating sales tax on imports may distort factor flows only.

Under more realistic conditions factor taxes are often imposed not by residents but by place of activity, whereas product taxes are usually combined with rebates and compensating taxes. Therefore Musgrave and Richman conclude that "reliance on the VT type of tax may be preferable on international allocation grounds, especially where PT (as against wage tax) differentials are concerned."[92]

V. *Tax Distribution over Time: Inter-Temporal Tax Incidence*

Specific problems are involved in the time dimension of incidence. Theoretical and empirical studies of inter-temporal tax distribution are still rare, though the classical shifting theory distinguishes long and short run incidence both assuming perfect and less than infinite elasticity of factors and supply of goods and even including population change. Specific time problems are linked to tax avoidance or evasion and to statutory decrees permitting losses and profits to be carried backward or forward or taxes to be paid on the basis of self-assessment in advance of final tax payments.

(1) Another type of short-run problem is concerned with the formal tax and budget incidence on various income groups over time: In an unpublished paper Prest discusses two ways of comparing tax effects over time. He illustrates the first case on the assumption that distortions in assigning tax burdens to specific income groups are constant from one year to another:

	Year 1	*Year 2*
Original Income (£)	500	500
Income Taxation (£)	25	75
Indirect Taxation (£)	50	75

Suppose we assume that income taxation and indirect taxation are allocated on the conventional assumptions. Even if we feel it is inappropriate to add these burdens (and so say that net income is £425 in year 1 and £350 in year 2), it is still possible to argue that the deterioration in this man's position is £75 (£25 indirect tax and £50 direct tax) between the two years. Of course, absolute errors of allocation may not be constant between the two years but this is at any rate a weaker assumption than the conventional ones.[93]

The second method is the calculation of disposable income for each group. The change in disposable income between the two years is deflated by a price index appropriate to that group. In spite of conceptual and statistical difficulties Prest attempts the following empirical calculations:

TABLE IV–7

Index of the Ratio of Post-Tax Real Income per Head to Pre-Tax Money Income per Head, U.K. 1959–64

Income Range (£ per annum)	*1959*	*1962*	*1963*	*1964*
Less than 500	100	89	88	86
500–979	100	90	88	86
1000–1479	100	88	85	81.5
Over 1500	100	97	99	96.5

He states that

between 1959 and 1964 the rate of post-tax real income to pre-tax money income changed in substantially different ways for the two upper income ranges, both being in contrast with the similarity of the change for the two lower income groups. These movements clearly reflect not only the changing pattern of direct taxation but also the differing movements of prices for the four income ranges, which in turn reflect not only indirect tax rate changes but also many other influences as well. This is clearly a limitation to this kind of approach though, in fact, further examination of the figures seems to show that by far the most important component of the movements shown in [Table IV–7] was the changing ratios of post-tax to pre-tax money incomes, rather than the price changes.[94]

(2) The long-period incidence is linked to capitalization of taxes and intergeneration distribution of the tax "burden."[95]

Inter-temporal incidence of the budget measures the distribution of taxes and expenditure benefits to the income or consumption of generations or over the life cycle or at any rate over a period of years. Here the effects of both budgetary revenue and expenditure are combined. The theory of public debt and the cost-benefit analysis focus on public investments, applying the principles of intergeneration equity and pay-as-you-use as well as discounting net benefits. Inter-temporal comparisons of social benefits and costs use a social-time-preference discount rate, a normative "interest" rate. Costs and benefits are converted into equivalent increases and decreases of consumption. The ratio represents government policy with respect to the relative desirability of consumption at different times. The conclusions should answer the questions: (1) Should public investment projects be financed by taxes or credit?[96] and (2) which project should be preferred from the point of view of incidence?

New investigations apply the cost-benefit analysis to classical (so-called) indivisible goods[97] estimating and calculating the costs and benefits to different periods and regions. Thus they introduce the redistribution effects linking efficiency and equity. But calculations of benefits accruing to various income groups over time are as rare as investigations into the effects of tax policy on changes in consumption and the distribution loss or surplus of various income groups. There is a wide field for research. However, in studies on inheritance or death duties, social insurance contributions and on tax capitalization the inter-temporal allocation of taxes is being considered.

(3) We will conclude this section by considering some empirical studies. Table IV–4 indicates the vertical redistribution of income in favor of lower income groups but it shows too, that this change of distribution hides an inter-temporal equalization or adjustment of incomes. The active population renounces its claims to the national product in favor of inactive members such as children, the aged and sick.

The pensioners' households paid relatively the same amount of taxes to finance the collective services of government as the other social groups but they contributed 20 per cent to the income transfers or social insurance payments which they received in 1960.

Another aspect of inter-temporal incidence on an individual basis is the timing of inter-generation wealth transfers related to taxation and interest. The central question is: Should wealth owners transfer their property as soon as possible in order to save tax by the lower effective tax rates on inter-vivos gifts? The results are obviously controversial.[98]

In his stimulating paper Prest examines government revenue burdens and/or expenditure benefits in relation to age. "If, for instance, a man with a given level of money income typically has a net tax burden of 10 per cent at age 60, it could be argued that the degree of redistribution over this period of years is considerably less than in any one year."

Prest is the first to attempt an empirical calculation. Since data concerning net burdens on or benefits to specific persons throughout their lives are not available, he uses different age groups at the same point of time.

TABLE IV–8

Direct Taxes and Transfer Payments by Age, U.K. 1965

	Income Range 1		*Income Range 2*	
Age Group	*Weekly household income per head (shillings)*	*% reduction (−) or addition (+) due to government*	*Weekly household income per head (shillings)*	*% reduction (−) or addition (+) due to government*
Under 30	118	−7.7	154	−9.3
30–40	102	−5.2	145	−8.4
40–50	103	−0.9	151	−8.9
50–60	113	+13.1	141	−6.3
60–65	—	—	159	−6.2
65 and over	120	+29.5	—	—

Source: Family Expenditure Survey *Report,* 1965

As one might expect *a priori,* the author concludes

> there is an increasing tendency for government transfer outpayments to increase relatively to tax inpayments as age increases. Government intervention also improves the position of income range 1 relatively to income range 2 at all age levels for which comparisons can be made. It must be emphasized that no account is taken here of indirect taxes. Also the elimination of differences in income and family size is rough and ready; and there are plenty of criticisms which can be made in respect of the basic data (e.g. sample size). But the results are at least suggestive.[99]

Notes

1. Among others, W. Leontief, *The Structure of the American Economy, 1919–39: An Empirical Application of Equilibrium Analysis* (New York, 1951); and *idem* "Methode der Input-Output Analyse," *Allg. Stat. Archiv,* Vol. XXXVI, 2 (1952).
2. As real production is assumed to be constant we may also speak of money flows if we allow for the fluctuations in the value of money.
3. For instance, while Rolph (*The Theory of Fiscal Economics, op. cit.,* p. 56) treats all contributions including the indirect taxes and the subsidies as transfer payments, most theorists hold the opposite view as do R. F. Stone ("Functions and Criteria of a System of Social Accounting," *Income and Wealth,* Series 1 [Cambridge, England, 1951], p. 178), S. Kuznets ("Government Product and National Income," *Income and Wealth,* Series 1 [Cambridge, England, 1951]) and C. S. Shoup, (*Principles of National Income Analysis* [Boston, 1947]); their reasons for differing vary, however.
4. The effects of increased demand on real or nominal income require a number of periods. So far, we have ignored the intermediate periods of the multiplier adjustment by assuming a so-called "instantaneous multiplier," a multiplier k of l. We shall come back to this question later.
5. This modification is relevant for all successful forward shifting. Of course, the state may exempt the consumer goods which it buys itself from taxation, thus lowering revenues and expenditures by the same amount. In this case the value of money has not changed for the state.
6. If monopolistic suppliers raise prices, however, before the increase in demand, a credit-financed maintenance of real consumption is a quite realistic assumption.
7. See Figure V–1.
8. See the empirical studies of Musgrave and others, *op. cit.,* and Tucker, *op. cit.,* as well as the study by Jecht, *op. cit.*
9. Due, *Incidence of Sales Taxation, op. cit.,* and "A General Sales Tax and the Level of Employment: A Reconsideration," *NTJ,* II (1949), 122–130.
10. J. F. Due, "Sales Taxation and the Consumer," *AER,* LIII (1963) 1078–1084.
11. J. M. Buchanan, *Fiscal Theory and Political Economy* (Chapel Hill, 1960); R. A. Musgrave, *Theory, op. cit.;* E. R. Rolph, "A Proposed Revision of Excise Tax Theory," *JPE,* LX (1952), 102–117; E. R. Rolph and G. Break, *Public Finance* (New York, 1961).
12. J. F. Due, *Incidence of Sales Taxation,* p. 1079.
13. R. A. Musgrave, *Theory,* p. 249.
14. J. F. Due, *Incidence of Sales Taxation,* p. 1081.
15. See chapter 7.

16. If we assume that the entrepreneurial income consists of wages, interest and risk premiums.
17. See the following section.
18. R. A. Musgrave, "On Incidence," *loc. cit.*, p 305.
19. Here, too, the question arises why the firms did not exploit the market situation before the tax.
20. H. G. Brown, "The Incidence of a General Output or a General Sales Tax," *loc. cit.*, and E. R. Rolph, "A Proposed Revision," *loc. cit.*, p. 102 *passim.*
21. He avoids in this way, as did Edgeworth, the question whether taxes should be treated as costs or not.
22. It appears practically more usual that expenditures are pre-financed which are formally covered by taxes but which can be actually undertaken only after the receipts have come in. Such a cash and credit policy eases the first step to forward shifting considerably.
23. E. R. Rolph, "A Proposed Revision," p. 130.
24. *Ibid.*, p. 109.
25. *Ibid.*
26. G. F. Break, "The Incidence of Consumption Taxes," *Proceedings NTA 1961,* pp. 627–628.
27. H. M. Somers, "Theoretical Framework of Sales and Use Taxation," *Proceedings NTA* 1961, p. 609.
28. *Ibid.*
29. D. T. Smith, "Value Added Taxation in Relation to Income, Excise and Sales Taxation," *Excise Tax Compendium* (1964), p. 89.
30. See Smith, p. 90. A. F. Friedländer "Indirect Taxes and Relative Prices," *QJE,* LXXXI (1967), 125, recently analyzed the most important indirect taxes (Retail Sales Tax, Wholesale Sales Tax, Turnover Tax, Manufacturer's Sales Tax) with respect to neutrality.
31. C. S. Shoup, "Theory and Background of the Value-Added Tax," *Proceedings NTA* 1955, p. 7. Though they are not so important with regard to shiftability, we should mention also the two variants of the consumption concept of the value-added tax. The consumption type of value-added tax may be expressed in a formula alternative to that given above. Instead of allowing deduction of cost of equipment in the year of purchase and disallowing depreciation in subsequent years the formula may read as follows: disallow deduction of cost in year of purchase; allow depreciation in subsequent years; and in addition, exclude from value added in subsequent years the interest earned by the investment.

    In other words, the consumption concept may be restated in just the same terms as the income concept, with the further provision that income earned by the investment shall be excluded from value added. This formula may be designated the *interest-exclusion variant* of the consumption-type concept. The variant described earlier may be called the *deduction variant.* See Shoup, pp. 11 and 12.

32. J. F. Due, "The Value-Added Tax," *Western Economic Journal,* III (1965), 170; J. F. Due, "Should the Corporation Income Tax be Replaced by the Value-Added Tax?" *Proceedings NTA 1964,* pp. 431–439.
33. D. H. Eldridge, "Equity, Administration and Compliance, and Intergovernmental Fiscal Aspects," *The Role of Direct and Indirect Taxes in the Federal Revenue System* (Princeton, 1964), p. 146.
34. Due, "The Value-Added Tax," p. 167.
35. Italics added. See also W. H. Oakland, "Automatic Stabilization and the Value-Added Tax," *Studies in Economic Stabilization,* A. Ando, E. C. Brown and A. F. Friedländer, eds. (Washington, D.C., 1968), pp. 41–60.
36. C. K. Sullivan, *The Tax on Value Added* (New York and London, 1965), pp. 263–264; see also E. R. Rolph, "A Proposed Revision" pp. 102–117; J. A. Stockfisch, "The Capitalization and Investment Aspects of Excise Taxes under Competition," *AER,* XLIV (1954), 287–300; R. A. Musgrave, *Theory,* chapters 15 and 16. Musgrave and Stockfisch, however, arrive at divergent positions concerning the price effects of a sales tax restricted to investment goods.
37. J. F. Due, "The Value Added Tax," pp. 167–169. Note, too, the article by D. K. Stout, "Value Added Taxation, Exporting, and Growth," *British Tax Review* (1963), pp. 314–335, and more recently W. H. Oakland, "The Theory of the Value-Added-Tax, II—Incidence Effects," *NTJ,* XX, 3 (1967), 270–281; and the critique of C. S. Shoup, "Consumption Tax, and Wages Type and Consumption Type of Value-Added Tax," *NTJ,* XXI (1968), 153–161.
38. Due, "The Value Added Tax," pp. 167–169.
39. *Ibid.*
40. *Ibid.*
41. Shoup, "Theory and Background," p. 11.
42. R. A. Musgrave, "Excises in the Federal Tax Structure—A General Appraisal," *Excise Tax Compendium* (Washington, 1964), p. 20; and Eldridge, p. 146.
43. Eldridge, p. 146.
44. W. H. Oakland, "The Theory of the Value-Added Tax: I—A Comparison of Tax Basis, II—Incidence Effects."
45. Since the increased earnings are also taxed proportionally, a *greater* effort is necessary to offset the decrease of the initial wage caused by tax.
46. For an exact analysis of production effects due to an increase of money, credit and demand under the given conditions see R. Nöll von der Nahmer, *Der Volkswirtschaftliche Kreditfonds, Versuch einer Lösung des Kreditproblems* (Berlin, 1934).

47. With an unbalanced budget the following changes occur: *ceteris paribus* if the public expenditures are less than the tax revenues, $C_T < T$, no shifting or compensation by production effects occurs. If $C_T > T$, shifting and an additional (nominal and real) gain results.
48. See W. J. Baumol and M. H. Peston, "More on the Multiplier Effects of a Balanced Budget," *AER*, XLV (1955), 140.
49. Rüstow has analyzed a multiplicative increase of income in his contribution to Föhl's theory. However, this does not lead to a modification of the incidence. With an instantaneous tax multiplier assumed by Rüstow ($k = 1$) gross profits of 10 billions immediately increase to 40, net profits from 2.5 to 10, the profit tax from 7.5 to 30 and borrowing falls from 7.5 to 0. If we consider the time sequences the process is as follows:

Periods	*Gross Profit*	*Net Profit*	*Profits Tax*	*Borrowing*
1	10	2.5	7.5	7.5
2	17.5	4.375	13.125	5.625
3	23.125	5.781	17.344	4.219
4	27.344	6.836	20.508	3.164
.	.	.	.	.
.	.	.	.	.
∞	40	10	30	0

See also H. C. Recktenwald, *Entwicklung, . . . op. cit.*, pp. 284 ff.
50. Most macro-economic investigations ignore this question. Föhl did not even touch the problem although the title of his studies suggest it (which Föhl later admitted, "Steuerparadoxon," *loc. cit.*, p. 114, footnote 1).
51. M. Krzyzaniak, "The Long Run Burden of a General Tax on Profits in a Neoclassical World," *loc. cit.*, pp. 472–495.
52. G. Zeitel, *Die Steuerlast in der Bundesrepublik Deutschland* (Tübingen, 1959); G. Göseke, "The Effects of Redistribution on Size Distribution of Personal Income and Household Net Income in Germany in 1955 and 1959," in *Income Redistribution and the Statistical Foundations of Economic Policy*, ed. Colin Clark and G. Stuvel, *Income and Wealth*, Series X (London, 1964), pp. 220–247; K. D. Schmidt, U. Schwarz, and G. Thiebach, *Die Umverteilung des Volkseinkommens in der Bundesrepublik Deutschland—1955 und 1960* (Tübingen, 1965).
53. The composition of government purchases of goods and services, however, is assumed to be constant, because its changes cause specific effects. See, e.g., A. T. Peacock and I. G. Stewart, "Fiscal Policy and the Composition of Government Purchases," *PF*, XIII (1958), 135–145; and M. Robine, "De la décomposition des quantités globales aux multiplicateurs du budget équilibré," *Revue de Science Financière*, 1964, pp. 203–274 and 472–520.

54. Antonio Pedone, "The Budget and the Intersectoral Income Distribution," Institut International des Finances Publiques, mimeographed paper given at the Congrès de Prague, 1967, p. 2.
55. W. Leontief, "Output, Employment, Consumption, and Investment," *QJE,* LVIII (1943–44), 290–314, and "Wages, Profit and Prices," *QJE,* LX (1946–47), 26–39.
56. Pedone, pp. 2–3.
57. L. A. Metzler, "Taxes and Subsidies in Leontief's Input-Output Model," *QJE,* LXV (1951), 433.
58. Pedone, p. 5. It is possible to introduce production functions which do not imply fixed and constant technical coefficients or to refer to some kind of demand functions. But the form of these more realistic production and consumption functions will be based on considerations which are external to the structure of the model.
59. (1) Constancy in the composition of output in the basic system, (2) neutrality of technical progress, and (3) uniformity of the profit rate in the sectors.
60. Metzler, pp. 433–434.
61. See e.g., E. R. Rolph, "A Theory of Excise Subsidies," *AER,* XLII (1952), 515–527.
62. Metzler, p. 434.
63. Pedone, p. 4.
64. See the analysis of some types of relations in Pedone, Appendix 1.
65. L. Johansen, *A Multi-Sectoral Study of Economic Growth* (Amsterdam, 1964), and M. Morishima, *Equilibrium, Stability and Growth. A Multi-Sectoral Analysis* (Oxford, 1964).
66. Pedone, pp. 8–9.
67. O. Morgenstern and G. L. Thompson, "Private and Public Consumption and Savings in the Neumann Model of an Expanding Economy," *Ky,* XX (1967), 387–409.
68. See C. S. Shoup, ed., *Fiscal Harmonization in Common Markets,* 2 vols. (New York and London, 1967).
69. W. G. Sundelson and S. J. Mushkin, *The Measurement of State and Local Tax Efforts,* Social Security Board, Bureau Memorandum No. 58 (1944); R. A. Musgrave and W. Daicoff, "Who Pays the Michigan Taxes," in Michigan Study Staff Papers (Lansing, Michigan, 1958), pp. 131–183; O. H. Brownlee, *Estimated Distribution of Minnesota Taxes and Public Expenditures* (Minneapolis, 1960); University of Wisconsin Tax Study Committee, *Wisconsin's State and Local Tax Burden* (Madison, 1959); C. E. McLure, Jr., "The Interstate Exporting of State and Local Taxes: Estimates for 1962, "*NTJ,* XX (1967), 49–77.
70. W. Albers, "Finanzzuweisungen und Standortverteilung," *Schriften des VfS, NF,* XXXII, 253–286; H. Timm, "Finanzpolitische Autonomie untergeordneter Gebietskörperschaften (Gemeinden) und Standort-

verteilung. Ein Beitrag zur ökonomischen Beurteilung des Finanzausgleichs," *Schriften des VfS, loc. cit.* pp. 9–60; K. Littmann, "Finanzpolitik, Räumliche Gleichgewichte und Optima. Kreislauf-theoretische Betrachtungen über die Wirkungen der staatlichen Aktivität auf die räumliche Faktorverteilung," *VfS, NF, loc. cit.*, p.61.

71. McLure, p. 50.
72. McLure, p. 52.
73. McLure, p. 63. We emphasize that McLure estimates the formal incidence of the differential type.
74. See H. Möller, "Das Ursprungs- und Bestimmungsland-Prinzip," unpublished study (University of Munich, 1963).
75. European Coal and Steel Community, High Authority, *Report on the Problems Raised by the Different Turnover Tax System Applied Within the Common Market* (Tinbergen Report), 1953.
76. *Report of the Fiscal and Financial Committee* (Neumark Report), The EEC Reports on Tax Harmonization (Amsterdam, 1963.)
77. G. Bombach, *Das Problem der optimalen internationalen Arbeitsteilung bei unterschiedlicher Struktur der Steuersysteme* (Düsseldorf, 1962), p. 23.
78. R. H. Parks, "Theory of Tax Incidence: International Aspects," *NTJ*, XIV (1961), 190–197.
79. McLure, "Commodity Tax Incidence in Open Economies," *NTJ*, XVII (1964), 187–204.
80. H. Shibata, "The Theory of Economic Unions: A Comparative Analysis of Customs Unions, Free Trade Areas, and Tax Unions," in Shoup, *Fiscal Harmonization*, I: *Theory*, 239, 241, and 242.
81. Shibata adds: "This general tax case should be differentiated from cases of special excises in which a country may succeed in shifting a part of its tax burden to other countries by imposing particularly heavy taxes on a few selected goods for which the demand of the rest of the world is highly inelastic, while domestic supply of the goods is either inelastic or can be controlled by monopolistic practices. This special case is often referred to as a rationale for the export tax."
82. Shibata, pp. 247–248.
83. See A. Dale, *Tax Harmonization in Europe* (London, 1963), chapter IV for a full discussion of the actual tax policies followed in the Common Market nations.
84. Neumark Report, p. 126.
85. A. F. Friedländer, "Indirect Taxes and Relative Prices," pp. 125–139.
86. O. Eckstein and V. Tanzi, "Comparison of European and United States Tax Structures and Growth Implications," *The Role of Direct and Indirect Taxes in the Federal Revenue System* (Princeton, 1964), pp. 219, 223.

87. W. S. Salant, "The Balance-Of-Payments Deficit and the Tax-Structure," *RESt*, XLVI (1964), 131.
88. *Ibid.*, pp. 132–134.
89. R. A. Musgrave and P. D. Richman, "Allocation Aspects, Domestic and International," *The Role of Direct and Indirect Taxes*, p. 123.
90. Musgrave and Richman, p. 101.
91. Musgrave and Richman, pp. 105 and 106.
92. Musgrave and Richman, p. 106.
93. A. R. Prest, "The Budget and Interpersonal Distribution of Public Finance," in International Institute of Public Finance, *The Budget and the Distribution of National Income* (New York, 1968), pp. 80–96.
94. *Ibid.*
95. See chapters II and VI–5; for more details on inter-generation incidence and the path of incidence see H. C. Recktenwald, *Das Kapitalbudget in finanz-und volkswirtschaftlicher Sicht* (Tübingen, 1962).
96. We can compare the intergeneration redistributive effects of tax finance and debt finance, thus measuring the differential debt incidence; see J. G. Head, "The Theory of Debt Incidence," *Rev. Dir. Fin.*, XXVI, 2 (1967), 175–213; R. A. Musgrave (*Theory*) has developed the concept of inter-generation equity.
97. H. C. Recktenwald, "Effizienz und Innere Sicherheit," *Ky*, XX (1967), 607–641.
98. W. Vickrey, *Agenda for Progressive Taxation* (New York, 1947); C. S. Shoup, *Federal Estate and Gift Taxes*, (Washington, 1966); H. M. Hochman and C. M. Lindsay, "Taxation, Interest and the Timing of Inter-Generation Wealth Transfers," *NTJ*, XX (1967), 219–226.
99. A. R. Prest, "The Budget and Interpersonal Distribution," p. 95.

5
Micro-Economic Tax Incidence

In this chapter we shall mainly examine how market form and behavior and the manner in which taxes are imposed influence the shifting process and the final incidence as far as individual firms and industries are concerned. Since tax shifting is intimately connected with the process of price formation, it is necessary to consider the determining factors of price and quantity sold which influence supply and demand. We will try to determine how shifting works in a variety of markets in three different periods, namely with sales from given stocks (in the so-called market period), in the short and in the long run. Again we start with general categories of taxes, not with concrete taxes of particular countries and periods. The bases for assessment are:

(a) The unit of goods produced or sold (quantity or unit tax).
(b) the receipts (ad valorem tax, for example a turnover tax).
(c) the surplus or net profit
(d) a fixed levy independent of quantity, receipts or surplus, (for example head tax, property tax).

Further, we shall start from a tax rate which noticeably influences the income of the taxpayer, so that the tax-conscious citizens are affected permanently in their behavior. They expect their tax to continue in time. The other specific effects of taxation, namely of the rates, of the progression and technique of levying will be discussed in another section.

I. *Shifting Possibilities by Private Households*

In the macro-economic incidence analysis we have already dealt in detail with the ability of a private household to shift its taxes. Its opportunities to do so are considerably less than those of firms. The differences between the individual categories of households (wage and salary earner, recipient of social security payments) may be considerable. The elasticity of the labor supply and the position on the particular labor market are decisive. Forward shifting through wage increases succeeds under monopolistic conditions only if a sharp credit cut prevents a price rise of consumption goods or lags behind the realized wage demands. On the other hand, consumer credits, dissaving or reduced cash holdings have, as a rule, an unfavorable effect on the households because of the increased demand after taxation.

II. *The Impact of Market Structure and Market Behavior on Incidence*

1. The Shifting Process under Perfect Competition

In a market of perfect competition no individual buyer or seller can influence prices though all together determine the price through their demand and supply. The market is cleared at the equilibrium price. Moreover, there are no personal, temporal, spatial preferences. If, for example, a seller attempts to raise the market price, he loses all his customers to other sellers since, in the judgement of the buyer, the goods are homogeneous. For this there must be sufficient knowledge of the market (market transparency). Finally, perfect competition implies absence of government regulation or collusion by private persons.

In the short run such a competitive market is in equilibrium when short run marginal costs and marginal revenues of all sellers are equal to the market price. Most investigations start with the assumption that the long run market equilibrium is reached when the lowest average costs (including a normal profit) of each seller are equal to the market price. Differences in cost among firms are largely eliminated in this case and all capacities are fully utilized.

(*a*) *Forward Shifting of a Unit Tax in Various Periods*

In such a market, how does supply and demand in different planning periods adjust to a "disturbance" of market equilibrium when sellers have to pay a tax on *quantities* sold? Who ultimately bears the tax?

First, the tax causes the marginal and average cost of all suppliers to rise equally by the amount of the tax. But the individual seller cannot himself—as some studies erroneously assume—immediately raise the price because of his higher costs since by assumption he has no influence on the market and the demand for his product is perfectly elastic. If he did, he would lose old customers to his competitors who have not changed their price. The following market adjustments will occur:

If the price estimates of all suppliers remain unchanged total supply decreases because the reservation price will have fallen by the amount of the tax. As a consequence and because of competition the market price rises. How much the price will increase depends essentially on the intensity of total demand. These adjustments do as a rule not occur instantaneously but over a more or less extended period. They can be observed within the individual periods until there is a new equilibrium.

(*b*) *Adjustment of Supply without Changes in Production*

If an existing amount of goods which cannot be increased in the short-run is to be sold within a certain period, the price will rise only to the level at which the market can be cleared. In this very short-run adjustment the suppliers will bear all or most of the tax, especially when perishable or fashionable goods are involved, or when difficulties with liquidity exist. If the goods can be stored (wine) the tax can be shifted forward through a speculative withholding until the next "market period." Such speculation is quite dangerous and only successful if the (expected) price on the future market rises high enough to cover the additional interest and storage costs (including higher risk premiums). In general and *ceteris paribus* the sellers pay and bear the greater part of the tax so that their profits diminish and possible losses occur.

(*c*) *Short-Term Incidence*

Since marginal and average costs have increased by the amount of the tax, with market price remaining relatively unchanged, however, profit necessarily shrinks, so that marginal production becomes unprofitable. If the suppliers do not expect a change in future demand, production in the short run is reduced until marginal cost and price are again equal. Since the suppliers produce under approximately equal conditions, they reduce their output uniformly so that no firm needs to close down. The market price rises as a result of diminished total supply. The new short-term equilibrium is now above the previous competitive price. In this way, at least part of the tax could be shifted to the buyers. The price increase from P_1 to P_2 (Figure V–1) shows the direction and amount of the successful shifting and at the same time the distribution of incidence between buyer and seller.

(*d*) *Long-Term Incidence*

But the new market price is still not as high as the long-run marginal and average costs, and not all production costs are covered. Over a long period no firm can sell at prices which do not cover a part of the costs (namely fixed costs). Therefore the suppliers have to reduce their capacities almost uniformly until total cost equals diminished total revenue. Such a reduction of capacity is difficult in modern industries since the invested capital is not sufficiently divisible or mobile. Moreover, the conditions on the supply markets are also relevant. Under conditons of perfect competition, the taxed firms can only adjust their demanded quantity, but cannot directly change the price. If factor supply is relatively elastic, the affected factors are eliminated. They either remain unemployed or move to untaxed markets. Backward shifting is successful if the factor supply is inelastic. So market price increases in the long-run or factor price decreases until the tax is completely or at least to a large extent shifted. The following diagram shows how supply adjusts in various periods to the market "disturbance," and who bears the forward shifted tax in each period.[1]

The long-run equilibrium price rises from P over P_1 and P_2 to P_3. The incidence is shown at each point of time, that is to what extent the tax is borne by the suppliers and the demanders.

The extent of the final reduction of production and with it of price increase and forward shifting depends in the last analysis on the adaptabilty of supply and demand and on the shapes of the cost and revenue curves.

(*e*) *Shifting under Dynamic Competitive Conditions.*

This "ideal type" of a shifting process, however, still needs two qualifications. To start with, the real transition from one equilibrium to another is not so smooth as we assumed in our simplified model.

FIGURE V–1

Shifting of Unit Tax—Pure Competition

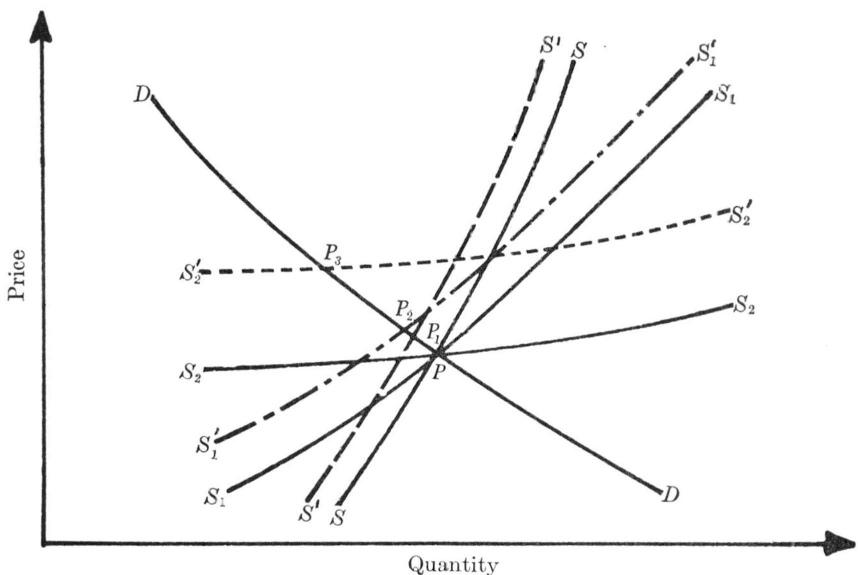

DD = Demand (unchanged in the whole period)
SS = Supply in the market period
$S'S'$ = Same supply after tax
S_1S_1 = Short-run supply
$S'S'$ = Same supply after tax
S_2S_2 = Long-run supply
$S_2'S_2'$ = Same supply after tax

Firms produce under unequal cost conditions. Inefficient marginal enterprises whose revenues no longer cover their current costs are eliminated, while others increase their output or appear on the market because of technical innovations.

As such a market tends towards long-run equilibrium, the reaction of the individual suppliers to the tax will not be uniform; in addition to marginal costs, differential profits will influence the short-run elasticity of supply. Thus part of the supply can temporarily be kept fixed which will increase the pressure on the marginal seller, more so than in the case of a uniform reduction of marginal production (or even a common price increase). Firms with high differential rents may attempt to maintain the pressure of the tax on the weaker competitors at least temporarily by paying the tax out of profits and by continuing to offer the same quantity at the unchanged market price. Thus the sellers may sometimes bear the tax in order to hasten the elimination of marginal producers.

The second qualification concerns market behavior. As quantity adapters under perfect competition suppliers have, theoretically, only the choice of limiting their supply if they intend to shift the increased cost resulting from the tax to the consumers. But such a reaction appears very unrealistic indeed. If the individual seller cannot directly influence the market price, he will at least try, contrary to theory, either to increase his sales in order to maintain, if possible, the total profit he made before the tax was imposed, or to increase the prices directly, together with the other tax-burdened producers. The first mode of behavior leads to further losses, at least if, with unchanged demand and constant factors, the market stagnates. The second mode of behavior, which is entirely realistic, can considerably change the process of shifting. It is, however, questionable whether this kind of price policy with its decidedly monopolistic element is still to be considered within the framework of perfect competition. We shall deal with this problem when we discuss the market form of polypolistic competition.

(*f*) *The Possible Backward Shifting of a Unit Tax*

Backward shifting can succeed only if factor supply is relatively inelastic. In such a case a drastic reduction of demand will reduce the supply of factor services only slightly even with falling factor remunerations. The production of the taxed goods will be more or less constant. If the total supply is fixed, incidence is divided evenly among the factors involved in the production of the good and the least cost combination remains unchanged. In the case of labor, its geographic immobility and specialization is offset by the monopolistic position of trade unions in maintaining wages in the face of falling employment. On the other hand contractual arrangements with factor owners, e.g. trade unions, make backward shifting impossible.

(*g*) *Final Incidence*

Let us sum up the results of the analysis of market adjustment. In a market under perfect competition a specific unit tax can burden (a) the profits of the tax paying firms, (b) the incomes of the purchasers and (c) the remunerations of the factors of production. The extent to which incomes of the three groups are reduced and with them the incidence, depends upon the relative elasticity of supply and demand. The adaptability of supply tends to increase in the long-run. Quite often, a portion of the tax is borne by the suppliers at the beginning of the shifting process, and a partial or total shifting to the consumers succeeds only through a gradual adjustment of supply.

(*h*) *General Rule on Tax Shifting*

If we compare the equilibria on a competitive market before and after a unit tax has been imposed, without considering the adjustment path, the incidence may be clearly shown in Figure V–2.

(a) The producers consider the tax a part of costs; they add therefore the tax to the supply price so that the supply curve SS′ is shifted upward parallel by the amount of the tax (Ep) to ss′. Since demand is assumed to be unchanged, the new equilibrium price rises from P to p, and the quantity which can be sold at this price decreases from OQ to Oq. The producers have successfully shifted forward exactly half of the tax. The rectangle CKpR ($\frac{Ep}{2} \times Oq$, half of the tax multiplied by the quantity sold) shows the amount of the tax shifted forward and the rectangle FEKC, the portion borne by the producers, which they either have to pay or which they may completely or partially shift backward to factor owners. The relation of the slopes[2] of the supply and demand curves determines the incidence of the tax.[3] The same result holds on the factor market.

(b) Because of the decrease of the market sales from Q to q the Treasury loses a tax yield of KPTL (= the product of tax rate and lost sales). If the quantity sold had remained unchanged, the government would indeed have received a yield amounting to FEpR and KPTL (= *lucrum cessans* of the Treasury). These amounts are of special practical interest for tax policy. For, budgetary policy and particularly expenditure policy are essentially influenced by the correct estimate of tax receipts.

(c) The area EPp measures the loss which results from diminished exchanges in the welfare of all market participants. The supply situation has worsened. The producers who merely collected the tax have suffered a reduction in their gain from exchange or differential rent of

FIGURE V–2

Shifting of Tax on Output—General Case

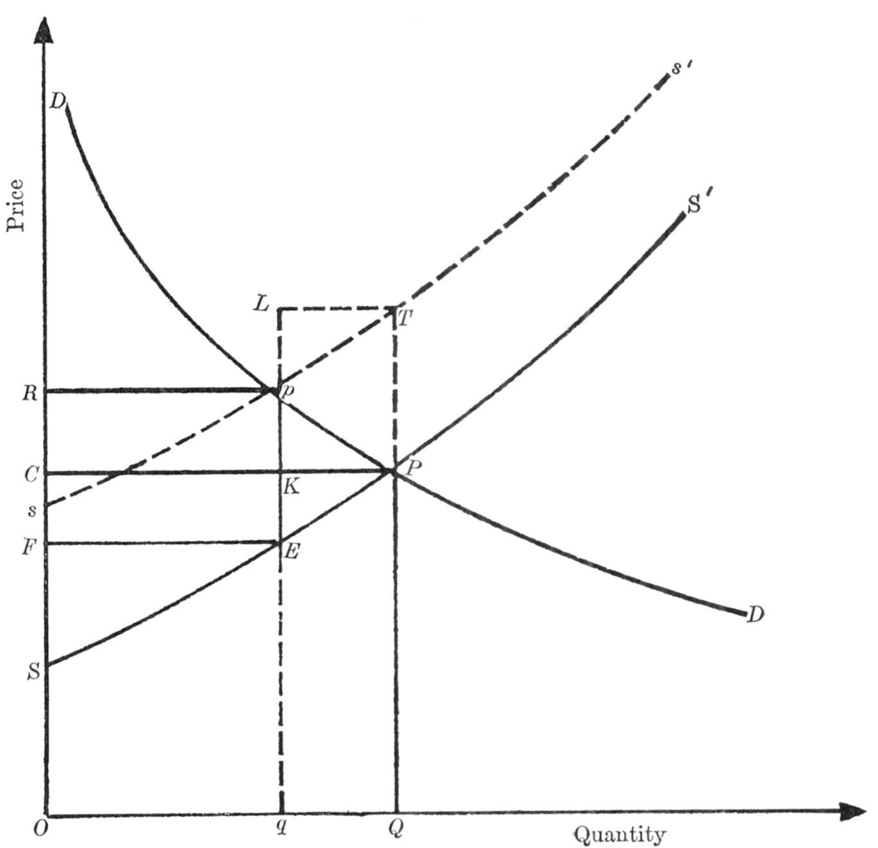

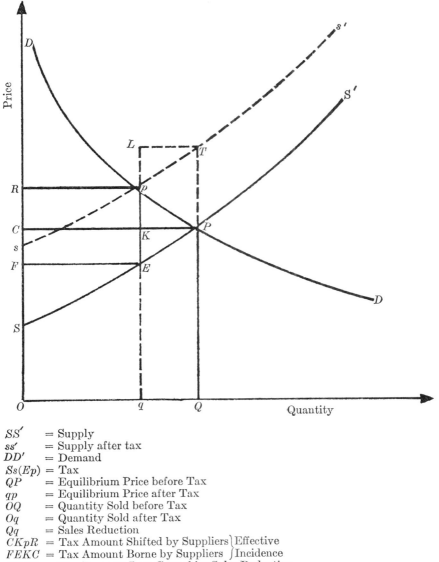

SS'	= Supply
ss'	= Supply after tax
DD'	= Demand
Ss(Ep)	= Tax
QP	= Equilibrium Price before Tax
qp	= Equilibrium Price after Tax
OQ	= Quantity Sold before Tax
Oq	= Quantity Sold after Tax
Qq	= Sales Reduction
CKpR	= Tax Amount Shifted by Suppliers } Effective
FEKC	= Tax Amount Borne by Suppliers } Incidence
KPTL	= Tax Revenue Loss Caused by Sales Reduction

EPK and purchasers of KPp. The extent to which this economic loss is compensated by the effect of tax-financed public expenditures will be discussed in another context.

Figures V–3 to V–8 illustrate the incidence of a unit tax on markets with varying degrees of elasticity of supply and demand. The diagrams are derived from Figure V–2, hence a further explanation is unnecessary. The shaded rectangle is the portion of the levy which was shifted forward to the consumer; the unshaded rectangle the portion borne by the sellers; x is the quantity and y the price.

While in Figure V–3 the elasticity of demand in the range Pp is almost zero and that of supply is relatively large, so that forward shifting with a slight reduction in sales succeeds nearly completely, Figure V–4 shows the opposite case.

In the extreme cases, if demand is entirely fixed, the buyers bear the tax, and with entirely inelastic supply the sellers bear it.

The quantity sold does not change in these cases. The examples can be applied *mutatis mutandis* to the factor market. Clearly a parallel shift downward of the demand curve by the amount of the tax, with a relatively fixed factor supply (Figure V–4) leads to an almost complete backward shifting, without any noticeable fall in sales.

Figures V–5 and V–6 illustrate the more normal degrees of the elasticities of supply and demand.

In Figure V–7 supply and demand react relatively elastically to the tax. As a result, market sales decrease sharply so that the industry may even collapse. Finally, Figure V–8 illustrates the effects of various tax rates on incidence and production under particular given conditions.

(*i*) *Excursus: A Measure of Forward, Backward and Cross Shifting*

Since forward shifting via price increase diminishes individual income as does backward shifting by reducing factor earnings, we may measure the tax incidence by the total change of real income.

Following Musgrave's proposal[4] to measure budget effects of this kind we may express the individual incidence by means of the following functions:

(1) A change of product prices affects the uses side of income. If we assume that money income after taxation is constant and total income is spent only on two goods, a and b, the gain Δr is valued by the quantities *before* tax.

FIGURES V-3–V-8

Shifting of Tax on Output

Different Elasticities of Supply and Demand

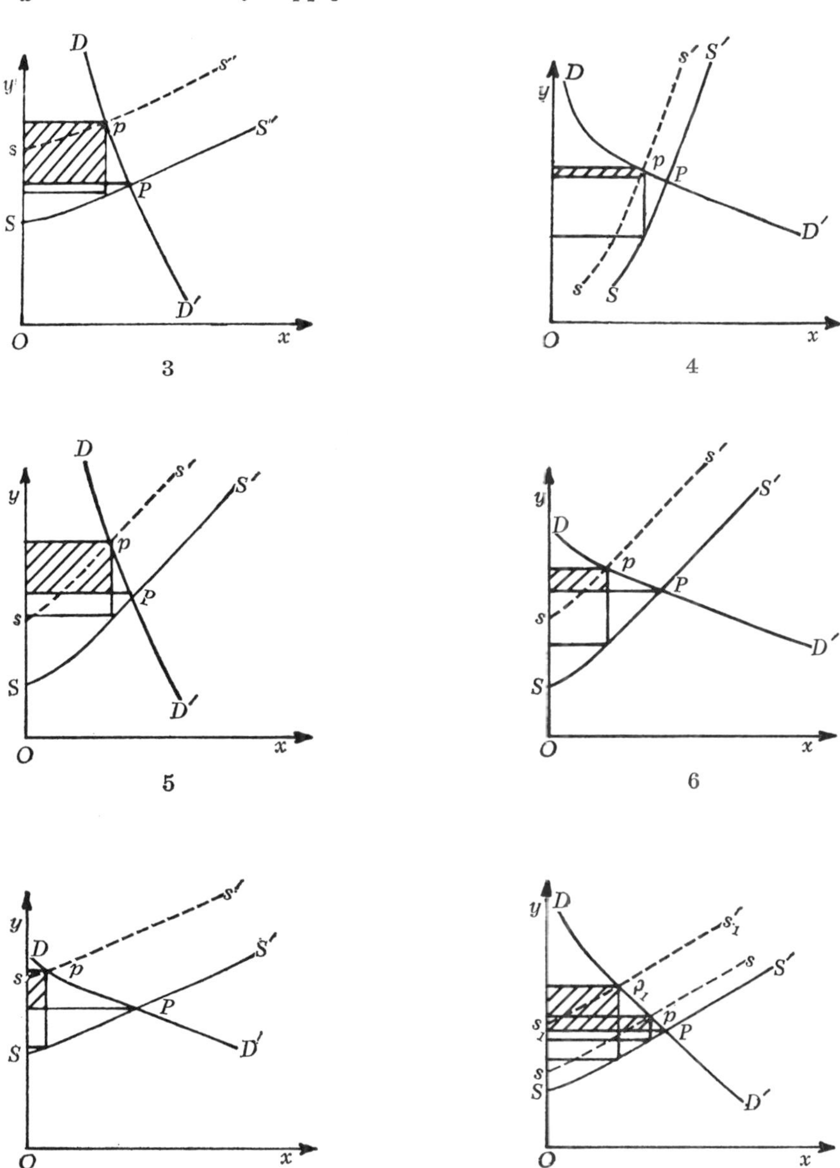

$$\Delta r = \Delta p^a q^a{}_1 + \Delta p^b q^b{}_2.$$

The loss is valued by the quantities *after* tax.

$$-\Delta r = \Delta p^a q^a{}_2 + \Delta p^b q^b{}_2.$$

(2) The change of net return may lead to an adjustment of individual services on the sources side. If w is the net wage rate and h the work hours, the change in real income (Δr) *is* $\Delta r = \Delta w h_1$ *or* $\Delta w h_2$ depending on whether we choose the hours worked before (h_1) or after (h_2) taxation.

(3) If we consider both income sides, i.e. the total change under varying money income, we may measure the total tax induced change of real income in index form

$$\Delta r = \left(\frac{w_2}{w_1} - \frac{P_2}{P_1}\right) w_1 h_1$$

where P_1 and P_2 are price averages weighted by quantities after tax. and respectively

$$\Delta r = \left(\frac{P_1}{P_2} - \frac{w_1}{w_2}\right) w_2 h_2$$

where P_1 and P_2 are price averages weighted by quantities after tax.

(j) *Incidence of a Tax on a Surplus*

Under conditions of perfect competition the surplus or net profit of a firm as the difference between total costs and gross revenue is the *result* of market price formation. And since a tax on this surplus neither affects the marginal costs nor the marginal revenues it influences neither price nor quantity, at least in the short-run. Ricardo has stated these relations for rent of land. If net revenues are greater than the tax, it can neither be shifted forward nor backward. The incidence falls completely on the net profit of the taxed firms.

We arrive at the same generalization if we start from the taxed market. Since under the pressure of perfect competition the market price will eventually be equal to the costs of the marginal producer or of the price-determining marginal product and since this producer works without net profit, the surplus tax exclusively affects the so called intra-marginal competitors who in turn are not in a position, under these assumptions, to raise the price. Since the suppliers aim at the highest net profit after taxation, they will seek better profit possibilities. If the tax is general, a cost-increasing transfer of resources is not worthwhile since the proportional and even more so a progressive tax does not make other industries more attractive. On the other hand, a special tax on surplus would, at least theoretically, allow long-term shifting.

This orthodox theory of the general non-shiftability of a surplus tax on a market of perfect competition and pure monopoly is the basis for the thesis that the modern income and corporation tax rests entirely on the taxpayer.

Do such unsuccessful marginal suppliers exist in reality and do their marginal costs or products actually determine the market price? These assumptions are being questioned in the modern literature. Thus Black[5] rejects the statistical proof of the existence of price determining "no profit firms" which Coates[6] attempted in the Colwyn Report. Actually the suppliers are singly or jointly not so powerless in the real markets as the theory assumes. Their influence on price may, together with other factors, allow a shifting of a net profits tax *under certain conditions.* But these are no longer conditions of pure but of imperfect (monopolistic) and oligopolistic competition where the profits tax may be "anticipated" and shifted by joint action either via higher prices or lower factor remunerations, *provided* other subjective and objective conditions permit it. Consequently, the view of some "practitioners" has a sound core. But the testimony of businessmen before the Colwyn Commission that surplus taxes would as "cost" taxes be invariably shifted to the consumer are, in this generalized form, naive and just as untenable as the opinion that excise and turnover taxes would be paid and borne by the firms. Apart from exaggeration in the first case, the desire to shift taxes is simply equated with its success.

(*k*) *Shifting of a Lump-Sum-Tax*

Such a tax raises fixed but not marginal costs so that price and quantity remain unaffected in the short-run. In the long-run, however, fixed costs must also be covered, so that marginal producers are eliminated when backward shifting fails and forward shifting becomes possible.

2. Shiftability under Conditions of Pure Monopoly

In a purely monopolistic market a single seller faces the total atomistic demand. From the viewpoint of the consumers the taxed good is homogeneous. The monopolist does not have to fear competition through substitution, particularly since there is no possibility that new sellers will enter the market because of his high profits. Intervention by government or sellers organizations is also not to be expected. The monopolist possesses absolute control over prices. His attempt to maximize profits is therefore limited only by demand and his costs. He sets price or quantity autonomously after feeling out the demand, so that marginal costs and marginal revenue are equal and his profit is maximized. When a pure monopolist has to pay a unit tax, he will try to evade the burden as much as possible. He will therefore compare present profit less tax with possible net profit after increasing prices or reducing factor remunerations by the whole or part of the tax. If present net profit is greater than the potential one, he will have to bear the whole tax; if not he can, through a price change, partially or completely shift the tax forward to consumers.

Therefore, the monopolistic adjustment to a specific or unit tax depends primarily on the relevant costs and the form of demand for the monopolistic good in each planning period. Let us first look at this adjustment from the cost side. If a monopolist sells from a given stock to be sold completely within a given time (market period) he will, depending on the elasticity of demand have to pay all or much of the tax out of his monopoly profit. If the product can be stored and transferred to the next production period, both the expectation about future demand and his additional costs of holding inventories will determine his price policy and with it the shifting.

If the monopolist produces continuously with unchanged size of plant the short-term adjustment depends decisively on the relevant marginal cost. Before we investigate the possible cases more closely, the incidence of a unit tax will be illustrated on the basic model.

The vertical line through the intersection of the marginal cost and marginal revenue curves determines the monopoly price C at which the quantity OQ is sold. The rectangle $FKCR$ (= product of unit profit KC and quantity sold $OQ = CR$) is the monoply profit before taxation.

If we now vary the marginal cost curve in order to analyze the effect upon the distribution of the tax, we can draw the following conclusions:

(a) If marginal costs in the relevant area of production are constant[7] and if demand (average revenue) falls evenly (Figure V–10), the incidence falls equally on both sides of the market.

(b) Rising marginal costs in the relevant curve segment allow, other

FIGURE V–9
Shifting of Product Tax—Monopoly

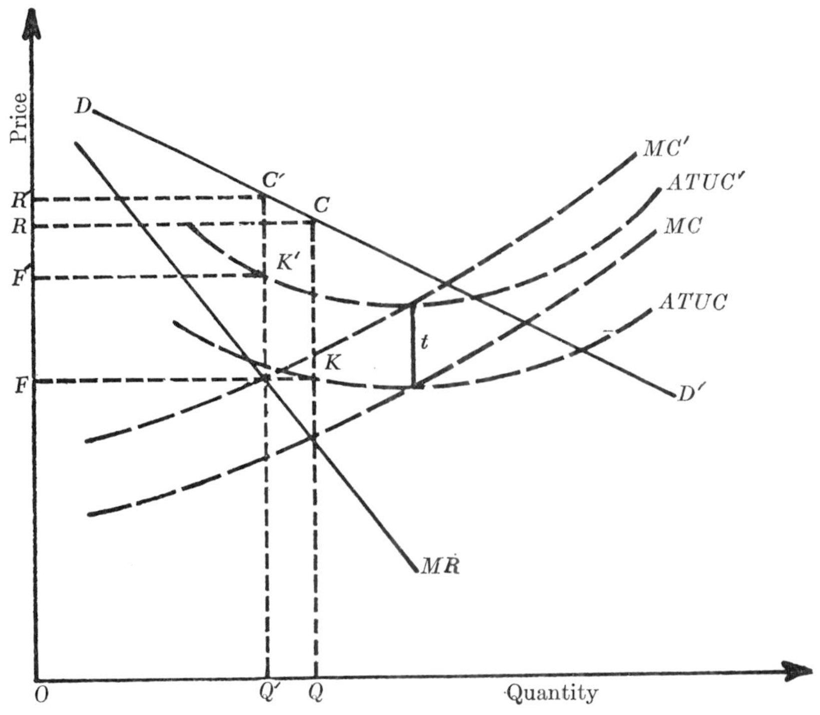

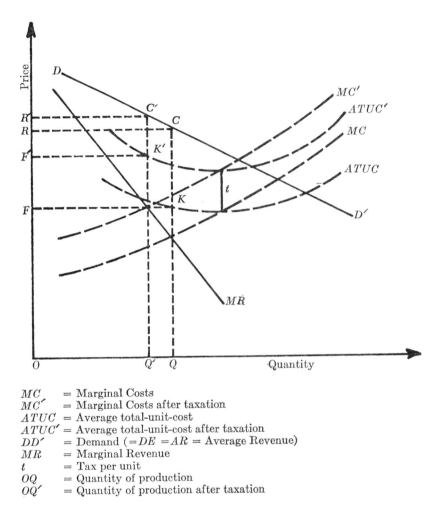

MC	= Marginal Costs
MC′	= Marginal Costs after taxation
ATUC	= Average total-unit-cost
ATUC′	= Average total-unit-cost after taxation
DD′	= Demand (= *DE* = *AR* = Average Revenue)
MR	= Marginal Revenue
t	= Tax per unit
OQ	= Quantity of production
OQ′	= Quantity of production after taxation

things being equal, a shifting of less than half of the levy, since marginal costs decrease with decreasing production (Figure V–9). The extent of the shifting depends on the slope of the marginal cost curve.

(c) However, if marginal costs fall with increased production, an assumption which may be quite realistic, the monopolist can increase

FIGURE V–10

Incidence of Product Tax—Different Marginal Costs

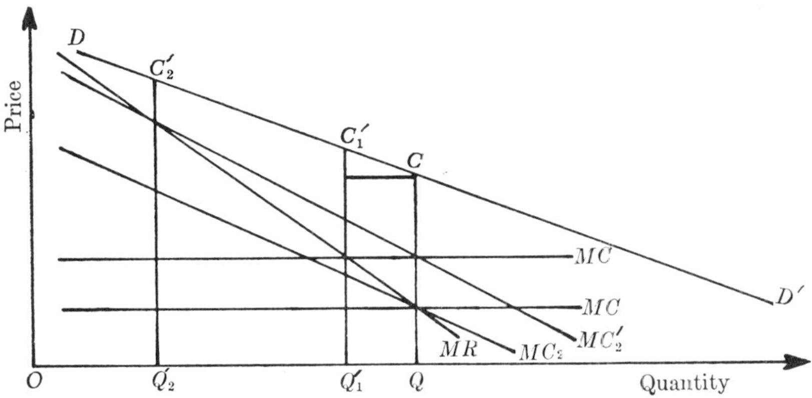

his price by more than half of the tax (Figure V–10). The more sharply they decrease the greater is the shifted amount. If marginal costs decrease more sharply than demand falls, the price increase may even exceed the tax.[8]

(d) The extreme case of fixed capacity of the monopolist is occasionally found in the literature.[9]

In this case the monopolistic firm bears a moderate unit tax entirely, since price and the quantity produced and sold remain the same, as shown in Figure V–11. The marginal cost curve *MC* shifts vertically at the capacity limit, *Q*, so that marginal costs after the tax *MC′* equal marginal revenue at the same (Cournot) point *P*.

As to the slope of the demand curve, the same statement holds true: The flatter the demand curve, the more the sold quantity will fall. This influences monopoly profit and with it the extent of shifting.[10] The many possible combinations between different marginal costs and elasticities of demand are outside the scope of this book.

In general, a monopolist knows a sales and supply market better than the great number of producers in the competitive market. His reactions to a tax on quantity sold will therefore be immediate. The more urgent the monopolist's need to sell, the greater his tax burden for any given elasticity of demand. In the most important real cases a unit tax is partially shifted, especially when the supply market is not a monopoly market. Unlike with a competitive supplier, that portion

FIGURE V–11

Commodity Tax—Incidence at Limited Capacity

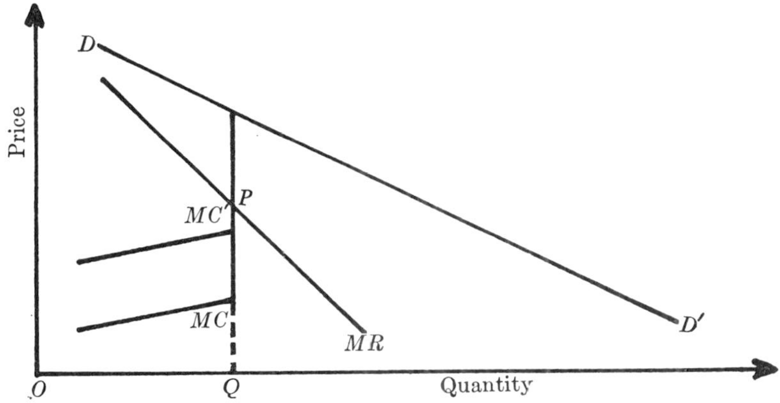

of the tax which after a period of adjustment cannot be shifted forward, will continue to be borne by the monopolistic enterprise since it is useless to move even part of the capital into other, less taxed industries as long as its profit after tax is higher than in other branches. As a rule this can be assumed. It is not worthwhile to investigate the long-run adjustments of such a pure monopoly market. In a world of substitution possibilities and government intervention, monopolies of this kind can hardly exist in the long run, and a short-term policy of maximal market exploitation which disregards government interventions, outsiders, future successes and technical progress is possible only for a limited time. As soon, however, as the monopoly price is not uniquely determined but lies somewhere between the competitive price and the price of highest profit, the otherwise subtle static monopoly and dyopoly theories lose much of their relevance for the analysis of long-run incidence.

(a) *Incidence of an Ad Valorem Tax under Monopoly Conditions*

If the tax is linked to the value of the produced or sold goods, the monopolist can also increase the price in order to shift the tax partially forward. It is merely controversial whether an ad valorem tax (expressed as percent of the sales price or gross revenue) causes a greater price rise than a correspondingly high unit tax. While Meyers[11] insists that in the latter case the monopoly price would increase more than in the former, Brown[12] proves in a practical example, that the effect can be the opposite. Fagan and Jastram believe that no difference in price increases is necessary.[13] Contrary to this opinion von Mering unambiguously demonstrates by means of a simple diagram that, depending on the amount of marginal costs, either the unit or the ad valorem tax leads to a greater price increase or that the amount shifted is the same in each case.[14]

It seems practically much more important that if an ad valorem tax enters into the price calculation, the price must necessarily be raised by more than the tax if the tax is to be completely shifted. Thus, if the sales tax is 4 per cent we have to apply the shifting formula $\frac{100 \times 4}{100 - 4}$, so 4.17 per cent of the pre-tax price must be added.

RA = average revenue curve = 100-x, RM = marginal revenue curve, CC' = marginal cost curve which is constant at 40.

The tax on total revenue amounts to 50 per cent, the tax per unit 35. Under these conditions $RM = 100 - 2x$ and the monopoly price before the tax $PQ = 70$. A gross revenue tax of 50 per cent lowers the average revenue curve to $R'A = 50 - \frac{x}{2}$, with the corresponding marginal revenue curve $R'M = 50 - x$. Consequently, the price rises to $P_1Q_1 = 90$. A product tax of 35 per unit which amounts to 50 per cent of the original monopoly price of 70, would reduce the original average cost curve RA by the constant amount of 35. As a result its ordinate would be $R''A' = 65 - x$, corresponding to the marginal revenue curve, $R''M' = 65 - 2x$. Obviously the monopoly price is now $P_2Q_2 = 87.5$, that is to say, it is less than in the case of a gross revenue tax.

At the same time Figure V–12 shows that in the case of a constant marginal cost curve of 35, the tax-induced price increase would be the same in both cases. If marginal costs are less than 35, the monopoly price would rise more sharply with a product tax than an ad valorem tax. The opposite hold when marginal costs are higher than 35.

Since in practical taxation the ad valorem tax is generally calculated on the selling price, we have the simplest form of a tax on a tax. The ad valorem tax thus tends, in principle, to increase the price more than

FIGURE V–12

Tax on Real and Money Output—Monopoly

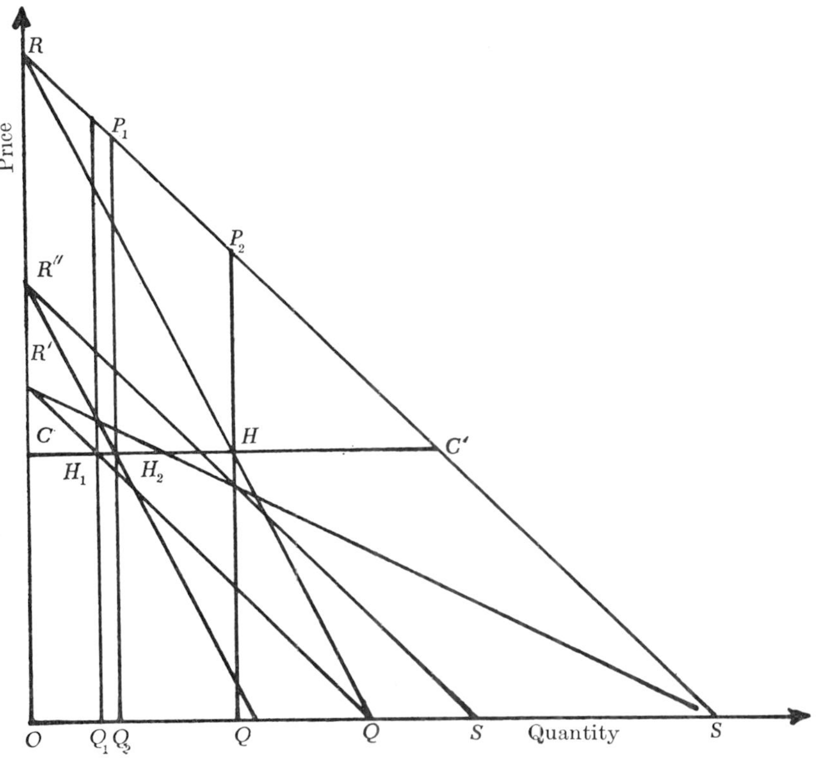

a unit tax. In general all "cost" taxes encourage shifting since the relation between tax and unit price is made explicit, strengthening the desire to shift.

(*b*) *Taxation of Pure Monopoly Profits*

A monopolist whose profit is subject to a proportional tax, is forced to bear the tax. For his net revenue is proportionally reduced at each level of production; he therefore maximizes his profit at the old level of production and sales, though the absolute value falls. The incidence affects only him. The following diagram shows these interrelations.

FIGURE V–13

Incidence of Profits Tax—Monopoly

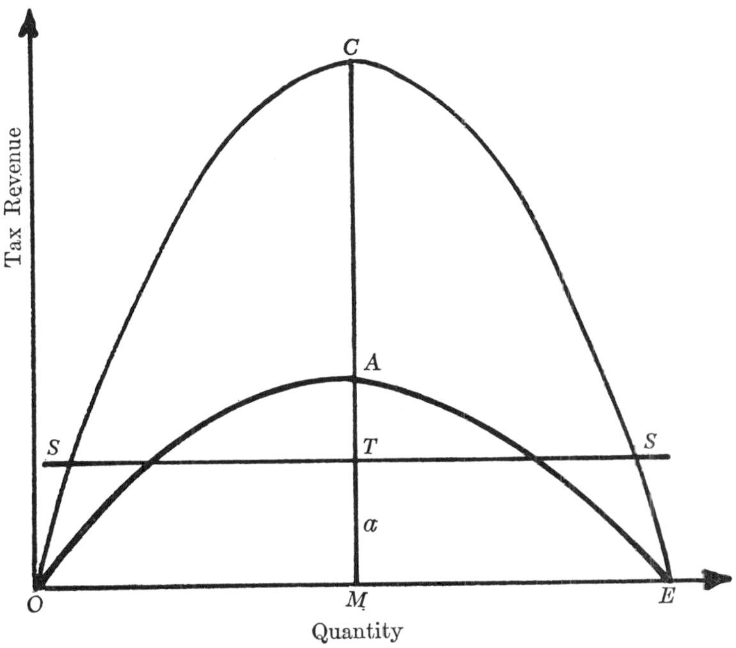

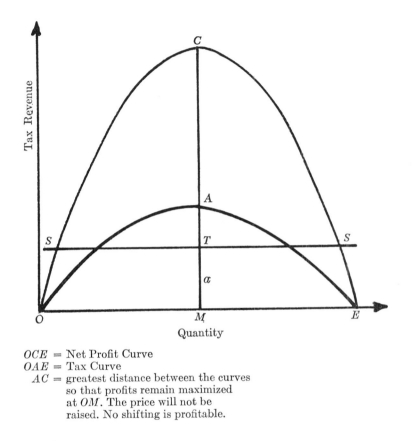

OCE = Net Profit Curve
OAE = Tax Curve
AC = greatest distance between the curves so that profits remain maximized at *OM*. The price will not be raised. No shifting is profitable.

(*c*) *Incidence of a Fixed Tax*

A tax independent of the quantity sold or revenue (for example a poll or property tax) diminishes net profits by the same amount at any level of production. Thus maximum profit is reached at previous sales. Incidence is unambiguously determined, as long as the tax does not exceed total profits. In Figure V–13 the distance between the revenue curve *OCE* and the tax curve *SS*, expresses the net profit of a monopolist, who is producing without costs, after the imposition of the fixed tax a. It is greatest at *CT*, the quantity *OM* being unchanged.

Since the tax does not affect marginal costs, the result is the same also for the case in which the costs of the monopolist are considered.

3. Incidence in Markets of Monopolistic and Oligopolistic Competition

In today's industrialized economies neither pure competition nor monopoly are typical market forms. Instead we have markets in which the individual or a whole group influences the price directly, while at the same time being exposed to a more or less strong competition from others. In principle, individual influence on the price may be the result either of product differentiation or a small number of sellers and buyers or of both. Hence a multiplicity of market structures is possible. Market behavior will also vary. It does not always correspond to a particular market form.

We begin with the tax effects on a market in which a large number of sellers offer an economically heterogeneous good. On the basis of geographic advantage, difference in quality, personal commitments or immediate possibilities of delivery the individual supplier fixes the price for his limited market area; he assumes he can keep a particular group of customers even if he increases his price, and that he can increase the sale to a certain extent if he lowers it. He chooses the price at which his net revenue is maximized. The possible substitution among goods increases the elasticity of demand for his product, so that his price is set near the monopoly or the competitive price depending on the degree of competition by substitution.

(*a*) *The Market Adjustment of the Monopolistic Competitors*

A unit tax on such a market will probably lead to a general price increase. Unlike under pure competition, the seller will adjust the price rather than the quantity. This reaction agrees largely with reality, in which there is typically a tendency to direct price changes under conditions of polypolistic competition, rather than to reduce quantities. The price changes will be the more uniform the more equally the actual or expected profits of the taxpayers are taxed. In spite of different efficiencies, production methods will be more or less the same, as soon as the number of firms in one branch has reached a certain size. The cost differences gradually cancel each other and profits become "normalized." Increased sales can usually only be obtained by increased advertising costs. Some advantages based on production processes generally serve to secure continued sales. The lack of exact knowledge about cost and demand as well as the method of calculation can also contribute to making the behavior of the competitors similar. The tax itself may even promote a common reaction. Reduced demand may affect the individual monopolistic competitor almost equally. Thus each cost-increasing tax contributes to the increase of excess capacity in markets of imperfect competition which, due to monopolistic elements or imperfect price competition, can exist even in the long-run.

If, however, demand is sensitive to price changes, the tax discriminating, and collusion about prices difficult, the individual cannot increase his price by the amount of the tax since he would lose a considerable number of his customers. The stronger the competition of any kind and the more the tax affects the competitors differently the less successful a common forward shifting will be, especially when the money supply is inelastic.

Figure V–14 illustrates this case of a unit tax where, in a market of polypolistic competition, the taxed producer pays out of his profits.

The producer bears the tax without reducing his sales; because the optimum quantity of production remains *Q*, determined by the kink *A* in the individual sales curve. If point *F* of the cost curve which gives the limit of capacity lies below *A*, the sales optimum moves to the right to maximum capacity. For the present case of incidence this change is insignificant.

(*b*) *Shifting under Conditions of Oligopoly*

Under conditions of oligopoly and weak product differentiation, the possibility and extent of shifting depend largely on the market behavior of the few sellers. As we have already pointed out at the beginning of this section, the oligopolist possesses a market influence which enables him to pursue within limits a monopolistic price policy, but only with careful attention to the reactions of the other oligopolists. If all oligopolistic firms have a common interest in peaceful market behavior then the individual possesses, within a more or less limited framework, a certain freedom of action. Only if he offends against the "esprit de corps," for example, against the conventional, often tacitly accepted behavior of the group to undertake major price changes only together, does a power struggle of the entire group against the offender

FIGURE V–14

Incidence of Output Tax—Polipolistic Competition

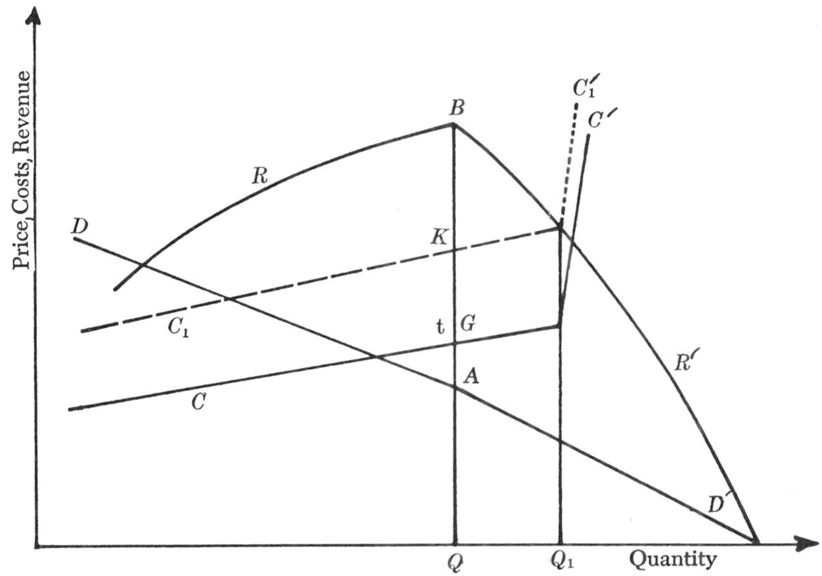

CC' = Total Costs before Unit Tax
RR' = Total Sales
DD' = Sales
Q = Limit of Sales
Q_1 = Maximum Capacity
GB = Maximum Profit before Tax
KB = Maximum Profit after Tax
GK = t = Reduction of Profit
C_1C_1' = Total Costs after Unit Tax

against group "discipline" set in. A tax affecting all oligopolists uniformly will probably help bring about or strengthen existing solidarity of behavior and common reactions. But even when cooperation has not been good, such a tax may, under the assumed circumstances, actually stimulate concerted action.

Under such oligopolistic conditions, a unit tax can be shifted. Since the costs of each supplier rise by the tax, they all find it advantageous to increase the price without having to fear counter measures by competitors. As long as the price is below the level at which total profits of the group are maximized there are no further losses. Since in reality the oligopoly price lies between the monopolistic and the competitive price—in order to keep new competitors away from the market and because cooperation is imperfect because of distrust of the other oligopolists (whose interests are after all different)—tax shifting leads to a fuller utilization of the monopolistic position. This price increase represents a genuine forward shifting because it would not have been possible before the common tax burden under given conditions.

Figure V–15 shows the result of tax shifting if the oligopolists act in concert. The sales curve of the individual oligopolist is relatively flat above the conventional price (P). This means that demand is relatively elastic in this area, because competitors react hesitatingly

FIGURE V–15

Shifting of Output Tax—
Oligopoly with Kinked Demand Curve

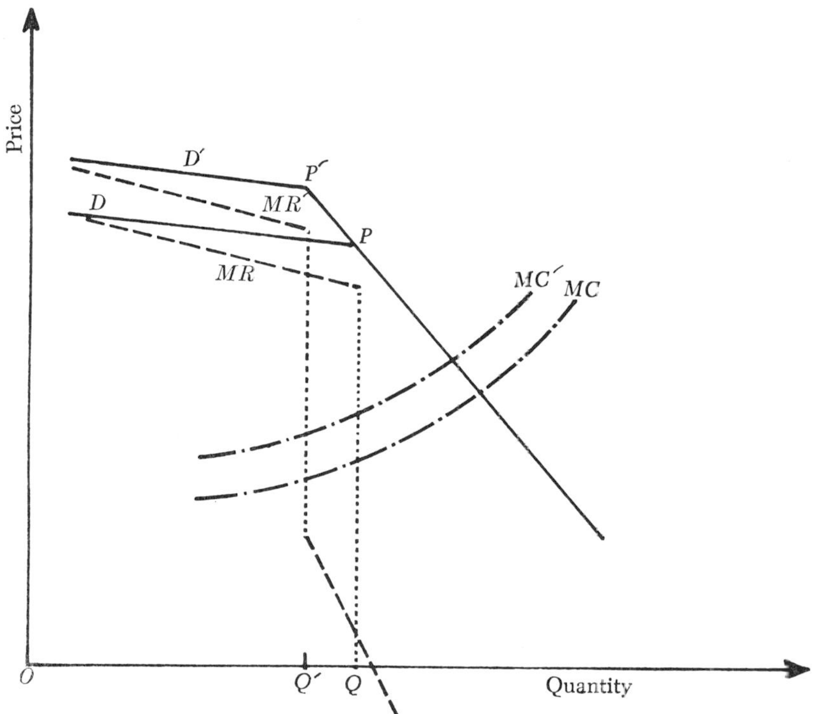

to a small price increase. The sales curve is relatively inelastic below the conventional price, since any substantial important price cut will lead to an immediate underbidding by the other members of the group, so that a price reduction would not be profitable. Thus, at the conventional price the individual sales curve is kinked. The taxing of market sales now increases the costs of the individual producers, and since all oligopolists who expect similar behavior by the other competitors increase the price by the tax, the price and with it the kink in the sales curve is shifted upward from *P* to *P′*. In these circumstances there will be a new "stable" equilibrium.[15]

(*c*) *Price Leadership and Differing Market Behavior*

When a firm has established a leading position in an oligopolistic market its strategies are generally considered reasonable and are tacitly accepted. Under such price leadership the leading firm may attempt to shift the tax forward to the consumers, since it can count on the agreement of the entire group. All members find the adjustment "reasonable" because of their increased costs and will follow it. To the extent to which a monopolistic position is approximated in this manner, a partial forward shifting succeeds. Otherwise the effects are the same as in pure monopoly, if the tax does not lead to a price war as a result of decreased sales. In addition, other price strategies which strengthen the common action of the oligopolists—as for example pricing based on average costs—facilitate tax shifting because the uncertainty of the members' reactions is eliminated or at least diminished.

But even great uncertainty about the expected reactions of competitors towards price policy or great product differentiation will probably not prevent a direct price rise, since the unit tax generally is regarded as a uniform cost increase.

Hardly ever will the tax lead directly to a price war, which would in the short-run prevent a forward shifting. If knowledge of sales is imperfect, it may be assumed that the adjustment of supply *after* shifting will lead to a kind of ruinous competition which would eliminate some individual producers.

Finally, the possibility is not to be excluded that in a tense and unsettled market situation (for example at the beginning of a depression) individual oligopolists may not be frightened by the risks of a costly power struggle and may use the tax increase as an occasion for a price war by answering with a drastic price reduction.

But these cases are quite rare. Generally, a tax on oligopoly products will, under "normal" conditions of equilibrium, lead to a common price increase and thus to a tax shifting onto the consumers. The possibility of a price increase based on the imperfect monopoly position is the characteristic defense against a tax. If demand is relatively inelastic, the tax can be shifted without difficulty. If, however, demand is elastic, the oligopolists bear a part of the tax which they pay out of their profits, and thus no firms are eliminated. In this case too, taxation tends to create excess capacities which can be maintained in the long-run, a situation which is undesirable from the standpoint of the economy as a whole, since it leads to high prices and unused means of production.[16]

4. Summary

As the step-by-step analysis of the elementary interrelations of incidence has shown, market form and behavior as well as the type of the tax affect differently the possibility, direction, amount and course of shifting.

(a) In markets of monopolistic and oligopolistic competition the tax can be shifted without the necessary elimination of marginal enterprises or capacities. Even relatively elastic demand leads only rarely to the liquidation of firms as excess capacity may continue even in the long-run due to imperfect competition.

(b) The more equally the actual and expected profit of the taxpayers is affected, the more uniformly and directly is shifting attempted. Since with monopolistic competition the differences in efficiency are, as a rule, not significant, and since average cost calculation prevails and marginal firms also usually earn a profit, the tax affects the firms almost uniformly, which also favors the opportunities for shifting.

(c) How much of the tax can be shifted depends also on whether the market price is closer to the monopoly or the competitive price.

(d) If oligopolists act in concert, there exists even the possibility that more than the tax may be shifted, since a common price increase permits a more intensive exploitation of the monopolistic position than before. With absolute monopoly the opposite is the case, since the maximum profit has, as a rule, already been reached before.

(e) A detailed analysis of the adjustment process over time under perfect competition and pure monopoly indicates: (1) The conclusions of previous incidence theories are necessarily limited and one-sided. Thus the assumption is logically impossible and completely unrealistic that the textbook competitor, who already supplies only minimal amounts, will reduce his supply *just a little* in order to shift the tax. (2) Eventually supply will adjust to the tax, usually *after* the price has been raised. Practically, however, this process is closely linked to dynamic developments, in which case the monetary situation becomes increasingly relevant. (3) The long-term incidence of a tax on a monopoly is similar in reality to that of a tax on an oligopoly, since the actual monopoly price is seldom fixed without consideration of government interference, substitution or other possible competition as well as future technical development.

Thus market form and behavior influence shifting considerably. Hence a thorough knowledge of the *empirical* market is necessary for the analysis of practical incidence problems.

III. *Dynamic Micro-Incidence—Recent Developments*

The main characteristics of neoclassical micro-incidence theory are the change of the level of income (profits or factor earnings, or consumer surplus) via price changes as a measure of shifting and, in the long-run, the reduction of the capital stock (disinvestment) in the taxed form or industry in order to shift the burden. More recently Schlesinger, Musgrave, Krzyzaniak, Hall, and Gordon have in empirical studies proposed to take the rate of return on capital (i.e. relative factor shares) instead of the absolute level of income (i.e. profits or the share of profits) as a measure of shifting. These dynamic analyses allow also for growth in the economy and changes in the productivity of capital and labor.

We will deal with these approaches in chapters VI and VIII and concentrate here on the theoretical background of tax shifting in a growing firm. We will use in general the Musgrave-Krzyzaniak measure of shifting, i.e. the ratio of the return on private capital to the tax liability and we shall compare this model to a simple micro-economic growth model previously published by M. Rose.[17] The growth rate of a firm (w) is measured by its capital and it corresponds to the growth rate of the capital supply to it (k) and capital input (v):

$$w = k = v$$

In the case of self-financing through profits or credit financing the company's rate of growth consists on the capital supply side of the following items:

(1) $$k = s\frac{R - ihk}{K(1 - h)} \quad \text{or}$$

(2) $$k = s\frac{r - ih}{1 - h} = sg.$$

where
R = gross profit
K = total capital
s = ratio of self-financing out of profits
i = rate of interest
h = ratio of credit financing
r = rate of return on total capital
g = rate of return on equity

Thus the rate of growth is the product of self-financing and the rate of return on equity.

By substituting $r = (p - c)\ \beta$ into equation (2) we get

(3) $$k = \frac{\beta(p - c) - ih}{1 - h} = sg.$$

where
p = price of the product
c = unit cost
β = coefficient of capital productivity.

p: The five variables of equation (3) are determined as follows:

The price of the product p is assumed to be a function of turnover (U). If v is equal to the rate of growth of turnover we get:

(4) $$p = p_0 - b_1 v \text{ where:}$$
p_0 = equilibrium price
b_1 = a constant, and
$U_t = U_{t+1} = U_{t+2}$

c: Unit costs are determined by

(5) $$c = l\frac{M}{X} + Z\frac{V}{X} \quad \text{where:}$$
l = wage rate
M = employment
V = capital input
Z = capital consumption as fraction of V
X = output

$$\text{Let } \frac{X}{M} = \alpha = \frac{X}{V}\frac{V}{M} = \beta\epsilon, \text{ where:}$$
α = productivity of labor
ϵ = capital intensity.

Substituting into equation (5) we get

$$c = \frac{l + z\epsilon}{\alpha}. \tag{6}$$

When all variables are constant over time, equation (6) becomes the new line (6a):

$$c = \frac{\bar{l} + \bar{z}\bar{\epsilon}}{\bar{\alpha}} = \bar{c}\,.\text{[18]} \tag{6a}$$

The interest rate i is assumed to be constant, i.e.

i: $i = \bar{i}$.

h: h is assumed not to exceed a specified marginal value $\bar{h}$.

s: The lower limit of s is given by the minimum interest on equity.

The maximum rate of growth can now be written as:

$$w = sg = s\frac{\bar{\alpha}p_0 - (\bar{l} + \bar{z}\bar{\epsilon} + \bar{i}h\bar{\epsilon})}{\bar{\epsilon}(1 - h) + s\bar{\alpha}b} \tag{7}$$

We have already mentioned that the measure of shifting *Ig* may be derived from the equation

$$Ig = 1 - \frac{g(1 - \pi)g\pi}{\pi g_\pi}, \text{ where}$$
π = tax rate.

Since r is determined in the Rose model by w, *Ig* may be expressed by the following equation:

$$I_g = \frac{\alpha(w_\pi)[p(w_\pi) - c(w_\pi)] - \alpha(w)[p(w) - c(w)]}{\pi\alpha\,(w_\pi)\,[p(w_\pi) - c(w_\pi)]}. \tag{8}$$

All expressions give the equilibrium adjustment to the tax π. If *Ig* is zero, the entrepreneurs have to pay the whole tax. If *Ig* is one, the tax is shifted completely. If

$$\alpha(w_\pi) = \alpha(w) \text{ and } c(w_\pi) = c(w),$$

Ig can be easily transformed into the well known neoclassical measure of shifting I_p:

$$I_p = \frac{p\,(w_\pi) - p(w)}{\pi[p(w_\pi) - c(w_\pi)]}.$$

Thus, in the long-run and under certain assumptions the neoclassical measure of shifting becomes again important. However, this case is only one of several possible constellations of the growth process.[19]

We can now deduce the degree of shifting and the effective incidence of a tax on profits, output and turnover in our model. The effective incidence may be measured by the relative decrease of the firm's growth rate (m) due to the tax.

1. In the case of a proportional profits tax π the rate of growth becomes:

$$w = sg\pi\,(1 - \pi) = \frac{s(1 - \pi)[\bar{\alpha}p_0 - (i + \bar{z}\bar{\epsilon} + \bar{\iota}\bar{h}\bar{\epsilon})]}{\bar{\epsilon}(1 - h) + s(1 - \pi)\,\bar{\alpha}b_1}. \tag{9}$$

On the assumption that formal and effective incidence are the same, i.e. if the tax is not shifted, the relative decrease of the growth rate after tax (m_π) is equal to the tax rate (π). The rate of growth to be chosen after the imposition of the tax is shown in the following graph:

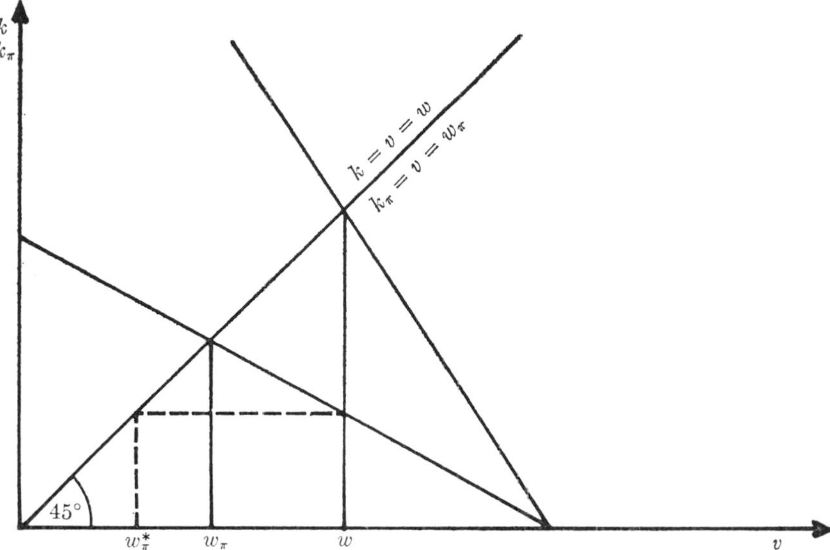

It is easily seen, that the relative decrease of the rate of growth $\left(m_\pi = \frac{w - w_\pi}{w}\right)$ is smaller than the tax rate $\left(\pi = \frac{w - w^*}{w}\right)$. Unlike in the neoclassical model the firm can shift part of a profits tax.

Equations (8), (9), and (7) show that

(10) $$I_g = I_p = \frac{\bar{\alpha} s b_1}{\bar{\epsilon}(1-\bar{h}) + \bar{s}\,\bar{\alpha}\,b_1}.$$

This means that the possibility of shifting a tax on profits is independent of the tax rate. On the other hand, it increases more than proportionately with the rate of growth (decreased m_π), the ratio of self-financing out of profits, and the ratio of credit financing. For increasing rates of s and h, these relationships can be pictured as follows:

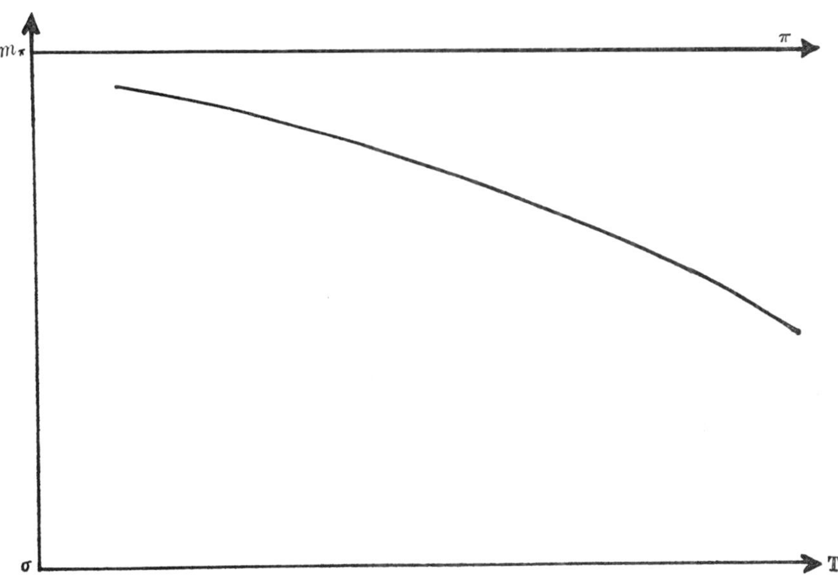

2. A turnover tax at the rate y decreases the initial equilibrium rate of growth by:

(11) $$s\frac{yp(w)X}{K(1-h)} = s\frac{yp(w)\bar{\alpha}}{\bar{\epsilon}(1-\bar{h})}.$$

3. The formula for the effect of a tax on output on the rate of growth is:

(12) $$s\frac{\eta X}{K(1-h)} \text{ where } \eta = \text{tax per unit.}$$

A comparison of the three taxes leads to the following results:

(a) Since equation (10) applies to all three taxes, it follows that the shifting possibilities are independent both of the tax type and the tax rate.

(b) Depending on the assumptions of the model the tax on profits has the highest, and the tax on output the lowest effective incidence. That is:

$$m_\pi > m_y > m\eta.$$

Notes

1. Expectations of future demand and price developments may delay shifting in the short-run.
2. For the sake of simplicity (excluding problems of point and arc elasticity) and on account of the limitations of the results, we express the ability to adjust or price sensitivity of supply and demand absolutely in terms of the slope of both curves.
3. The simple analytical proof is given, among others, by A. Cournot (*Researches into the Mathematical Principles of the Theory of Wealth*) and by von Mering (*Die Steuerüberwälzung, op. cit.*, pp. 58–59). If $f(a)$ is the supply function, $g(a)$ the demand function and t the unit tax, then the quantity sold before taxation can be expressed by the root of the equation $f(a) = g(a)$, and the quantity a_2 sold after imposition of the levy with the root of the equation $f(a) + t = g(a)$. The market price after tax would be $f(a_2) + t = g(a_2)$. The incidence is thus: $I = \frac{f(a_2) - f(a_1)}{g(a_2) - g(a_1)}$. If the tax is sufficiently small, a Cournot premise and object of much controversy, and if the functions are linear, then the following equations hold approximately: $g(a_2) = g(a_1) + (a_2 - a_1)\, g'(a_1)$; $f(a_2) = f(a_1) + (a_2 - a_1)\, f'(a_1)$; so that the incidence is expressed in $I = \frac{f'(a_1)}{g'(a_1)}$.
4. Musgrave, *Theory, op. cit.*, pp. 217–221.
5. Black, *Incidence of Income Taxes, op. cit.*, p. 9 *passim*.
6. W. H. Coates, "Incidence of Income Tax," in *Report of the Committee on National Debt and Taxation* (Colwyn Report) (London, 1927), Appendix XI.
7. A case dealt with by many earlier investigations, however, under the assumption of average costs.
8. See Joan Robinson (*Imperfect Competition, op. cit.*, p. 76 *passim*), who extensively analyzes the short-run shifting, without considering the practical significance of the examples. We limit ourselves to this brief discussion and refer the reader to the verbal, mathematical and geometrical arguments (with numerous examples) of Brown ("Incidence

of a General Output or General Sales Tax," *loc. cit.*, p. 96 *passim*), von Mering (*Die Steuerüberwälzung*, p. 41), Fasiani (*Elementi, loc. cit.*, p. 204) and in the earlier works of Cournot, p. 63 and F. Y. Edgeworth, II (London, 1925), 86. However, some of these writers base their analyses on long-run average cost curves.

9. As an example, Otto von Mering's article, "Steuerüberwälzung" (The Shifting of Taxation), *HdS*, X, 178, should be mentioned.
10. If the elasticity of demand is the same while the marginal cost curve is constant, the monopolist will adjust his price only by the amount of the tax, since an adjustment to the respective degree of elasticity would not bring a profit. If the elasticity rises degressively (progressively), price increases will cause rising (falling) profit losses. See Robinson, pp. 14, 76, *passim*, and von Mering, *The Shifting and Incidence of Taxation* (Philadelphia, 1942), pp. 40 *passim* and 243; and C. S. Shoup, *Shifting and Incidence Theory: Taxes on Monopoly* (New York, 1950).
11. Albert L. Meyers, *Modern Economic Problems* (New York, 1939), p. 43.
12. Brown, "Incidence," p. 136 *passim*.
13. Elmer D. Fagan and R. W. Jastram, "Tax Shifting in the Short Run," *QJ*, LIII (1939), 584.
14. von Mering, *Shifting and Incidence, op. cit.*, p. 36 *passim*. His diagram which is reproduced in the text illustrates these relations.
15. See among others H. L. Hall and C. J. Hitch, "Price and Business Behavior," *Oxford Economic Papers* (Oxford, 1939), No. 2, p. 2 *passim;* and W. Fellner, *Competition among the Few* (New York, 1949).
16. See Edward Hastings Chamberlin, *The Theory of Monopolistic Competition*, 8th ed. (Cambridge, Massachusetts, 1962), p. 109.
17. M. Rose "Wachsende Unternehmen unter dem Einfluss der Besteuerung. Ein Beitrag zur mikro-ökonomischen Steuerinzidenztheorie," *FA*, XXVIII, 1 (1968), 1–25.
18. This equation implies a Leontief production function with constant returns to scale.
19. With growing firms, the neoclassical measure of shifting always leads to misleading results when labor productivity and unit costs are affected by the tax.

6

Distributional Effects: Empirical Analyses of Formal (Legal, Statutory or Intended) and Effective Incidence

I. *Shifting of Particular Taxes*

1. Corporation Income or Profits Tax

(a) The Deplorable Situation.

Who bears the corporate income tax? This question is one of the most controversial issues in taxation as both the Föhl[1]-controversy in *Finanzarchiv* and the Symposium[2] on business taxation at Wayne State University reveal. Economists and business men alike differ strongly among themselves on the shifting of this tax. To illustrate the situation I need only quote some representatives of these divergent views. While Föhl holds that the corporate profits tax is fully (Boulding,[3] almost entirely) shifted and the government simply uses the corporation as a tax collector, Goode supports the orthodox theory. The initial or short-run incidence of the corporate income tax seems to be largely on corporations and their stockholders. He sees little foundation for the belief that a large part of the corporate tax comes out of wages or is passed on to consumers in the same way that a selective excise tax tends to be shifted to the buyers. His view corresponds to Harberger's opinion on long-run incidence.

More recently Goode perfectly describes the confusion in the incidence discussion as follows:

> This does not mean simple observation of overall results (e.g. deduce full everyone to choose whatever assumption best fits his own predilections or policy program. Economists' recent skepticism about the incidence of the corporation income tax reflects a rebellion against previously accepted theories. At the micro level, the assumption that firms attempt to maximize

> profits has been questioned. At the macro level, there has been increased willingness to accept the hypothesis that any increase in costs or in taxation will provoke a general rise in the price level and that this will be made possible by an accommodating monetary policy.[4]

Instead of theorizing Musgrave rightly recommended empirical testing.

> This does not mean simple observation of overall results (e.g. deduce full shifting from the fact that the gross rate of return doubled from the mid-twenties to mid-fifties, or conclude no shifting from the fact that the profit share showed little change) but a serious effort to isolate the effects to tax rate changes on the relevant variables.[5]

(*b*) *Short-Run Incidence*

Although up to now the pure theory of tax shifting and incidence has predominated, recently, empirical and statistical research has considerably reduced the gap between theory and the applicability of the results for governmental and entrepreneurial policy.[6] Since the short-run price effects of the tax are of decisive importance for efficient fiscal policy, the incidence of the relatively high corporation tax moves to the center of empirial considerations. E. R. Schlesinger has analyzed the shifting of corporate income tax, considering also stability and economic growth.

1. Since it seems almost impossible to determine statistically the short-term shifting of the corporation income tax, Schlesinger suggests a different way to estimate, at least approximately, the order of magnitude of shifting. Using the shiftability of other business taxes for comparison and utilizing knowledge of market structure, he argues as follows: Because the shifting process itself leads to increased tax receipts, this comparison is difficult. If, for example, a specific tax of two dollars per unit is placed on an untaxed profit of four dollars, the result would be, with complete shifting, a price which is two dollars higher than before the imposition of the tax, the tax receipts likewise amounting to two dollars. If the corporation tax is computed at fifty percent of the value, a price increase of two dollars would result in tax receipts of three dollars per unit, which would result in a tax on the consumers of only 66 percent compared to 100 percent with a shifted specific tax.

The slightly abridged Table VI–1 illustrates these relationships, and gives an idea of the order of magnitude of shifting.[7]

TABLE VI–1

Consumer Incidence, at Different Tax Rates, of Each One Billion Dollars of Total Tax Revenues under Various Assumptions of Comparative Corporate-Income Tax Shiftability

(In Millions of Dollars)
(shortened)

Total Comparative Price Effect[a]	*Corporate Income Tax Rate*[b]			
	15%	*38%*	*52%*	*57%*
25.0%	$ 241	$ 228	$ 221	$219
50.0%	465	420	397	389
75.0%	674	584	540	525
100.0%	870	725	657	637
149.3%	1,220	953	840	807
161.3%	1,299	1,000	877	840
208.3%	1,587	1,163	1,000	952

[a] The comparative total price effect (x) is defined as the ratio, in percentage terms, of *A*) the price increase which would be associated with the shifting of the entire corporate-income tax to *B*) the price increase that would have accompanied full shifting of a specific tax of an equivalent amount per unit of sales.

[b] The percentage share of total tax collections falling on the consumer is equal to the increase in unit price (xT) divided by total tax collections per unit ($rP + rxT$), where r is the corporate-income tax rate. P is the profit margin, and T is the specific tax. However, since for the sake of meaningful comparability r must be defined as equal to T/P (see note 1), this expression can be simplified to $x/1 + xr$.

Schlesinger also compares the incidence of higher and lower tax rates.[8] He summarizes these results in Table VI–2.

If one takes market structure into account, the shifting results can be modified by economic sectors.

Schlesinger concludes that for a fiscal policy which maintains stability and economic growth "the quantitative importance of the effects of any shifting are so minor that they can be safely ignored in forecasting and policy-making. The critical issue, from a broad fiscal-policy standpoint, is the existence of the corporate-income tax itself, and not its shiftability."[9] Thus Schlesinger doubts the practical significance of all analyses and their results as to the degree of shiftability in the short and long-run. According to conventional doctrine the

TABLE VI–2

Consumer Incidence, at Different Tax Rates, of Each One Billion Dollars of Marginal Tax Revenues under Various Assumptions of Comparative Corporate-Income Tax Shiftability
(In Millions of Dollars)

Comparative Marginal Price Effect[1]	*Corporate Income Tax Rate*			
	15%	*38%*	*52%*	*57%*
25%	$ 59	$ 53	$ 51	$ 50
50	222	185	167	162
75	473	369	323	305
100	803	586	499	484

[1]The comparative marginal price effect is defined as the ratio, in percentage terms, of A) the price increase which would be associated with the shifting of an increase in the corporate-income tax to B) the price increase which would have accompanied full shifting of an increase in a specific tax of an equivalent amount per unit of sales.

corporation tax cannot, as a rule, be shifted in the short-run if the capital stock remains relatively constant. From a long-run viewpoint, shifting depends on a series of factors such as the form of the corporation and profit elasticity of the supply of capital.

2. Musgrave and Krzyzaniak's empirical study (the K-M study) focuses on the rate of return earned on capital instead of on the absolute level or the share of profits as the measure of shifting.[10] The corporation tax rates are predetermined with a one-year lag or without any lag. Shifting in manufacturing and other industries is measured by the regression coefficients between the rates of return and of the tax. Variables such as accelerated depreciation and inflation as well as various concepts of capital are considered in different experiments.

In two models they examine the dependence of the rate of return on the (in their opinion) most important independent variables.

$$\text{Model A: } Y_{gt} = a_0 + a_1C_{t-1} + a_2V_{t-1} + a_3I_t + a_4L_t + a_5G_t + a_6L_{t-1} + U_t$$

$$\text{Model B: } Y_{gt} = b_0 + b_1C_{t-1} + b_2V_{t-1} + b_3I_t + b_4Z_t + b_5G_t + b_6\,Z_{t-1} + U_t$$

C consumption expenditure standardized by division by GNP
G Federal purchases, standardized by division by GNP
I ratio of tax accruals other than corporate tax, minus government transfers to GNP
L standardized tax liability
U stochastic variable
V ratio of inventory to sales in manufacturing
Yg gross rate of return
Z statutory tax rate
t represents time

The models differ only in the tax variables. In model A the standardized tax liability is:

$$L_t = \frac{T_t}{K_{t-1}} \qquad \frac{\text{tax liability, accrual base}}{\text{capital stock}}$$

$$= Z_t^* \cdot Y_{gt} \qquad \text{effective tax rate} \cdot \text{gross rate of return}$$

In model B we have only the legal or statutory rate, Z_t. The effective tax rate in model A is more appropriate than Z_t, but it is a dependent variable in the system.

Y is a function of the selected variables estimated by multiple correlation. The factors $a_1(b_1) \ldots a_6(b_6)$ are regression coefficients.

$$S_t = \frac{Y_{gt} - Y'}{Z_t^* \cdot Y_{gt}} \qquad Y' = \text{priming of } Y \text{ variables indicates their estimated value for zero tax.}$$

If we insert the shifting measure in model A we get

$$S_{g,t} = \frac{Y_{g,t} - Y'_t}{L_t}$$

and as therefore $Y_{g,t} - Y'_t - a_4L_t$, we get $S_{g,t} - a_4$. The gross shifting measure thus is the estimated coefficient of the tax variable.

In model B we get $S_{g,t} = \frac{b_4}{Y_{g,t}}$. Here the extent of shifting depends inversely on the rate of return.

The result of the standard model indicates a full shifting, in one case even of 134 percent.[11]

Break summarizes the criticisms expressed at the Wayne State Symposium on business taxation. He arranges the major attacks on the K-M's overshifting thesis into three groups:[12]

TABLE VI–3

Estimated Degrees of Shifting

	General observations, rate-of-return indicator		*Model A*	
	1955–57 with 1927–29	*1955–57 with 1936–39*	*All years*	*Postwar*
All Manufacturing				
Equity	124	136	123	108
Total Capital	134	134	134	121
Equity, with inflation correction	n.c.	99	101	78
Equity, assets above $50 million	124	121	121	117
Equity, assets below $50 million	141	129	129	42
Other Groups				
15 largest firms, price leaders	147	111	111	111
15 largest firms, price followers	140	89	89	118
26 Steel companies	n.c.	157	123	122
12 Textile companies	n.c.	21	123	175

(1) The validity of the theoretical model is doubted.

Goode notes that one of the dependent variables, the rate of return on corporate capital, is subject to large errors of measurement which may have a significant effect on the empirical estimates obtained, and both Slitor and Goode complain about the imprecision in the definition of the variable used to measure effective tax rates. By including excess profits taxes in its numerator and the losses of deficit companies in its denominator, they argue, the tax variable fails to isolate the rate changes that can logically be expected to induce corporate attempts at tax shifting. Still more disturbing, however, are the questions raised concerning the three non-tax independent variables used in the basic K-M model. To Slitor the prior-year change in the ratio of consumption to GNP is only a "pseudo-accelerator," and Goode wonders why, if the variable does represent the acceleration principle, it was not defined as the ratio of the change in consumption to GNP, or as the rate of change in GNP or in some other general measure of economic activity. The second independent variable, the prior-year inventory to sales ratio in manufacturing, is a plausible measure of the pressure of costs on profit margins, but, understandably, Goode concludes that ". . . on economic grounds, the one-year lag is curious." The third variable, the current-year ratio to GNP of federal, state and local non-corporate taxes, minus government transfers to domestic recipients and grants-in-aid to state and local governments, is perhaps the most perplexing of all. On the one hand, it might represent the impact of rising (or falling) governmental operations on profits and hence have a positive coefficient, and on the other, it might reflect the negative influence on corporate profits of higher non-corporate taxes, government expenditures being taken as given. In the K-M study it is the latter result that apparently emerges.

(2) The second set of criticisms concerns multicollinearity, a familiar econometric problem. Are the tax effects really isolated from the effects of other variables that influenced corporate profit rates in the period and were also correlated with corporate tax rates? How sensitive is the estimated size of their tax rate coefficient to the specification of the empirical model?

On neither question is there a meeting of the minds of the disputants. Slitor does test the validity of his criticisms by using an "economic pressure" variable to supplant or supplement the independent variables used by K and M in their basic model, but the results he obtains, indicating a drop in the shifting measure from 134–141 percent to 87–99 percent, are ambiguous. They do, to be sure, show a considerable degree of instability in the shifting coefficient, but they do little to refute the K-M conclusion that the corporate profits tax is fully shifted in the short-run. In addition, the disputants argue inconclusively over whether or not inclusion in the model of an unlagged pressure variable creates a simultaneous-relations problem and hence results in biased statistical estimates.

(3) A third category of criticisms focuses on the plausibility of the results.

To Slitor shifting on such a scale ". . . long- or short-run, defies credulity and Goode finds it hard to believe, as do I, that had corporate tax rates remained constant between 1936–39 and 1955–57, the before-tax rate of return on the total capital of manufacturing corporations would have fallen between the two periods. Yet the K-M model predicts, for example, that if 1955–57 tax rates had applied in 1936–39, the before-tax rate of return would have been 16.66 percent, compared to an actual rate of 7.46 percent in 1936–39 and one of 16.33 percent in 1955–57. Similarly unorthodox is the K-M "ratchet effect" under which profits tax changes fail to reduce corporate income on the way up but do augment on the way down. The latter finding, however, is based on a single, and rather special, statutory tax rate decrease: the pre-announced removal of the Korean excess profits tax in 1954—and hence, in the words of Slitor, ". . . it hangs by a statistical thread." Another aspect of the general plausibility test concerns the "price umbrella" effect that is implied by full and rapid shifting of corporate tax increases. Here the argument is that profitable firms, by increasing their sales prices and gross profit margins in order to shift the tax, will provide inefficient firms with a better economic environment in which to continue to operate. Slitor tests this hypothesis by relating changes in the relative size of the deficit corporation group in manufacturing to tax rate changes for four periods between 1926–29 and 1957–60. The results, however, are inconclusive because of uncertainty as to how much of the negative correlation found should be attributed to the tax rate changes rather than to other factors.

3. In a recently published empirical study Gordon investigates the short-run incidence of the corporation income tax in U.S. manufacturing.[13] He states that the growing productivity of capital has improved the corporate rates of return in the same way that wages increased with the rising average productivity of labor. On the average, firms were not able to go beyond this and shift the increased tax between 1925 and 1962. Gordon attempts to avoid the inconsistency between the rate of return and income share measures of tax shifting in the K-M study. He uses a model of markup pricing behavior, specifying productivity as an input and thus obtaining consistent tax shifting coefficients relative to *both* the corporate rate of return and the income share.

Musgrave and Krzyzaniak have refuted Gordon's critique.[14] They state that Gordon also fails to integrate satisfactorily the tax variable into a structural system as part of the price equation. His model, like that of M and K can thus not be used to explain the mechanism or direction of shifting: It measures only total incidence.

4. The result of Hall's econometric study on short-run shifting of the corporation income tax is along traditional lines. Hall characterizes his method as follows:

> In contrast to previous attempts involving comparison of such variables as profit margin on sales, profit rates on invested capital, the profit share of income originating in the corporate sector, another attempt to investigate short-term shifting appeared desirable, and a new approach which deals directly with wages and profits as productive contributions of labor and capital appeared to offer promise.[15]

Hall's analysis refers to the years 1919–59. He applies a production function of the Cobb-Douglas type to data on output, capital employed and labor input. The results of his statistical study more nearly confirm the thesis of non-short-run shifting than that of full or over shifting.

5. Goode's views on incidence are somewhere in between and reflect skepticisms about methods, figures and facts:

> My conclusion is that the case for short-run shifting of a large fraction of the corporation income tax remains unproved. My own inclination is to continue to employ the working hypothesis that little short-run shifting occurs and that, with a given capital stock, changes in the corporate tax rate affect mainly profits.
>
> My hypothesis is that short-run changes in corporate profits reflect mainly changes in the economic environment, particularly the rate of capacity utili-

zation and the degree of inflationary pressures. The level and rate of change of government expenditures contribute importantly to capacity utilization and inflationary or deflationary pressures and are also associated with statutory and effective corporate tax rates.[16]

(c) *Long-Run Incidence*

1. A. C. Harberger considers the long-run effects of the corporation tax of greatest theoretical and practical interest.[17] He uses a general-equilibrium framework with the same variables of relative factor prices and income distribution as writers in the field of international trade theory. At the end of his study he draws some inferences about the probable incidence of this tax in the United States.

His overall conclusion confirms the traditional opinion that capital probably bears very close to the full tax burden. All plausible alternative sets of assumptions about the relevant elasticity lead to this result. Even if we assume either that the tax substantially affects the rate of saving or that savings (supply of capital) are interest elastic, the general result would be modified only slightly. It would by no means support the opinion that large fractions of the tax fall on consumers and/or laborers.

2. J. C. Cragg, A. C. Harberger, and P. Mieszkowski confirm Harberger's results using an entirely different approach.[18] They operate within the Krzyzaniak-Musgrave framework incorporating only cyclical and wartime variables. In an introduction they emphasize the difficulties arising from the K-M model in determining the incidence of the corporation income tax from empirical evidence. A variety of interacting forces other than the corporate income tax change may operate secularly and cyclically on the distribution of income as we have shown in Figure I–1 and Figure II–1.

The three authors conclude that capital bears almost the entire burden of the corporate income tax (90 to 120 per cent) thus asserting that K-M's shifting results are not valid.

In a (unpublished) note to *IPE* Musgrave and Krzyzaniak refute the Cragg-Harberger-Mieszkowski results. Furthermore in a recent paper Krzyzaniak deals with the central problem of all modern empirical attempts to build up a model for measuring the shifting process: Whether tax rates are endogenous or not.[19]

3. Krzyzaniak has recently published a further empirical approach to long-run shifting.[20] Compared with K-M's short-run analysis he develops four neoclassical growth models and two indicators to

measure shifting: the rate of capital return and the share of profits in total national income. He examines the effects both of partial and general profits taxes using as do Hall and Harberger, Cobb-Douglas and CES production functions. The elasticity of substitution between products both of the taxed and untaxed sectors (partial profits tax) and factor inputs (general profits tax) plays, of course, a decisive role. Since in the long run taxation will reduce saving and investment, he concludes that a corporate income tax is shifted to a large extent.

If we compare Krzyzaniak's assumptions with our observations and experiences in all western countries we may doubt his fundamental premise that profits taxes will diminish the saving and investment rates. In spite of heavy profit taxation in most industrialized countries, net investment and hence growth rates are, in historical perspective, extremely high. Obviously K's theory of investments used in his assumption does not fit reality.[21]

Nevertheless and in spite of much skepticism and criticism of methods and results, further empirical testing of the Harberger, Musgrave and Krzyzaniak type is sorely needed.

2. Personal Income Taxation

(*a*) *Hinrichs' Empirical Study*

Since the basic problems are similar to those of the corporation income tax we shall deal with only two empirical studies. The analysis of H. H. Hinrichs[22] merits special attention because the author refers to D. Dosser's[23] dynamic theory of incidence and applies it for the first time to American data.

The result is surprising: The incidence of the American income tax forms a U-curve. While the burden in the income groups from \$100,000 to \$200,000 is dynamic-regressive compared to the groups from \$50,000 to \$100,000, the incidence is dynamic-progressive as compared to the groups under \$50,000. The burden on incomes over \$200,000 is dynamic-regressive compared to all groups up to \$25,000.

(*b*) *The Legal Incidence of U.S. Federal Income Tax—Pechman's Sample*

Pechman's tax file computes the effective tax rates throughout the income scale on the assumption that the current nominal tax rates

TABLE VI–4

Dynamic Incidence of Federal Income Tax on Income Classes between 1957 and 1959

Adjusted Gross Income Classes (000)	*1957–1959 Increase in Realized Income With Tax*[1]	*1957–1959 Increase in Realized Income Without Tax*[2]	*Dynamic Incidence Coefficients*[3]	*Dynamic Incidence*[4] *between classes*
$500 up	49.21%	122.35%	.4022	
				Regressive
200–500	40.42	112.68	.3587	
				Regressive
150–200	26.61	92.95	.2863	
				Regressive
100–150	37.79	110.67	.3415	
				Regressive
50–100	29.42	89.04	.3304	
				Progressive
25– 50	19.32	56.14	.3441	
				Progressive
15– 25	27.87	55.06	.5062	
				Progressive
5– 15	17.47	33.19	.5264	

Notes: Based on all taxable returns, *Statistics of Income, 1957 and 1959.*

1) $(R^a_{59} - R^a_{57})/R^a_{57}$ with R being "realized income" (adjusted gross income plus the excluded half of net long-term capital gains); and "a" being "after taxes less credits."

2) $(R^b_{59} - R^a_{57})/R^a_{57}$ with "b" being "before taxes."

3) Represents equation (1) over equation (2) or the share of the income growth remaining after the imposition of the tax.

4) The dynamic incidence between income classes is regressive if

$$(g^s_a)(g^f_b)/(g^s_b)(g^f_a) < 1$$

with "g" being the growth rate of income R and "s" and "f" representing the "more slowly" and "faster" growing income classes (without taxes), i.e., if the dynamic incidence coefficient of the "faster" growing class is greater than that of the 150—200 class is regressive compared to the 100—150 class due to a lower coefficient combined with a lower income growth rate.

(without the surtax) would apply successively to (1) total income of the taxpayer before any exclusions, exemptions or deductions; (2) total income less the personal exemptions; (3) total income less exemptions and personal deductions; and allowing for (4) the capital gains provisions, and (5) income splitting for married couples. He

FIGURE VI–1

Influence of Various Provisions on Effective Rates of the U.S. Individual Income Tax; Taxable Returns, 1964 Act

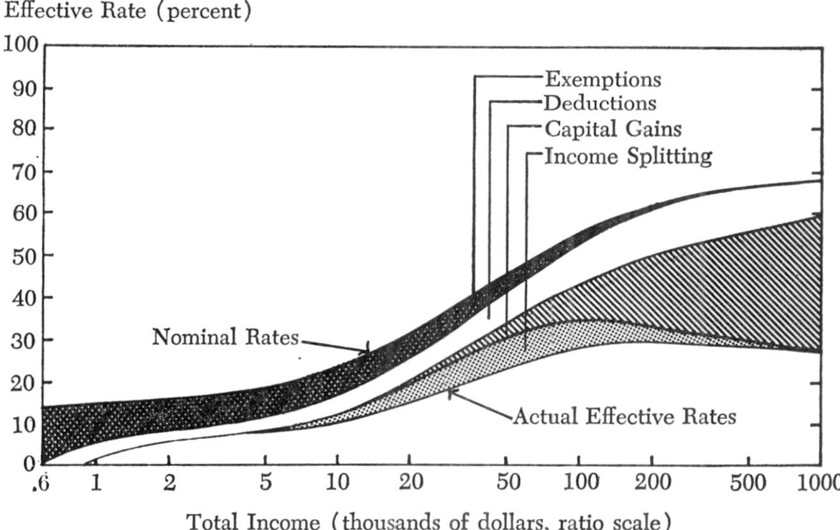

Note: Calculations based on the 1962 file.

measures by this computer program the legal incidence of tax "erosion." The results of the calculations are shown in Figures VI–1 and 2.

In spite of much skepticism (Kaldor, Recktenwald, Roskamp, Turvey) and criticism (Gurley)[24] the U.S. Treasury Department has also used Pechman's sample for tax legislative purposes. The Canadian Royal Commission on Taxation (Carter Report) developed a similar file to estimate the distributional effects of its widesweeping reform recommendations. Computer application of a similar tax model to Germany and Great Britain is going on.[25] The Brookings Institution prepared the file to provide the basis for quick estimates of individual income tax yields through simulation on high-speed electronic computers.

(c) *The Formal Incidence of a Negative Income Tax*

With a negative income tax, the distribution of the whole tax burden becomes more equalized. Lampman, Friedman, and Tobin re-

FIGURE VI-2

Average & Marginal Tax Rates of the U.S. Individual Income Tax, Taxable Returns, 1954 & 1964 Act Rates

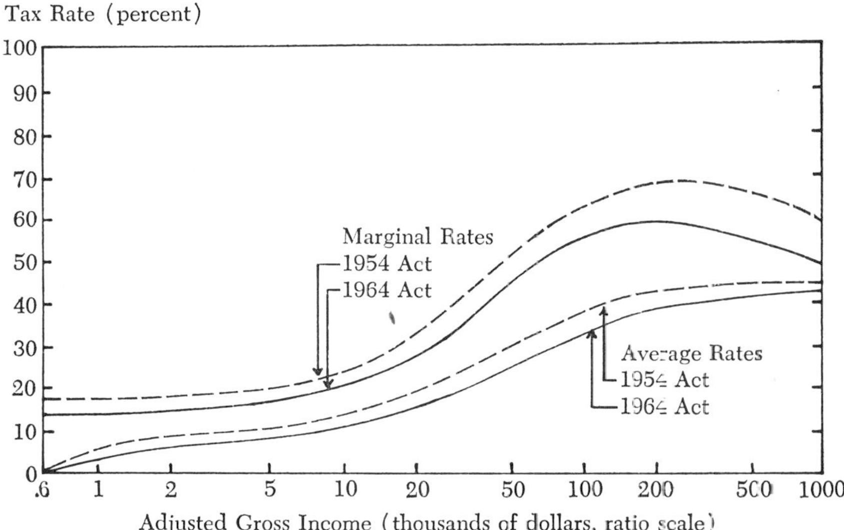

Note: Calculations based on the 1962 file.

cently have proposed assistance to the poor by means of a subsidy or negative income tax.[26] The subsidy declines as income rises and becomes zero at an income of about $3,500 per year.

The Berlin Senate had already paid a negative income tax in 1962 in order to increase the labor supply as a part of the overall effort to encourage Berlin's economic development. But the Berlin plan had the opposite effect on income distribution. The absolute amount of transfer rises as income rises. The supplemented income limit is 1,591 DM per month.[27]

In a recent study Tobin, Pechman and Mieszkowski have designed a workable plan for a negative income tax.[28] In this proposal formal or statutory incidence of tax payments, tax reductions and net benefits is measured by the disposable income (DY) after tax and allowance which corresponds to total income of a family (Y) before taxation and exceptions.

Figure VI-3 illustrates the legal incidence. The solid line OAB shows the relationship between DY and Y under the present tax law for a married couple with two children filing joint returns. After start-

FIGURE VI–3

Legal Incidence of a Negative and Positive Income Tax 4-Person Family, 50 Per Cent Rate of Offsetting Tax

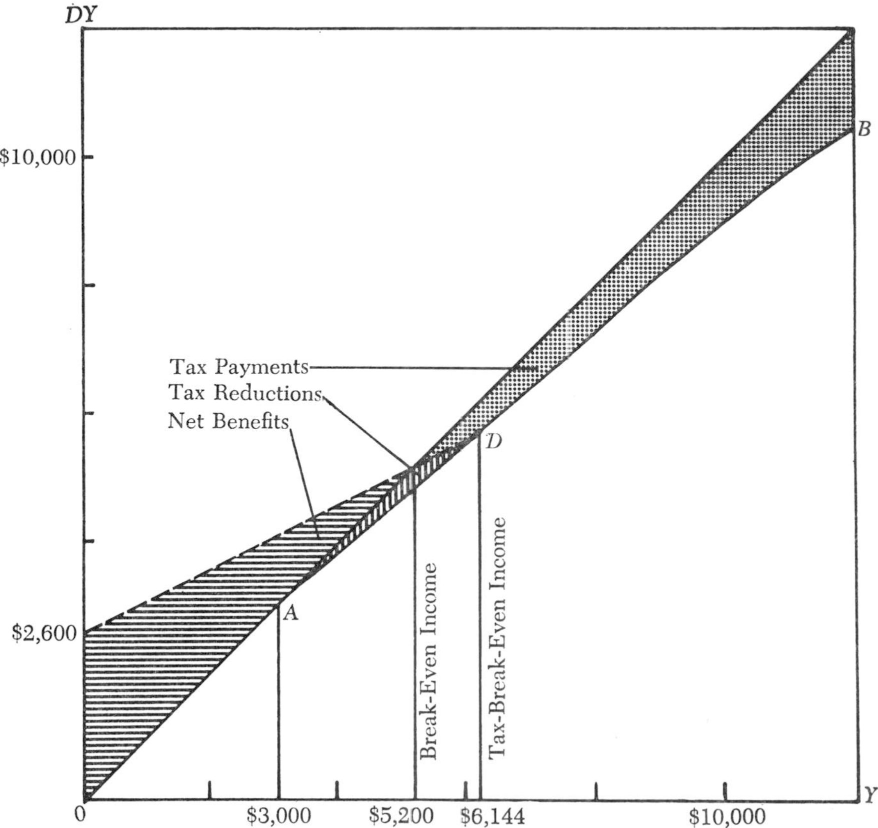

ing from the origin with a slope of 1, since four-person families with income below $3,000 pay no tax, OAB then takes on successively lower slopes as income increases and progressively higher tax rates apply. The total tax is the vertical distance between OAB and the 45-degree line.

The plan providing a 50 per cent rate of offsetting tax is to substitute the relationship CDB for OAB. Below $6,144 families will have larger disposable incomes than they do now. Those with no income will get an allowance of $2,600. Those with incomes below the break-even level of $5,200 will get some net benefits—and this group includes some families, namely those between $3,000 and $5,200, who now pay tax. Families with incomes between $5,200 and $6,144 will pay a smaller tax than they do now; and those above $6,144 will not be affected.

The proposal wipes out all tax payments on incomes below $5,200 in order to avoid confiscatory marginal tax rates at that point giving

FIGURE VI–4

Total Positive Tax (+) and Total Welfare Payment (−), Based on Own-Income

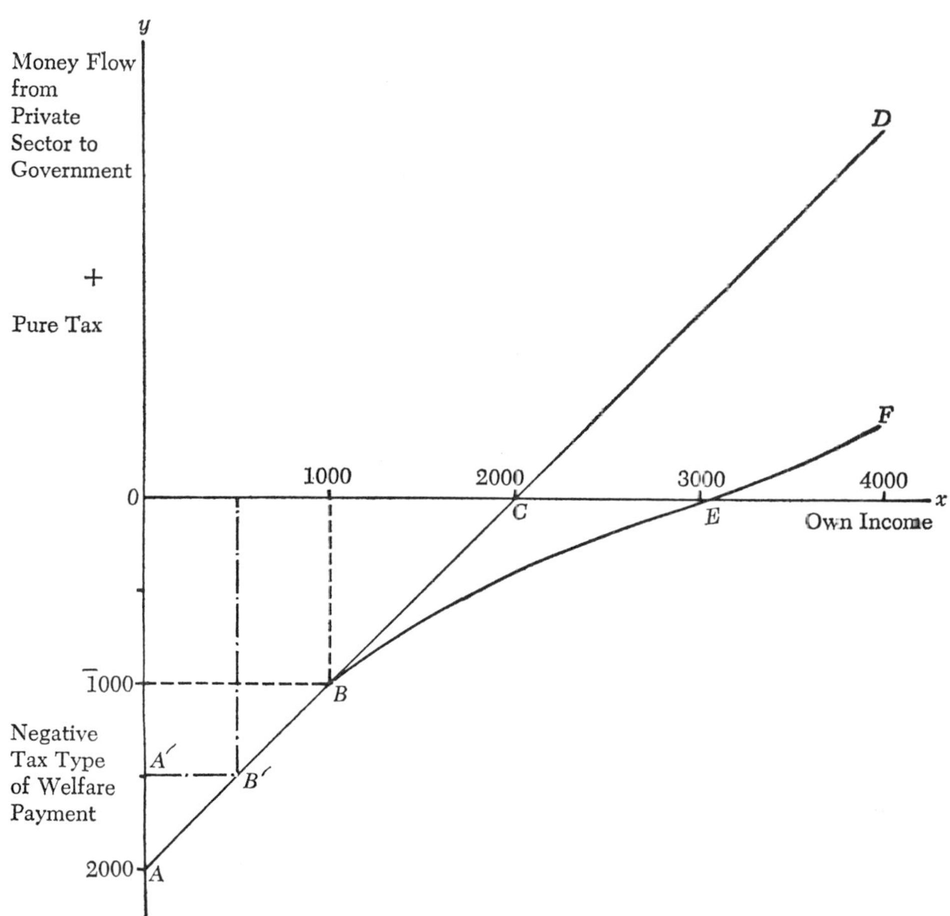

the family the option to remain under the negative income tax system until its disposable income is exactly the same under the positive and negative income tax. For a family of four persons, this point is reached at a "tax-break-even" of $6,144.

Most recently Shoup, Green, and Rolph have contributed to conceptual and analytical illustration by developing diagrams of similar types, combining negative taxes, welfare payments and subsidies.[29] The x-axis in the Shoup-diagram measures the household's own-income, the y-axis the money flows between household and government. The household's total income is the sum of own-income and payment from government, the region below the x-axis. Thus if own-income is $1,000, point B shows that the household receives $1,000, in welfare payment, raising its total income to $2,000. The slopes of the lines AD and AF measure the marginal tax rates. The 45-degree line represents an extreme case, where the household's disposable income is held to a fixed amount of $2,000, no matter how large or small its own income. If the positive tax will not begin until own-income is $3,000, the total welfare payment and the total positive tax can be represented by ABEF, or some other curve resembling it.

3. Sales or Consumption Tax

Empirical research work on the formal incidence of sales or consumption taxes is rare; a first attempt is Hansen's empirical analysis of the retail sales tax.[30] The object of the study is to ascertain from empirical data how the *initial* burden of the tax varies among consumer units of different incomes, size (vertical differentials), race and other significant characteristics (horizontal differentials).[31]

"This comparison becomes possible after actual tax burdens are derived for these 'family' units by applying a typical sales tax[32] to several budget studies.[33] The result is a clear identification of the major tax differential among families with an attempt to quantify the magnitude of these tax inequities."[34]

Hansen has arranged the data by family income at nine income levels and by family size ranging from one to six-or-more. The result is, as one might expect: a regressivity, but one does not expect the vertical tax differential to be as large as Hansen concludes. For instance a family of four, living in the large cities of the North, paid effective rates varying from 9.6 (incomes under $1,000) to a low of 0.74 per cent for the group representing incomes in excess of $10,000, a significant and unquestioned regressivity, as Figure VI-5 reveals.

When all the budgetary data are presented in a summary without regard to area or family size, Figure VI-6 reveals that rates range from a high of 4.93 for the lowest income group to 0.89 for the high income group.

Besides regressivity Hansen's study of a typical retail sales tax provides "striking and conclusive evidence of perversity": In most cases the tax rate regression line rises as family size increases. "For incomes above $1,000 the spread in effective tax rates for a 2 per cent typical tax varies between 1 per cent and 1½ per cent. The derived data indicate that where single individuals pay an effective rate of approximately 1 per cent, the larger families pay at least 1½ per cent. Therefore, larger families of comparable income pay 50 per cent more in taxes."[35]

FIGURE VI–5

Effective Tax Rates under a Typical Retail Sales Tax for Families Varying in Size from One to Six-or-More, Living in Large Cities of the South

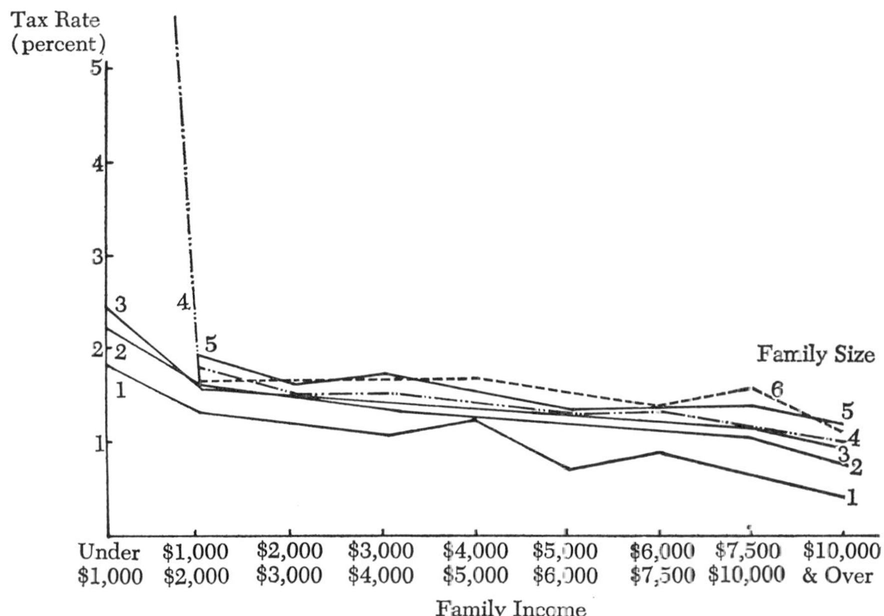

Source: Derived from *Study of Consumer Expenditures, Income and Savings*, Bureau of Labor Statistics and University of Pennsylvania, 1950, Vol. 1–18.

FIGURE VI–6

Effective Tax Rate at Nine Income Levels for American Families in All Large Cities

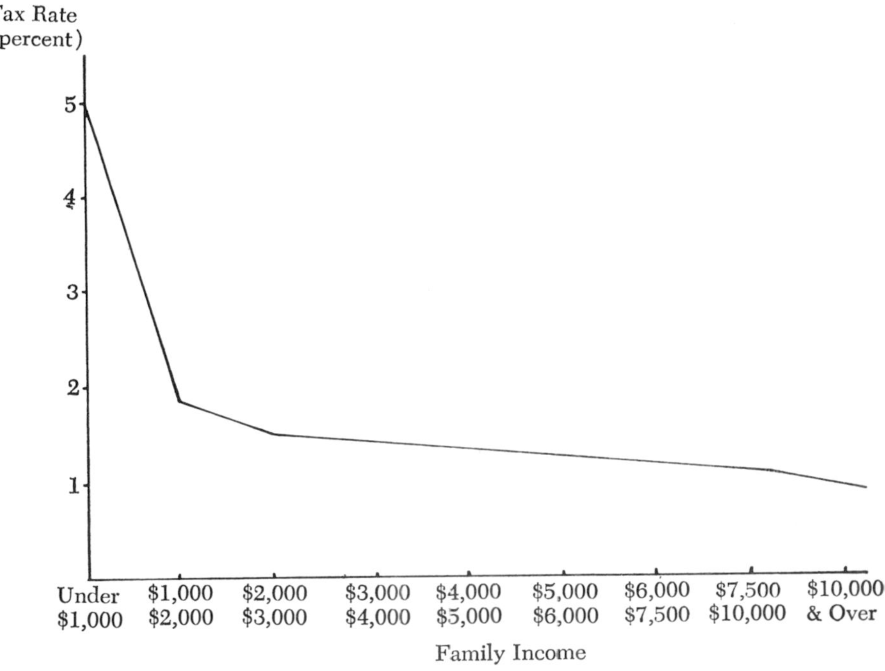

4. Value-Added Taxation

Since only France and the state of Michigan and, most recently, West Germany, levy a value-added tax, empirical studies are rare.[36] Besides, they do not consider incidence. When, in 1950, Japan intended to introduce a value-added tax, Bronfenbrenner attempted to analyze in a general way its effects in the light of the Japanese situation. He remarks about incidence:

> The shift (in the allocation of the tax burden) is in favor of firms making high profits with relatively low payrolls and much new capital. It is against firms making low profits (or losses), with high payrolls, or with large fixed capital investments if depreciation cannot be charged against value-added. Generally speaking we may say that the tax burden is shifted against big business, and in favor of medium and smaller enterprises, as the larger firms

> are the ones most heavily saddled with a payroll which Japanese customs render frequently supernumerary, and with old capital equipment which may remain ineligible for depreciation deductions. This would seem to be a point in favor of the tax in present-day Japan. However, the medium and small enterprises, being relatively unorganized, have remained almost silent, while the large firms have presented a most effective campaign of opposition.[37]

These more or less intuitive generalizations express the deplorable status of empirical work in this important field.

5. Property Tax

The wide variety of types of properties makes the analysis of property tax shifting difficult. To know whether property taxes are shifted or borne by owners it appears useful to subdivide the tax base into three categories:

(1) Real estate, consisting of land and all buildings and structures attached to it, as well as minerals and timber.

(2) Tangible personal property, consisting of all types of material wealth from business inventories and office furniture to automobiles, wrist watches, clothes, and other personal effects.

(3) Intangible personal property, consisting of claims of various kinds such as corporate stocks and bonds, mortgages, money, and deposits in savings banks and buildings and loan associations.[38]

(1) In the traditional view based on partial equilibrium analysis, taxes on land value or economic rent rest initially on the owners. Under competitive conditions, shifting is impossible because the supply of land is practically inelastic. Thus, an increase in taxes will reduce investment in land whose price will fall. In this case the tax is capitalized. Shoup gives the following numerical example of capitalization:

> If the rent of a parcel of capitalization is 5 per cent, then the value of the site is $20,000 with a zero tax rate ($1,000 – 0,5). Suppose a site value tax of 10 per cent is now applied. The value of the site will equal $1,000 divided by the interest rate plus the tax rate (.05 + .10) or $6,667. A 100 per cent tax rate would reduce the value to $487; a 500 per cent tax rate to $198.[39]

Since this chapter deals with empirical studies we will refer to the corresponding literature.[40] There are two empirical studies, an older one by Jensen, for the period 1919 to 1924,[41] and a more recent one by Daicoff,[42] for the period 1951 to 1957. While Jensen found strong confirmation of the orthodox capitalization theory for farmland, Daicoff's tests of the usually accepted doctrine in his regression analysis produced results which are inconsistent with this theory. It is evident that the "most relevant explanation for the results of the aggregate models seems to be in terms of service differential between jurisdictions. Within a jurisdiction this did not prove to be an adequate explanation; here the meaning of assessed values to the purchaser and the assessor may be the best explanation."[43]

(2) We turn now to the incidence of a tax on residential dwellings. They are consumer goods when occupied by their owners and investment goods when rented out to tenants.

In this field much empirical research has been done in the last few years. Netzer has summarized the results of empirical studies of residential and non-residential property taxes. Table VI-5 shows the results of five studies for periods in the mid-1950's: taxes on residential property are markedly regressive when compared to money income before taxes. The three state-wide studies cover both rented and owner-occupied housing; the two individual-city studies cover only owner-occupied housing, but exhibit similar degrees of regressivity. A 1959 nation-wide study, based on a sample survey of approximately 2,400 families by the Survey Research Center of the University of Michigan, also found pronounced regressivity—for owners, for renters, and for both categories combined (See Table VI–6).[44] Like most empirical studies of property tax incidence by income class these analyses deal with *formal incidence,* i.e., they anticipate the result of the shifting process: in our case, residential property taxes rest on the occupants.

Tobier considerably modifies the regressivity by introducing a longer time period of income-receiving. On a one-year-income basis the high regressivity seems to be, in the greater part, a function of the income inelasticity of housing consumption expenditures in the short run.[45]

In this connection a recently published study by Sears deserves our interest.[46] The author tries to measure the formal differential incidence of a real estate tax.

(3) Much empirical research has been done on the personal property tax. Thomas F. Hady has published a comprehensive investigation of the incidence of a property tax.[47] In his study of the Minnesota property tax he estimates both the degrees of shifting and the average

TABLE VI–5

Residential Property Taxes as a Percentage of Money Income in Various Studies

Income Class	*All Residential Property Taxes*			*Taxes on Owner-Occupied Houses*	
	Minnesota 1954	*Michigan 1956*	*Wisconsin 1956*	*Lansing, Mich. 1955*	*Wichita, Kans. 1958*
Less than $1,000	5.11%	—	14.47%	—	—
$ 1,000–$2,000	2.16	5.05%	5.42	8.83%	16.1%
2,000– 3,000	1.38	2.71	3.39	—[g]	8.4
3,000– 4,000	1.07	2.02	2.75	5.00	4.8
4,000– 5,000	0.89	1.63	2.53	3.53[h]	3.8
5,000– 6,000	0.77	—	2.21	—	3.5
5,000– 7,000	—	1.51	—	2.86[i]	—
6,000– 7,500	0.67	—	2.18	—	3.1
7,000–10,000	—	1.21	—	2.25	—
7,500–10,000	0.57	—	1.97	—	2.8
10,000 and over	0.64	1.01	1.48	2.12	2.5
All classes	0.88	1.49	2.49	n.a.	n.a.

TABLE VI–6

Estimated Distribution of Nonresidential Property Taxes by Money Income Class, 1957, before Federal Tax Offset

Income Class	*Percentage Distribution*		*Percentage of Money Income*	
	Case I	*Case II*	*Case I*	*Case II*
Less than $2,000	7.7	8.2	3.8	4.1
$ 2,000–$3,000	8.8	9.3	3.3	3.5
3,000– 4,000	11.4	12.5	3.0	3.3
4,000– 5,000	14.7	17.2	3.0	3.5
5,000– 7,000	19.2	21.3	2.1	2.3
7,000–10,000	12.5	13.1	1.7	1.7
10,000–15,000	6.6	5.4	1.8	1.5
Over $15,000	19.1	13.0	3.6	2.5
All classes	100.0	100.0	2.6	2.6

money burden of various income groups. He proves that this tax burden may vary within similar income groups. He concludes with a comparison with other taxes.

If the property tax is deductible from another tax, such as the income tax, a change of the rates may affect receipts of other taxes which again means that a part of the property tax would be shifted to the government, for example, in the form of diminished income tax receipts. The details are shown in Table VI–7.[48]

The distribution of the property tax is based on three assumptions which support differing hypotheses on incidence. Hady applies three types of burden distribution, a most likely, a most regressive, and a most progressive one. He comes to the conclusion that despite different hypotheses, only slight differences appear.[49]

His over-all result is that the property tax is regressive over wide ranges. He also concludes that the tax does not burden equal incomes equally; on the contrary, the tax amount varies considerably. He doubts whether the postulate of fairness in taxation is sufficiently realized.

While Hady's study includes only tangible personal property, all other studies consider also intangible personal property. Netzer compares the four major analyses of nonresidential property taxes which have followed rather simple methods. They

> rely on sets of shifting assumptions plus series of proxy allocators to distribute the tax amounts assigned to particular sectors among income classes . . . nonresidential property taxes assumed to be shifted forward are distributed among income classes in proportion to consumer expenditures, either for all goods and services or for particular items of consumption. Business property taxes not shifted are distributed in proportion to business, farm, or property income. Personal property taxes on consumer-owned property are distributed on the basis of selected types of consumer expenditure . . . Where there are alternative sets of shifting assumptions which affect property tax incidence, the table presents the results on the basis of that set of assumptions treated by the relevant study as most probable. The studies differ in their treatment of federal income tax deductibility of state-local taxes which has led to differences in both the level and the shape of the distribution of property taxes by income class. The findings of the four studies, however, generally agree: nonresidential property taxes as a percentage of income trace a U-shaped curve, initially falling as income rises, but rising once again for the highest income groups.[50]

Netzer explains the main differences as follows: In the Minnesota study, the rise begins quite soon, at the $5,000 income level because the Minnesota study assumes very little forward shifting of business

TABLE VI–7

Summary of Incidence Assumptions

Description of Property	Incidence on						
	Federal Govern-ment	Residents of Other States	Con-sumer	Business Owners	Farm Owner Opera-tors	Farm Land-lords (non-opera-tors)	House-hold Goods Owners
	Per cent	Per cent	Per cent	Per cent	Per cent	Per cent	Per cent
Mined iron ore and direct products of blast furnaces	50	47.5	...	2.5	...	...	...
Household goods and boats	8	...	...	...	...	...	92
Business property:							
Retailers	37	3	60	...	...	...	...
Wholesalers	50	5	33¾	11¼	...	...	...
(Alternative allocation)	(50)	(5)	(11¼)	(33¾)	...	...	...
Manufacturers[1]	50	16.7	...	33.3	...	...	...
(Alternative allocation)	(50)	(16.7)	(8)	(25.3)	...	...	...
Agricultural property	20	...	...	...	53.6	26.4	...
(Alternative allocation)	(20)	...	...	...	(80)	...	...
Structure on railway lands, not owned by railways; privately owned structures on public lands in urban areas	37	...	31.5	...	31.5	...	...
Transmission and distribution lines of public utilities	50	...	50	...	...	...	...
Billboards and advertising devices	50	...	...	50	...	...	...
All other taxable property	37	...	63	...	...	...	...

[1]Includes oil refineries.

TABLE VI–8

Nonresidential Property Taxes as a Percentage of Money Income before Taxes in Various Studies

Income Class	*United States 1948*	*Minnesota 1954*	*Michigan 1956*	*Wisconsin 1956*
Less than $1,000	3.2%	4.3%	—	4.6%
$1,000– $2,000	1.8	5.3	3.7%	3.5
2,000– 3,000	1.6	3.2	2.3	2.8
3,000– 4,000	1.5	2.1	1.9	2.4
4,000– 5,000	1.4	2.0	1.5	1.8
5,000– 6,000	—	2.4	—	1.7
5,000– 7,000	—	—	1.4	—
5,000– 7,500	1.5	—	—	—
6,000– 7,500	—	2.4	—	1.6
7,000– 10,000	—	—	1.2	—
7,500– 10,000	1.8	3.2	—	1.6
Over $10,000	—	5.2	1.7	2.4
All classes	1.7	3.3	1.6	2.0

property taxes, business and property income is more unequally distributed than consumption spending, and taxes which fall heavily on business property tend to be progressive in character. In the other studies, in contrast, considerable forward shifting is assumed, and thus the rise in nonresidential property taxes as a percentage of income occurs only in the top, open-ended income class.[51]

Netzer's own empirical study on the allocation of 1957 property taxes by income class shows the same results, however, with only small modifications. He too makes alternative assumptions as to shifting and income concepts. Nearly everything depends on the assumed results of the shifting process, i.e., the effective incidence.[52]

6. Social Insurance Contributions

In a Dutch investigation on the incidence of taxation and social insurance contributions, R. Bannink uses a micro-economic conception of family structures, such as size, income and occupation of the head-of-the-family.[53]

(1) With regard to the size of family, the incidence of direct taxes (measured by income) drops off more sharply than the burden of in-

direct taxation, as family size increases. With regard to social insurance contributions the direct levy rises slightly and the indirect falls considerably, as family size grows.

(2) In a comparison of income classes Bannink concludes that the increase of indirect taxes is nearly proportional to growing income, while direct taxes rise more sharply. Total incidence is proportional to income up to the "income limit of welfare" (beyond which no direct levies are payable). If income exceeds this limit, the incidence of direct insurance contributions falls sharply, since above this point pension payments are the sole component of the contribution.

Tables VI–9 and VI–10 summarize the results of the incidence.[54]

It is interesting to note that the incidence of taxes and contributions is substantially the same for workers and employees.

In three empirical studies concerning the effective rates of Old Age Survivor Disability Insurance and Old Age Survivor Disability and Health Insurance taxes, Pechman, Deran, and Harvey[55] claim that these American social security taxes have different incidence. Assuming full backward or forward shifting of premiums, Pechman analyzes the formal differential incidence as Table VI–11 shows.

Pechman interprets the figures in the following conclusions which are similar to the result of Deran's study, using the same statistical materials.

> The OASDHI taxes seem to be progressive with respect to income up to about $4,000 of money income, proportional between $4,000 and $7,500, and regressive thereafter (Table VI–11). This pattern of tax incidence re-

TABLE VI–9

Combinations of Characteristics, Describing Family-Types.

Family-size	2	4	6	4		
Income-class	*f*3.000,— *f*4.000,—			*f*5.000,— *f* 8.000,— *f*6.000,— *f*12.000,—		
Occupational group of the head of the family	Manual workers			Clerical workers		
Code	A	B	C	D	E	F

TABLE VI–10

Absolute and Relative Incidence of Taxes and Premiums for Social Insurance, per Family-Type, 1954 and 1956.

Family-type	*B*	*A*	*B*	*C*	*D*	*E*	*F*
Year	*1954*	*1956*	*1956*	*1956*	*1956*	*1956*	*1956*
	In guilders						
Taxes							
Direct taxes	51	154	7	6	42	245	972
Indirect taxes	257	168	166	162	168	278	482
Total	308	322	173	168	210	523	1,454
Social Insurance							
Direct charges	225	224	217	199	227	345	251
Indirect charges	96	87	95	101	100	136	220
Total	321	311	312	300	327	481	471
	In 0.1 percents of family-income						
Taxes							
Direct taxes	14	45	2	1	11	44	99
Indirect taxes	72	49	46	44	45	50	49
Total	86	94	48	45	56	94	148
Social insurance							
Direct charges	63	65	61	54	61	62	26
Indirect charges	27	25	27	27	27	25	22
Total	90	90	88	81	88	87	48

flects the changing importance of covered earnings as incomes rise. In the lower part of the income scale, the ratio of covered earnings to total income increases; and, finally, the ratio begins to fall because the payroll taxes apply only up to $6,600, and because property income which is not subject to tax becomes increasingly important as incomes rise above this point.

On the basis of 1960–61 data, the current OASDHI taxes are more progressive than an equal-yield proportional tax on consumption up to about $7,500 of income, and at least as regressive above this point. The income tax is, of course, much more progressive throughout the income scale than the payroll taxes. These conclusions are the same whether the employer and employee OASDHI taxes are assumed to be borne entirely by the wage earners or whether it is assumed that only the employee tax is borne by wage earners and the employer tax is shifted to the consumer (compare the last two columns of Table VI–11 with the first two).[56]

Prima facie, the statement of Harvey seems provocative that, in general, effective tax rates increase at decreasing rates over the income range covered by the social insurance tax base. His results are shown in Figure VI–7.

TABLE VI–11

Effective Rates of OASDHI Taxes and of Alternative Methods of Raising the Same Revenue, by 1960–61 Family Money Income Classes, with 1966 Tax Rates

(In percentages)

	OASDHI Effective Rates		*Effective Tax Rates Assuming OASDHI Revenue Raised by*	
1960–61 Family Money Income Class (Dollars)	*Assuming Backward Shifting of Employer Tax*	*Assuming Forward Shifting of Employer Tax*	*1961 Income Tax*	*Hypothetical Proportional Consumption Tax*
1,000– 2,000	1.6	4.3	0.8	7.3
2,000– 3,000	3.3	4.9	1.4	6.4
3,000– 4,000	4.3	5.2	2.3	6.2
4,000– 5,000	5.7	5.7	3.4	5.7
5,000– 6,000	5.9	5.7	4.0	5.4
6,000– 7,500	6.0	5.6	4.6	5.2
7,500–10,000	5.5	5.2	5.1	4.8
10,000–15,000	4.9	4.7	5.8	4.4
15,000 and over	3.1	3.2	8.3	3.2
All classes	4.9	4.9	4.9	4.9

The chart shows the effective tax rates under current statutory provisions for males entering the labor force at age 25 and retiring on a primary benefit at age 65 after 40 years of continuous coverage as employed or self-employed persons. Separate curves are shown for employed and self-employed persons who are alternatively assumed to have fixed incomes and increasing incomes. Two pairs of curves are shown for employed persons: one is based on the assumption of complete backward shifting of the employer contribution and the other, complete forward shifting.[57]

Since contributions for social security are levied in Germany, the U.S. and other countries to the greatest part on the insurance principle, i.e. on a *quid pro quo* base, Harvey includes in his effective rates the premiums and the benefits attributable to the contributions. This is a fair procedure. Most research studies give a one-sided and therefore

FIGURE VI–7

Effective Social Security Tax Rates for Males (Beginning Covered Employment at Age 25 and Retiring at Age 65)

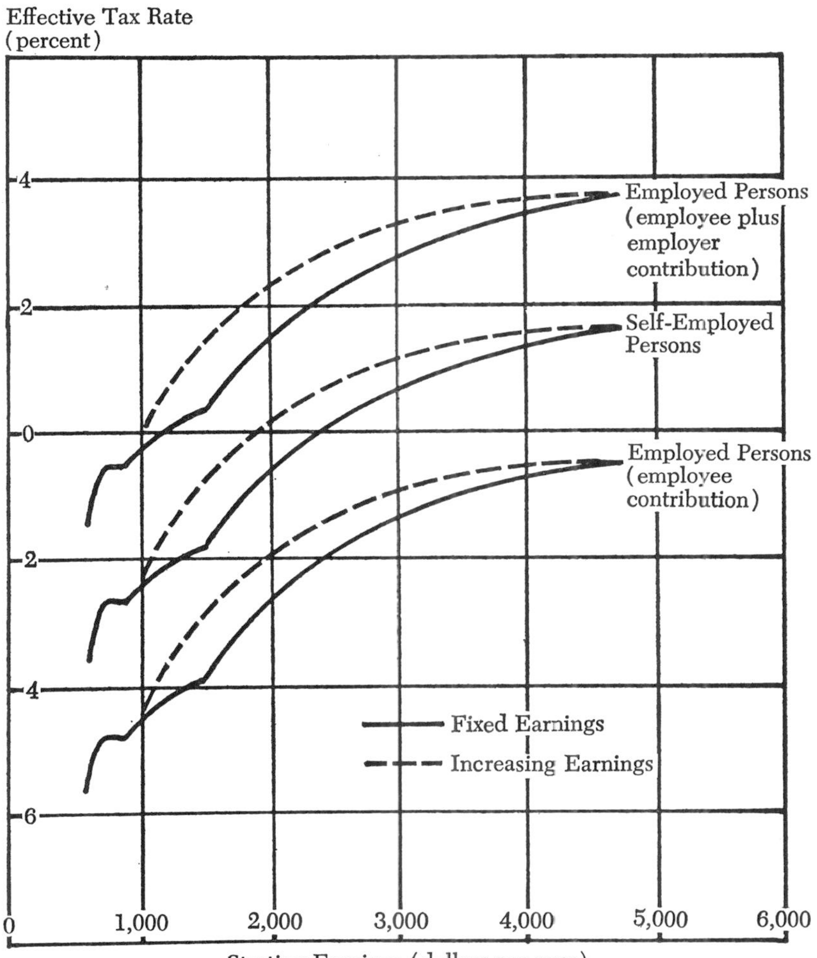

false picture of reality. Policy recommendations based on formal incidence of premiums or tax burdens and neglecting the appropriate benefits are of dubious value, if not dangerous, in the hand of nonexperts.

II. *Formal Incidence of Tax and Fiscal Systems*

1. Some Fundamental Problems

At the end of the thirties and the beginning of the forties comprehensive studies of the incidence of the tax system as a whole were published which remain basic to this day. The most significant ones are the pioneering contributions of Newcomer, Colm and Tarasov, Shirras and Rostas, and Barna.[58]

Any analysis of formal tax incidence at different income levels has to decide at the outset on the following assumptions and methods:

(1) The degree of tax shifting or the effective incidence. Many analysts choose as an assumption for this purpose neither legal nor intended incidence but arbitrarily a *mixtum compositum* that has become conventional. The corporate profits tax is expected to be (a) half passed back to stockholders and half shifted to consumers or (b) (less accepted) fully shifted forward to buyers. All taxes on "business costs" (indirect taxes and property taxes on company property) are estimated to be entirely shifted by price increases and all personal income taxes to rest on the taxed people.

It is evident that a premise of a fully forward-shifted corporation tax or backward shifting to factor incomes of other taxes would substantially alter the results.

(2) The income concept. Most studies disagree widely over the appropriate definition of income. But there is some progress on the international level as to what we wish to measure and as to the methods that should be used since the concepts in the national income and product accounts are more and more improved and standardized. We can mention briefly four alternative definitions of income: (a) the money income of a household or person before or (b) after personal taxes, (c) the aggregate income on the product side of the national accounts (income less taxes plus benefits) and (d) total income on the income side of the account (income before taxes). The appropriateness of the concept depends on the purpose of the study: do we want to measure the distributive effects of some types of taxes (or expenditure programs), the whole tax system, or the budget? Additional difficulties arise when we allocate taxes paid and benefits to households classified by size of income.

(3) The income "unit." There are several alternative ways to attribute

TABLE VI–12

Bases for the Allocation of the Tax Burden by Income Class in Previous Studies

Tax	*Basis of Allocation*					
	Adler (1947/48)	*Musgrave et.al. (1948)*	*Conrad (1950)*	*Bishop (1958)*	*Gillespie (1960)*	*National Tax Foundation (1961 + 1965)*
Individual income	*Personal taxes (P.t.)*	*P.t.*	*P.t.*	*P.t.*	*P.t.*	*P.t.*
Corporate income	Alternative methods on different incidence assumptions: 1. Total dividend income 2. Half total consumption, half dividend income	Three different incidence assumptions: 1. One third total consumption, one eight wage earnings, rest dividend income 2. Total consumption 3. Total dividend income	Two different incidence assumptions: 1. Total dividend income 2. One third total consumption, rest dividend income	Half dividend income, half total consumption expenditures	One third total consumption, two thirds dividend income	Two different incidence assumptions: 1. Total consumption 2. Half total consumption, half dividend income
Excises, customs and sales	Consumption expenditures (C.e.)	C.e.	C.e.	C.e.	Total consumption expenditures	Total consumption expenditures
Estate and gift	Highest income bracket, $7,500 income class and above	Highest income bracket, $7,500 income class and above	Highest income bracket, $7,500 income class and above	Highest income bracket, $15,000 income class and above	Highest income bracket, $10,000 income class and above	Highest income bracket, $15,000 income class and above

Property	Two thirds on personal property, one third on business property	business and farmer's property: consumption expenditures. Individual property: homeowners and renters	Property owners except for business property	Half housing expenditures, half consumption expenditures	Half housing expenditures, half consumption expenditures	Half housing expenditures, half total current consumption
Social Insurance: Personal contributions	not available	Wages and salaries	Wages and salaries	Wages and salaries	Wages and salaries	Social security, railroad and government retirement contributions
Employer contributions:			not available		Half wages and salaries, half consumption goods	Total current consumptions

Sources:

(1) J. H. Adler — "The Fiscal System, the Distribution of Income, and Public Welfare," in K. E. Poole (ed.), *Fiscal Policies and the American Economy* (New York, 1951), pp. 359–409.

(2) R. A. Musgrave, et. al. — "Distribution of Tax Payments by Income Groups: A Case Study for 1948," *NTJ*, IV (1951), pp. 1–53

(3) A. H. Conrad — "Redistribution through Government Budgets in the United States, 1950," in A. T. Peacock (ed.), *Income Redistribution and Social Policy*, (London, 1954), pp. 178–268.

(4) G. A. Bishop — "The Tax Burden by Income Class, 1958," *NTJ*, XIV (1961), pp. 41–55.

(5) J. W. Gillespie — "The Effect of Public Expenditures on the Distribution of Income: An Empirical Investigation," in R. A. Musgrave (ed.), *Essays in Fiscal Federalism*, (Washington, 1965), pp. 122–186.

(6) National Tax Foundation — *Tax Burdens and Benefits of Government Expenditures by Income Class, 1961 and 1965* (New York, 1967).

(7) U.S. Department of Labor — *Consumer Expenditures and Income, Survey of Consumer Expenditures 1960–61*, BLS Report No. 237–38, and Supplement 3. (Washington, 1965).

income. These range from individual to small group income classified by family size or by other categories.
(4) The meaning of taxes (and expenditures). If we study the distributive effects of a whole tax system or even a budget on the basis of national income accounts, all government receipts and expenditures should, of course, be considered. But we have to decide whether the costs and benefits of public investments should be allocated over time.
(5) The source of "aggregate" data. In most countries basic statistical data for allocating estimates are limited and of different quality, classification and period. The analyst must choose appropriate samples or data and periods (e.g. family expenditures by income group or type) to avoid the necessity of adjustments and up-dating.
(6) Allocation bases. A difficult task is to discover and select an adequate basis for the allocation of taxes (and expenditures) to an income group. Here we have to deal with the same problems of arbitrariness and adequacy as in (1) and (2). To illustrate tax allocation by income group we have compared in a survey the procedures used by six writers.

2. The German Tax Structure

More recently G. Zeitel has investigated the distribution of taxes in the German Federal Republic using the concept of formal incidence.[59] In his statistical work he begins with the question of how the tax payment, turnover, prices, and incomes or profits etc. in a past period have been formed under the influence of a *given* tax system.

In such types of studies all tax shifting processes are considered to be already finished. The central problem is to calculate what part different income groups have to pay to the government directly (income tax) or indirectly (sales tax). Zeitel's intention is, in our terminology to investigate the intended incidence and not the legal or effective tax distribution, thus avoiding the whole problem of shifting. Thus he attempts to calculate the tax amounts falling on production and trade firms and accumulated in the price paid by the final buyers.[60]

Since in Germany, unlike in the United States and Great Britain, basic data on distribution of income and tax payments are unavailable, Zeitel has to estimate tax burdens for specified family units representing various ranges in the income scale. Their income and expenditure schedules are fixed.

Regarding the distribution of the "entire tax burden," of special interest here, Zeitel comes to the questionable conclusion that in 1954 the tax system was progressive for households of two or more persons. Figure VI-8 illustrates the degree of progression of the tax system as a whole.[61]

The tax burden for all households begins to rise with about 20 per cent, and reaches over 65 per cent for the highest income groups. In the upper incomes progression increases more slowly and becomes weaker with growing household sizes.

If we knew the actual incidence of taxes and compared it with the tax distribution desired by the government, the difference would be a useful measure of the success or failure of the tax and fiscal policy.

Roskamp's Study. In a pioneering effort, Roskamp has recently produced a first study of the effective incidence of the West German tax

FIGURE VI-8

The Progressive Burden of the Tax System by Social Groups, West Germany, 1954

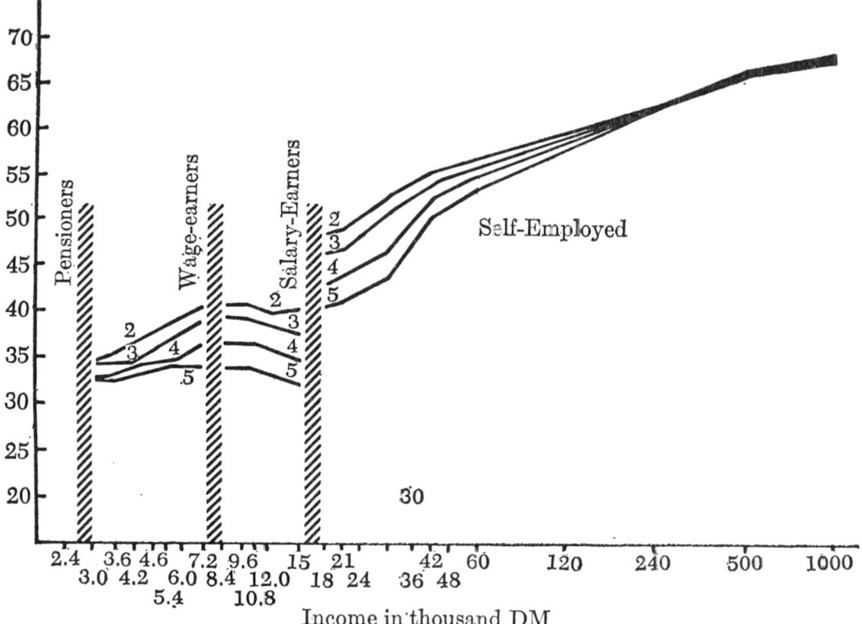

structure.[62] As in other analyses of this type he was confronted by three basic problems:

(1) First, to establish a household income distribution.[63]

(2) Next, to determine the expenditure structure of households in different income brackets.[64]

(3) Finally, and most difficult to allocate the various taxes to different income groups as we have explained in detail at the beginning of this chapter.

On the basis of the statistical results of (1) and (2) the possibility of shifting must be calculated under the economic conditions in each period. Of course all such investigations have to make crucial assumptions, and here lie the opportunities and weakness of the analyses. Are all theoretically important shifting factors considered and their effects more or less correctly evaluated? If we recall what a substantial influence the calculated income distribution has on the results, it is obvious that all statements on aggregate tax incidence should be treated with some caution. The formulation of some shifting hypotheses necessitates a great knowledge of the structure and working of a particular economy and requires some courage. Roskamp's incidence study no doubt benefited from the extensive earlier work of the author on the West German economy and in particular on fiscal efforts to foster capital formation during the early 1950's.[65] If there are shortcomings in aggregate tax incidence estimates it must also be recognized that they provide important information about actual and hypothetical total tax incidence. Modifications of the premises generate alternative incidence patterns.[66] In this way polar and in-between cases may be explored with respect to critical shifting assumptions. According to Roskamp the West German tax system in 1956 was not continuously progressive. He starts from the following hypotheses on shifting which he considers justified in the existing economic and fiscal conditions of 1956.[67] The *turnover tax* is fully shifted among households according to consumption expenditures. The *individual income tax* burdens "entrepreneurs," the large number of shop owners, business representatives, farmers and independent professionals. The tax is assumed to be non-shiftable. Roskamp argues, however, that many of the private companies with the legal form of OHG (general partnership) and G.m.b.H. (Society with limited liability), which employ as many workers as the corporations, adapt, to some extent, their behavior to the latter. Thus there is some forward shifting under the individual income tax in higher income brackets. Considering that the stable prices in 1950 were unfavorable to shifting, he considers a shifting of 20 per cent of the tax about right.

The *wage tax* on the other hand cannot be shifted. It is allocated to wage earners and salaried employees in different income brackets according to official tax statistics. The *corporation income tax* posed special difficulties. In the absence of any direct empirical evidence on the incidence of this tax in West Germany at the time of the study, Roskamp followed a lead by Musgrave in an earlier study for the United States and assumed that 40 per cent of the tax is shifted forward to consumers due to the then prevailing sellers' markets. A further 40 per cent is borne by capital. The remaining 20 per cent falls on wage earners, since some backward shifting succeeded with constant wages and increasing labor productivity.[68] Roskamp estimates that 55 per cent of the *Gewerbesteuer* (a type of local tax on business in West Germany) is paid, though not borne, by corporations and the rest by other firms. It is assumed that the corporations have shifted this tax fully. For the rest, 35 per cent was again shifted forward to consumers. Small business was assumed to bear only 10 per cent. The capital levy *Soforthilfeabgabe* (a special capital levy introduced to equalize the burden of war losses and help refugees after the last war) is estimated by the Ministry of Finance to be distributed by 70 per cent to industry, 10 per cent to agriculture and 20 per cent to house and land owners.[69]

Under these shifting assumptions the computed effective tax rates are as follows.

The effective tax rates (line 1) indicate a progression up to income class 3,600–4,800 DM. At higher incomes the tax structure is at first slightly regressive and then remains proportional. If we include the various tax exemptions and special tax provisions, the hypothetical ef-

TABLE VI–13

Estimated Effective Tax Rates in West Germany, 1950

	Household Income Bracket, 1,000 DM				
	0–2.4	*2.4–3.6*	*3.6–4.8*	*4.8–6.0*	*6.0+*
Effective Tax Rate	20.5	25.5	26.8	25.9	25.9
Hypothetical Effective Tax Rate	20.7	25.7	27.1	26.3	27.9

TABLE VI–14

Estimated Effective Tax Rates
(Tax as percent of incomes)

	Household Income Bracket, 1,000 DM				
	0–2.4	*2.4–3.6*	*3.6–4.8*	*4.8–6.0*	*6.0+*
Wage Tax	0.8	2.9	3.8	2.5	1.8
Personal Income Tax	0.4	0.7	1.0	1.3	5.0
Corporate Income Tax	1.1	1.4	1.5	1.5	2.4
Turnover Tax	6.0	6.4	6.2	6.9	5.0
Tobacco Tax	3.2	4.3	3.7	3.5	1.1
Real Estate Tax	1.6	1.4	1.5	1.4	1.2
Local Tax on Business	1.6	1.6	1.7	1.7	1.4
Immediate Aid Levy	1.2	1.2	1.7	1.4	3.7
All Other Taxes and Customs	4.5	5.6	5.7	5.7	4.3
Total	20.5	25.5	26.8	25.9	25.9

fective tax rates (line 2) shows similar patterns, yet the rates are throughout somewhat higher. Table VI–14 illustrates how the burden of particular taxes are distributed among income classes. The regressive effect of the turnover tax is as clearly indicated as is the progressive effect of the income tax.[70]

3. Federal and International Comparisons

(*a*) *Federal*

In independent studies R. A. Musgrave and I. J. Goffman have investigated the burdens of federal, state and local taxes by income groups in the U.S. and Canada.[71]

The effects of both tax systems are characterized by three common attributes: (1) the system of local and state (provincial) taxes is unambiguously regressive; (2) the federal taxes, most important in the two countries, are markedly progressive; and (3) the system of taxation as a whole is pronouncedly progressive.

More specifically, the American tax system shows four zones of progression: a slight one up to an income of $4500, a somewhat steeper progression up to $5500, a very weak progression up to $8000, followed by a rapidly increasing progression for higher incomes. The Canadian tax distribution is quite different. The lowest incomes lie

FIGURE VI–9

Burden of the U.S. Tax System by Income Class, 1954

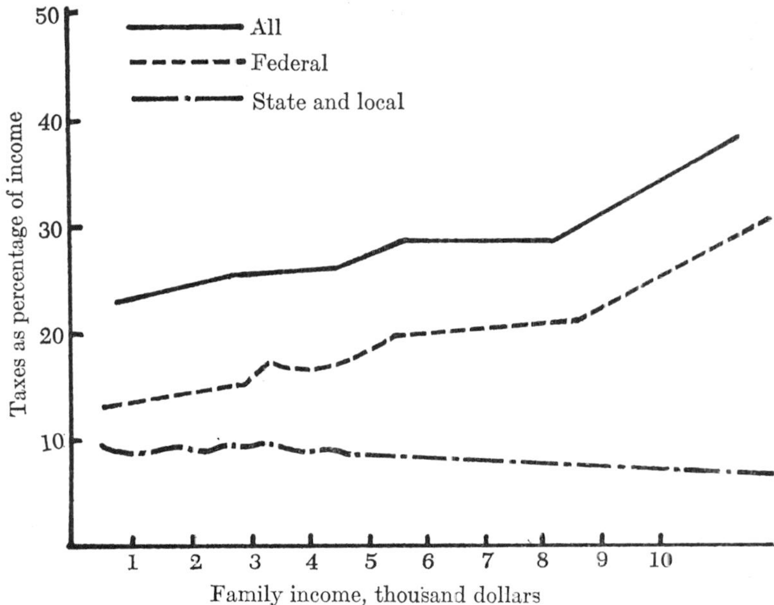

in a regressive zone. The incomes of $1500 to about $3500 are proportionally taxed. The progression for higher incomes is very steep.

(*b*) *International Comparisons*

As far as we know Clark and Peters attempted for the first time a broad international comparison of formal tax incidence.[72] For this purpose they have developed a technique of plotting the data of five studies attempting to answer the question: Do people at the same relative position in the income distribution in different countries pay different proportions of their incomes in taxation? This type of analysis permits limited comparisons of the formal incidence of taxation but in no way enables comparative studies to be made of the extent of redistribution. Usually Lorenz curves comparing the change in income distribution expressed in the Gini coefficient of inequality serve this purpose. Clark and Peters' method avoids the particular difficulty of

FIGURE VI–10

Effective Rates of Taxes by Level of Canadian Government, 1957

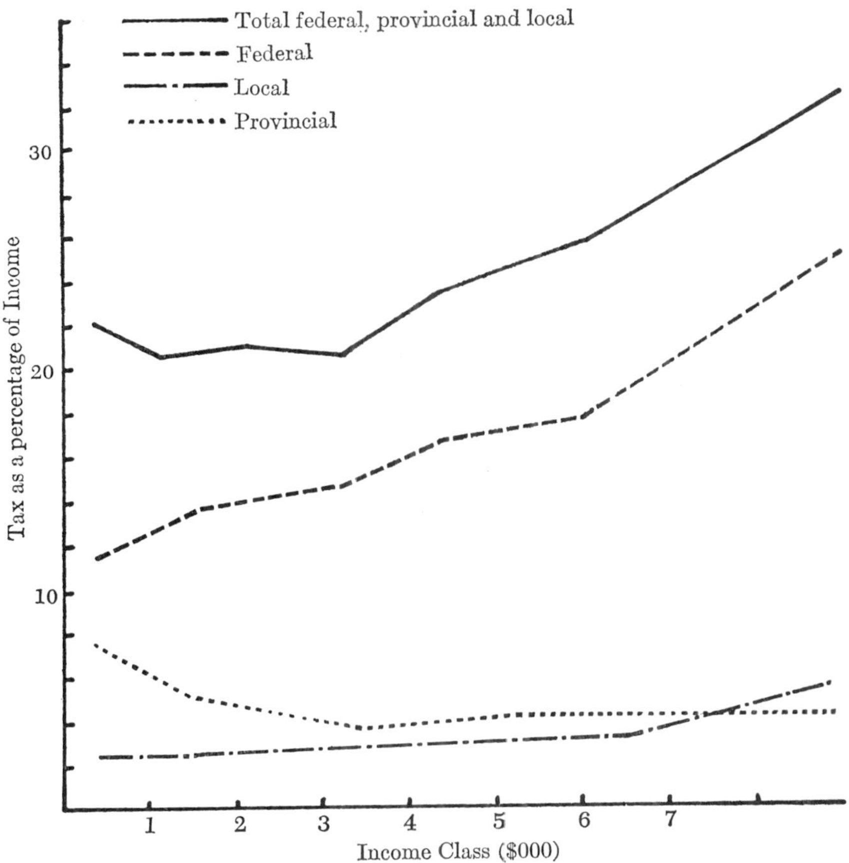

customary approaches in this international field by excluding the problem of the exchange rate.

Figure VI–11 compares the income tax and social security payments of Denmark, Germany, UK, and USA. It excludes indirect taxes. The incidence of direct taxes in the USA and UK are presented in a separate diagram which is not reproduced here. The two authors comment on the statistical comparison of the tax incidence in the four countries

FIGURE VI–11

Income Tax and Social Security Payments as Percentage of Income in Various Countries

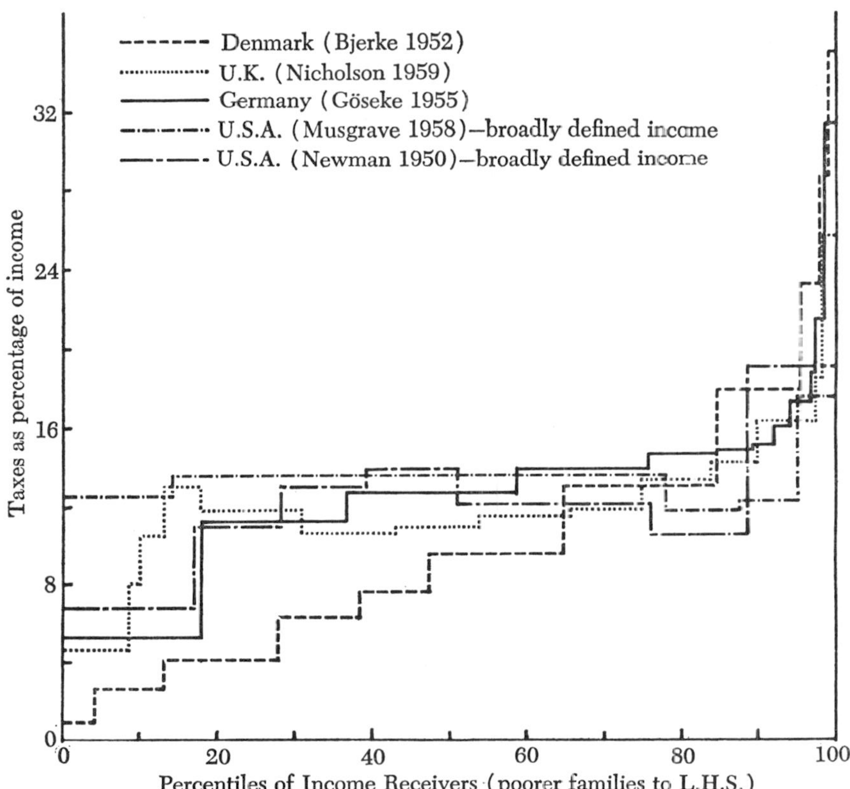

as follows. Beginning with Musgrave's data the "general picture which emerges, is of a broadly proportional system of taxation with a steep jump towards the upper end of the income range." From Newman's data they derived a somewhat different result. "There is some progressiveness at the lower end of the income scale covering the poorer 50 per cent of family units, followed by a dip in the percentage paid by the next 40 per cent of family units, with a more marked jump at the upper end than is recorded by Musgrave. This picture is little disturbed if alternative income concepts are used."

TABLE VI–15

Federal, State, and Local Taxes as a Percentage of Total Income for all Families by Income Class—1965[a]

Tax	Income class[b]									
	Under $2,000	*$2,000 to 2,999*	*$3,000 to 3,999*	*$4,000 to 4,999*	*$5,000 to 5,999*	*$6,000 to 7,499*	*$7,500 to 9,999*	*$10,000 to 14,999*	*$15,000 and over*	*Total*
Federal:										
Individual income	1.9	3.1	4.5	6.4	6.9	7.7	8.8	10.0	16.1	8.3
Corporate income	4.5	4.3	5.5	3.6	3.9	3.4	3.4	5.3	10.9	4.6
Excises and customs	3.3	3.1	3.3	3.1	3.0	2.8	2.6	2.4	1.5	2.7
Estate and gift	—	—	—	—	—	—	—	—	4.6	.5
Social insurance	3.2	3.4	3.8	4.1	4.0	3.8	3.5	3.3	1.7	3.5
Total	13.0	14.0	17.1	17.3	17.9	17.8	18.4	21.1	34.9	19.6
Total excluding social insurance	9.8	10.6	13.3	13.2	13.9	14.0	14.9	17.8	33.2	16.1

State and Local:										
Individual & corporate	.6	.6	.8	.9	.9	.9	1.1	1.2	2.2	1.1
Sales, excise, etc.	6.1	5.5	5.6	5.3	5.1	4.8	4.4	4.0	2.6	4.6
Property	6.9	5.2	4.7	4.2	4.2	3.8	3.5	3.3	2.4	3.8
Death and gift	—	—	—	—	—	—	—	—	1.3	.1
Social insurance	1.5	1.4	1.4	1.4	1.3	1.3	1.2	1.1	.7	1.2
Total	15.1	12.7	12.6	11.8	11.5	10.8	10.1	9.6	9.1	10.8
Total excluding social insurance	13.6	11.3	11.2	10.4	10.2	9.5	8.9	8.5	8.4	9.6
Total All Taxes	28.1	26.7	29.7	29.1	29.4	28.5	28.5	30.6	44.0	30.4
Total All Taxes (1961)	27.3	26.3	29.4	29.1	29.4	28.6	28.7	30.9	44.1	30.5
Total Taxes (1958)	28.3	26.3		25.9	25.7	23.9		24.0	35.9	27.4

a. The 1965 estimates are based on total taxes and income shown in the national income accounts for 1965. However, they take no account of the shift in the distribution of income from 1961 to 1965.

b. The income class limits are expressed in money income after personal taxes. "Personal taxes" consist mainly of Federal, state and local income taxes. The total income on which the percentages in the body of the table are based is a broad income concept equivalent in the aggregate to net national product.

Source: Tax Foundation, *op. cit.*, p. 20. The figures for 1958 are taken from an article by F. A. Bishop who was primarily responsible for the tax foundation study, "The Tax Burden by Income Class, 1958," *NTJ*, XIV (1961), 41–57. Since methods are improved only estimates could be compared.

> While the poorer 20 per cent and the richer 25 per cent of families grouped by income size are subject to progressive taxation, there is a rough proportionality in between these ranges. This aspect of proportionality compares very strikingly with that revealed by Musgrave's study of the United States though, as has been mentioned earlier, the Newman results are somewhat different.

The results based on German data cannot be regarded as comparable with the other information.

> As would be expected, the personal taxation pattern which is revealed is progressive, and very steeply so within the upper decile of income receivers. There are indications, however, that by 1959 (this data is not shown in the diagram) the system had changed to proportionality for the 70 per cent of income receivers between the poorer 20 per cent and the richer 10 per cent groups. The way in which the pattern would be affected if family units were used rather than income receivers, is, of course, impossible to predict.

Although the Danish data are limited at varying income levels, Clark and Peters have obtained comparable results by using other materials, revealing the existence of a progressive system of taxation with a steep progressiveness in the personal income tax structure.[73]

Obviously the common features of the five distributional results are both a different degree of progressiveness within the first and last two deciles of income earners and a broad proportionality between these ranges (except in Denmark). Since this tentative comparison excludes indirect taxes we may now incorporate their contribution considering their usually regressive effects.

We may add another interesting comparison of three national tax structures comparing formal tax incidence in America, Soviet Russia and Germany. Although the concepts and methods of Bishop, Holzman and a German collective study differ in some points, a rough comparison seems justified.

In a publication of the Tax Foundation the incidence of the American tax system in 1965 as a percentage of total income is summarized by groups in the following Table VI–15. We have added the corresponding figures of the total tax distribution for 1961 and 1958.

The major conclusion of this statistical estimate which is essentially similar to Musgrave's result for 1954, is a rough proportionality up to the income level of $10,000 (1958, $15,000) which includes most of the population.[74] Above this range the total tax burden rises sharply. As in most other studies the highest income class is open-ended covering all households with incomes of $15,000 and more. The tax burden of this group is 44 percent (1958, 35.9) as compared with an average for all families of 30.4.

A German statistical investigation for 1960, which we have put in relative figures and changed for our purposes, indicates a similar distribution.[75] The direct taxes as a percentage of disposable group income show a linear progression. In lower income classes fixed tax exemptions strengthen the indirect progression. Sales and consumption taxes affect only the highest income groups regressively, being proportional in the *lower* and middle ranges. Contrary to the American and

TABLE VI–16

Distribution of Taxes by Income Groups, Federal Republic of Germany, 1960

Disposable Income in DM/month	*Direct Taxes*	*Contributions to Social Insurance*	*Indirect Taxes*
		in per cent	
under 100 DM	—	0	100
100 to 200	—	5	95
200 to 300	2	15	83
300 to 400	3	27	70
400 to 500	7	43	50
500 to 600	9	47	44
600 to 700	10	46	44
700 to 800	12	45	43
800 to 1000	14	44	42
1000 to 1250	18	39	43
1250 to 1500	26	32	42
1500 to 2000	30	28	42
2000 and over	57	14	29
total	22	36	42

Canadian tax system the whole tax burden increases in the first two thirds of the income classes. In the last third there is a remarkable regression ending in a steep upward trend.

In a stimulating study Holzman attempts to compare the Soviet tax burden with the rate of taxation in the United States.[76] In order to allow a comparison he has to bridge the institutional gap by translating the American tax structure into the Soviet framework. He assumed that the incidence of indirect taxes is on consumers and that profits of business firms go entirely to the consumer.

TABLE VI–17

Average Rate of Taxation in the United States, 1949 (Billions of Dollars)

	Soviet Framework	*Western Framework*
Personal Income	206.1	206.1
Taxation of Household		
Direct Taxes	18.7	18.7
Indirect Taxes	21.3	21.3
Purchases of Government Bonds	4.3	
Social Insurance	5.7	
Corporate Profits Tax	11.0	
Undistributed Corporate Profits	9.8	
Sales of New Corporate Securities	4.6	
Total Taxes	75.4	40.0
Average rate of taxation	36.6	19.4

Source: F. D. Holzman, *Soviet Taxation* (Cambridge, Mass., 1962), p. 255.

The calculations in Table VI–17 indicate that (1) the rate of American taxation is lower under a capitalist institutional framework than under a communist one: 19.4 per cent instead of 36.5 per cent in 1949, and (2) the U.S. tax burden is apparently much lower than in the Soviet union where the rate is 68.7 per cent. Holzman states that the

> real burden of Soviet taxes is undoubtedly even greater, compared to the United States, than the figures would indicate, because of the much lower level of real national income in the USSR. However, awareness of the burden is probably obscured to some extent because most Soviet taxpayers have never experienced higher standards of living, and because so large a part of their income is taken away in the form of higher prices rather than as direct levies upon income. In addition, the Soviet ratio of marginal to average tax rates appears to be unusually low, a condition which tends to minimize the impact of such taxes.[77]

It is a pity that, despite methodological and statistical limitations, our knowledge of formal incidence in the Soviet tax system (as well

TABLE VI–18

Bases for the Allocation of the Benefits of Government Expenditures by Income Class in Previous Studies

Item	*Adler (1947/48) All levels of government*	*Musgrave (1958) State & local government*	*Gillespie (1960) All levels of government*	*Tax Foundation (1961 & 1965) All levels of government*
National defense and international affairs	income	income	number of families or money income, disposable income or capital income	number of families or money income or both
Education	per capita	income of families with school age children	number of students and wages and salaries	number of children under 18 and education expenses
Public welfare	inversely to income below $4,000	income below $3,000	public assistance payment	welfare payments
Labor	income	consumption expenditures and number of families or money income or capital income or property income	wages and salaries	wages and salaries
Veterans	consumer units with income below $5,000	n.a.	OASDI benefits and W.W.II veterans	unemployment and social security benefits
Agriculture	farm income	n.a.	food expenditures, farm income families and federal taxes	farm income
Highways	income	oil & gas expenditures and consumption expenditures	gas & oil expenditures, expenditures on goods transported and real property values	auto operation expenditures & consumption expenditures

TABLE VI–18

Bases for the Allocation of the Benefits of Government Expenditures By Income Class in Previous Studies (Cont'd.)

Item	*Adler (1947/48) All levels of government*	*Musgrave (1958) State & local government*	*Gillespie (1960) All levels of government*	*Tax Foundation (1960 & 1965) All levels of government*
Interest on Debt	holdings of liquid assets	same as labor	dividend income, and value of savings bonds	interest income
Insurance trust	consumer units with income below $4,000	same as labor	OASDI benefit payments, and unemployment compensation recipients.	unemployment and social security benefits

as the French or Italian tax structure) is as yet inferior. Holzman has attempted to consider Soviet taxation from the equity point of view but he himself calls the results of his pioneering study very tentative.[78]

4. Budget Incidence in the United States

Empirical analyses of tax systems focus on the burden or cost side of the budget. Distribution of benefits arising from the public expenditures are neglected.[79] Only a few studies include direct transfer payments, mostly as social security payments to households.

If we combine "cost" and benefits distributed to people in various income groups as the result of government activity we change the onesided picture of tax "burden" into one of net income redistribution under conditions of *assumed* effective tax incidence.

Fortunately much empirical work in the field of formal budget incidence has recently been done. The methods are improved compared with the pioneering studies of T. Barna, J. H. Adler, R. A. Musgrave, and R. S. Tucker. Here we meet, *mutatis mutandis*, the same fundamental problems concerning the tax system as discussed at the beginning of this section. Therefore it may be sufficient to emphasize the difficulties in measuring the effective incidence of benefits allocated to various income groups. For this purpose we add Table VI–18 as an

TABLE VI–19

Redistribution of Income through Federal, State, and Local Budgets in 1961

(1) Income Class[a]	(2) BLS Money Income before Personal Taxes[b]	(3) Taxes Borne[c]	(4) Benefits Received[d]	(5) Incomes after Redistribution (2 − 3 + 4)	(6)
					% of Income before Personal Taxes 5 : 2
	$000,000	$000,000	$000,000	$000,000	
Under $ 2,000	10,170	3,745	15,483	21,908	215.4%
$ 2,000 to 2,999	15,928	5,657	14,697	24,968	156.7%
$ 3,000 to 3,999	23,613	9,320	15,480	29,773	126 %
$ 4,000 to 4,999	34,260	13,410	16,365	37,215	108.6%
$ 5,000 to 5,999	42,389	16,899	17,772	43,262	102 %
$ 6,000 to 7,499	63,001	24,765	23,044	61,280	97.1%
$ 7,500 to 9,999	73,620	28,997	23,330	67,953	92.3%
$10,000 to 14,999	53,863	22,777	15,420	46,506	86.3%
$15,000 and over	31,239	19,063	7,378	19,554	62.5%
Total	348,083	144,634	148,968	352,419	101.2%

(a) The income class limits are expressed in money income after personal taxes. "Personal Taxes" consists mainly of Federal, State and Local income taxes.

(b) As defined by the US Bureau of Labor Statistics (BLS), money income includes wages and salaries, self-employment income, rent, profits from owned-businesses, interest, dividends, public unemployment and social security benefits, private pensions and annuities, public assistance, gifts of cash, and other items including alimony, royalties etc. It excludes "other money receipts" such as inheritances, occasional large gifts, lump-sum settlements of fire and accident insurance, and other "windfall" receipts. See the study of the US Bureau of Labor Statistics, Consumer Expenditures and Income, Survey of Consumer Expenditures 1960–61, (BLS Report No. 237–38 and various supplements, Washington, D.C. 1965 and 1966).

(c) Half of the burden of the corporate tax is assumed to be shifted to consumers and half is assumed to fall on shareholders.

(d) General benefit expenditures are assumed to be allocated half on the basis of number of families and half on the basis of family income.

example. It compares the different methods for allocating the benefits of public expenditures by income class applied in four studies.

Since one of the measures of total and group incidence is the Lorenz curve, we have calculated on the basis of the Tax Foundation figures the formal U.S. budget incidence for 1961. The three Lorenz curves show income distributions before and after government activity indicating the extent of redistribution in terms of the Gini-coefficient of inequality. Compared with Adler's results for 1946–47 the redistributive effects of the budget have become stronger. The degree of

FIGURE VI–12

Redistribution of Income through the Fiscal System, 1961

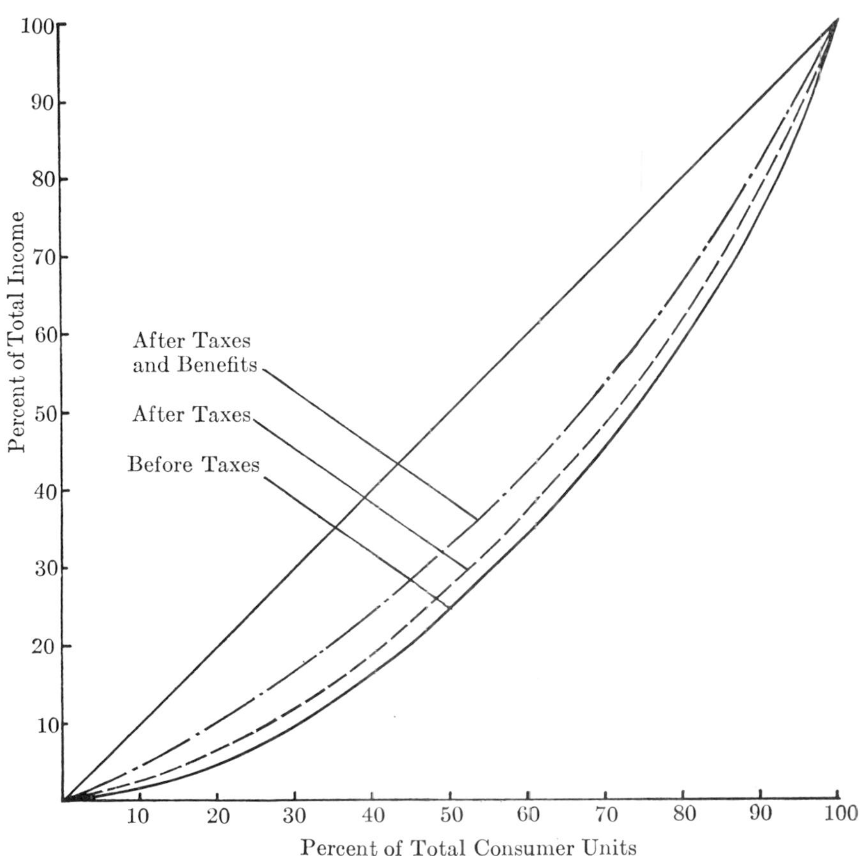

benefit deconcentration is much higher than the equalizing effects of taxation! In 1961 the redistribution curve lies nearer to the line of an egalitarian distribution than in 1946–47.

Unfortunately methods and concepts in the fields of formal incidence are too little standardized on the international level to allow comparison of the results of such studies with much profit.[80]

Notes

1. Carl Föhl, "Das Steuerparadoxon," *FA, NF,* XVII (1956), 1–37.
2. Krzyzaniak (ed.), *Effects of Corporation Income Tax* (Detroit, 1966).
3. K. E. Boulding, *The Organizational Revolution* (New York, 1953), p. 277.
4. R. Goode, "Rates of Return, Income Shares, and Corporate Tax Incidence" in *Effects of Corporation Income Tax,* p. 207. See, too, J. A. Pechman, *Federal Tax Policy* (Washington, 1966), p. 104.
5. R. A. Musgrave, "Discussion," *AER, P and P,* LIV (1964), 300.
6. Eugene R. Schlesinger, "Corporate Income Tax Shifting and Fiscal Policy," *NTJ,* XIII (1960), 17–28.
7. Schlesinger explains on page 21 how under similar price effects the burdening of the consumer changes with varying corporation tax rates.
8. *Ibid.,* p. 22.
9. *Ibid.,* p. 28.
10. Marian Krzyzaniak and Richard A. Musgrave, *The Shifting of the Corporation Income Tax* (Baltimore, 1963), pp. 13–41.
11. E. Schwartz, in *JF,* XIX (1964), 595, criticizes the periods while Goode, "Rates of Return," pp. 212–213, proves the assumptions and states: "(This) standard model includes, in addition to the corporate tax, three other variables that are supposed to account for changes in the rate of return on invested capital of manufacturing corporations:

    (1) the change in the ratio of consumption expenditure to gross national product (GNP);

    (2) the ratio of inventory to sales for all manufacturing establishments; and

    (3) the ratio of accruals of all federal, state, and local taxes other than the corporate income tax (minus government transfer payments) to GNP. The first two of these three variables are lagged one year. The corporate tax is usually represented by the effective rates of federal corporate income and excess profits tax for all manufacturing corporations, but the statutory rates of income and excess profits taxes are also used to some extent."
12. G. F. Break, Book Review, *AER,* LVII (1967), 646–647. The three subsequent quotations are from these pages.

13. R. J. Gordon, "Incidence of Corporation Income Tax," *AER,* LVII (1967), 731–758.
14. R. A. Musgrave and M. Krzyzaniak, "Incidence of a Corporation Income Tax in U.S. Manufacturing: Comment," *AER,* LVIII (1968), pp. 1358–1360.
15. C. A. Hall, Jr., "Direct Shifting of the Corporation Income Tax in Manufacturing," *AER, P and P,* LIV (1964), 258–271.
16. Goode, "Rates of Return," p. 228.
17. A. C. Harberger, "The Incidence of the Corporation Income Tax," *JPE,* LXX (1962), 215–40.
18. J. G. Cragg, A. C. Harberger, and P. Mieszkowski, "Empirical Evidence on the Incidence of the Corporation Income Tax," *JPE,* LXXV, 6 (1967), 811–821.
19. M. Krzyzaniak, "Are Tax Rates Endogenous? A Nightmarish Possibility for the Analysis of Tax Policies," in H. Haller and H. C. Recktenwald, eds., *Finanz-und Geldpolitik im Umbruch* (Mainz, 1969), pp. 175–196.
20. M. Krzyzaniak, "Effects of Profits Taxes: Deduced from Neoclassical Growth Models," *Effects of Corporation Income Tax,* pp. 17–106.
21. See my chapter 9.
22. H. H. Hinrichs, "Dynamic-Regressive Effects of the Treatment of Capital Gains on the American Tax System During 1957–1959," *PF,* XIX (1964), 73.
23. D. Dosser, "Tax Incidence and Growth," *loc. cit.*
24. J. A. Pechman, "The Use of Computers in Tax Research," Paper prepared for the JJPF Istanbul Congress, 1969. See Kaldor's, Recktenwald's and Roskamp's skepticism in the forthcoming Congress Report, and J. G. Gurley's sharp critique in his article, "Federal Tax Policy (A Review Article)," *NTJ,* XX (1967), pp. 319–327.
25. *Report of the Royal Commission on Taxation* (Ottawa, 1966). Nicholas Kaldor attempts to apply the model to Great Britain and the Institut für Wirtschafts-und Finanzpolitik, Erlangen, to West Germany.
26. R. J. Lampman, "Prognosis for Poverty," National Tax Association, *Proceedings* (September, 1964), and "Approaches to the Reduction of Poverty," *AER,* LVII (1965), 521–529; M. Friedman, *Capitalism and Freedom* (Chicago, London, 1962), and "Poverty, a Direct Approach," *Context II,* No. 1 (1964); J. Tobin, "Improving the Economic Status of the Negro," *Daedalus,* XCIV, No. 4 (1965).
27. See K. P. Kisker, "A Note on the Negative Income Tax," *NTJ,* XX (1967), 102–105.
28. J. Tobin, J. A. Pechman and P. M. Mieszkowski, "Is a Negative Income Tax Practical?", *The Yale Law Journal,* LXXVII, 1 (1967), reprinted by The Brookings Institution (Washington, 1967), pp. 6–7.

29. C. S. Shoup, "Negative Taxes, Welfare Payments and Subsidies," *Rivista di Diritto Finanziario,* XXVI, 4 (1967), 552–569; C. Green, *Negative Taxes and the Poverty Problem* (Washington, 1967); E. Rolph, "Controversy Surrounding the Negative Income Tax," *Institut International de Finances Publiques* (Congress of Turin, 1968).
30. R. R. Hansen, "An Empirical Analysis of the Retail Sales Tax with Policy Recommendations," *NTJ,* XV (1962), 1–16.
31. The horizontal tax differentials relating to racial or ethnic groups, to rural or urban families, when income and size remain unchanged, are omitted in this short review.
32. "The procedure for selecting those family expenditures to be taxed under the 'typical' retail sales tax needs clarification. The tax is a hypothetical one incorporating the provisions most commonly found in state retail tax law in the United States, 1957. On this basis, the following list of clothing, fuel, light and refrigeration, furnishings and equipment, household operations, toilet articles and preparations; radios, T.V., and musical instruments, automobile purchases and medical expenses. The 'typical' retail sales tax exempts from taxation many items in the family budget. The most significant exemptions are savings and expenditures for services." Hansen, pp. 1–2.
33. "The budgetary data are drawn from the Study of Consumer Expenditures, Incomes, and Savings, tabulated by the Bureau of Labor Statistics, U.S. Department of Labor for the Wharton School of Finance and Commerce, University of Pennsylvania, 18 volumes, 1956." Hansen, p. 2.
34. Hansen, p. 1.
35. Hansen, p. 4.
36. *Proceedings NTA 1955,* pp. 6–38; C. S. Lock, D. J. Rau and H. D. Hamilton, "The Michigan Value-Added Tax," *NTJ,* VIII (1955), 357–71; R. W. Lindholm, "An Approach to the Introduction of the Value-Added Tax by the Federal Government," *NTA,* 1965, pp. 517–31; C. K. Sullivan, *The Tax on Value Added* (New York and London, 1965); F. Forte, "On the Feasibility of a Truly General Value-Added Tax: Some Reflections on the French Experience," *NTJ,* XIX (1966), 337–361.
37. M. Bronfenbrenner, "The Japanese Value-Added Sales Tax," *NTJ,* III (1950), 312.
38. Rolph and Break, *Public Finance, op. cit.,* p. 327.
39. C. S. Shoup, "Capitalization and Shifting of the Property Tax," in *Property Taxes,* Tax Policy League (1940), pp. 187–201.
40. J. P. Jensen, *Property Taxation in the United States* (Chicago, 1931), pp. 53–75; D. Netzer, *Economics of the Property Tax* (Washington, 1966).

41. Jensen, pp. 69–75.
42. D. W. Daicoff, "Capitalization of the Property Tax" (doctoral thesis, University of Michigan, 1961).
43. *Ibid.*, p. 112.
44. Netzer, p. 747.
45. E. Tobier, *Residential Property Tax Incidence in Northern New Jersey.* Netzer critically summarizes the results of this study in his Appendix E, pp. 265–296.
46. G. A. Sears, "Incidence Profiles of a Real Estate Tax and Earned Income Tax: A Study in the Formal, Differential Incidence of Selected Local States," *NTJ*, XVII (1964), 340–356.
47. T. F. Hady, "The Incidence of the Personal Property Tax," *NTJ,* XV (1962), 368.
48. *Ibid.*, p. 374.
49. *Ibid.*, table on p. 377.
50. Netzer, p. 42–43.
51. *Ibid.*, and p. 44.
52. *Ibid.*, Appendix table D-1.
53. R. Bannink, "The Incidence of Taxes and Premiums for Social Insurance on Family Budgets," *PF,* XV (1960), 72.
54. *Ibid.*, pp. 86–88; the author defines incidence as the average amount of both levies (tax and social insurance contribution) which the family pays directly or indirectly (p. 74).
55. Pechman, *Federal Tax Policy,* pp. 166–168; E. Deran, "Income Redistribution under the Social Security System," *NTJ,* XIX (1966), 276–285; E. G. Harvey, "Social Security Taxes—Regressive or Progressive?", *NTJ,* XVIII (1965), 408–414.
56. Pechman, pp. 166–167.
57. Harvey, p. 412. See also E. Liefmann-Keil, *Oekonomische Theorie der Sozialpolitik* (Berlin-Göttingen-Heidelberg, 1961).
58. M. Newcomer, *Estimates of the Tax Burden on Different Income Classes: Studies in Current Tax Problems* (20th Century Fund, 1937); G. Colm, and H. Tarasov, "Who Pays the Taxes?", *loc. cit.*, and "Who Does Pay the Taxes?", *Social Research,* Supplement IV (1942), G. F. Shirras and L. Rostas, *The Burden of British Taxation* (New York, 1943); and T. Barna, *Redistribution of Incomes through the Fiscal System in 1937* (Oxford, 1945).
59. Compare Zeitel, *Die Steuerlastverteilung, loc. cit.*
60. *Ibid.*, p. 14.
61. *Ibid.*, p. 134 *passim.*
62. K. W. Roskamp, "The Distribution of Tax Burden in a Rapidly Growing Economy. West Germany in 1950," *NTJ* (1963), 20 *passim.*
63. Compare, among others, F. D. Holzman, "The Burden of Soviet Taxation," *AER,* XLII (1953), 548 *passim.*

64. I. J. Goffman, "Incidence of Taxation in Canada," *PF*, XIX (1964), 69.
65. Karl W. Roskamp, *Capital Formation in West Germany* (Detroit, 1965).
66. Goffman, *op. cit.*, from p. 54. See also, my section on the empirical incidence of taxes.
67. Roskamp, "The Distribution of Tax Burden," *op. cit.*, p. 24 *passim.*
68. For comparison, see the hypotheses of Goffman on the shifting of the corporation tax in Canada under very different economic conditions. Consumers bear 30 per cent, backward shifting to the wage earners is 15 per cent, and the actual burden of company profits is about 55 per cent.
69. Roskamp, "The Distribution of Tax Burden," p. 27. For a later, empirical econometric estimation of the effective incidence of taxes on business income in West Germany see, Karl W. Roskamp, "The Shifting of Taxes on Business Income: The Case of West Germany," *NTS*, XVIII (1965), No. 3.
70. Roskamp, "The Distribution of Tax Burden," p. 34.
71. Goffman, p. 47, and R. A. Musgrave, "The Incidence of the Tax Structure and Its Effects on Consumption," *Federal Tax Policy for Economic Growth and Stability,* Joint Economic Committee (1955), p. 98.
72. C. Clark and G. H. Peters, "Income Redistribution through Taxation and Social Services: Some International Comparisons," *Income and Wealth,* Series X, *op. cit.*, pp. 99–120.
73. Clark and Peters, pp. 108–112. This volume contains the five contributions quoted in this section.
74. If the income concept is changed to the product instead of the income view of national accounting, the tax distribution is more progressive. Tax Foundation, op. cit., p. 19.
75. Schmidt, Schwarz and Thiebach, *Die Umverteilung des Volkseinkommens, op. cit.*, p. 129.
76. F. D. Holzman, "The Burden of Soviet Taxation," p. 561 *passim.*
77. F. D. Holzman, *Soviet Taxation. The Fiscal and Monetary Problems of a Planned Economy* (Cambridge, Massachusetts, 1962).
78. *Ibid.*, p. 256.
79. Compare among others, Shirras and Rostas, p. xii.
80. H. C. Recktenwald, *Ein kommensverteilung und Steueraufkommen* (Mainz, 1971) and W. Hake, *Umverteilungseffekte des Budgets* (Göttingen, 1971).

7

Specific Effects of Tax Schedules upon Shifting

In addition to the market factors the autonomous tax structure exerts a significant influence on the possibility, direction and extent of shifting. The basis of tax assessment as well as the tax rate and the time and technique of taxation may affect the shifting process.

I. *Tax Schedule and Incidence*

However unimportant the absolute level of the tax rate may be in everyday economic life it plays an essential role from the standpoint of pure theory. In pure theory[1] the effect of any infinitely small tax can be recorded since to any infinitesimal change in price there corresponds a demand and a supply. This assumption is never realized in practice. On the one hand, the denomination of currency allows only certain discrete price changes, and on the other hand supply and demand react, as a rule, only to a significant change in price[2] and, moreover, this response is variable. If we have a minor tax, it can easily be added to the price as long as consumers do not react to small price changes, i.e. as long as the price elasticity of demand in this area is zero.

Under these circumstances, the seller may shift a tax, which otherwise he would bear himself because of the danger of losing sales. More frequently, however, the producers may bear the tax themselves even though objective and subjective shifting conditions prevail because the tax is so small. Shifting does not take place especially with goods to whose prices the public has become accustomed (e.g. with brand products). In the last example it is not even likely that a shift of the tax burden by means of a decrease in quality or in weight would occur.

This situation explains, among other things, the often surprisingly smooth adjustment[3] of the market to a small tax change, particularly when the rate of increase is not too high and the tax burden in general stays within reasonable limits.

Also, when the tax is levied at an extremely high rate, the tax payers respond in the short-run for the most part contrary to theory. Although the psychological resistance of buyers to shifting are minor when the legislator intends the tax to be borne by them, and particularly when the tax may be explicitely indicated, the sellers may as a rule hesitate to add the tax in full to the price, because they fear a considerable loss in sales. For this reason, for example, German manufacturers objected very strongly to a proposed Federal Consumption Tax (*Bundesaufwandsteuer*).

The effect of the tax rate on incidence can be summarized thus: the lower the tax per unit relative to the remaining costs, the greater the probability that the market will adapt itself very quickly, since supply and demand do not respond to price in certain areas. On the other hand, the higher the tax rate schedule, the more difficult is the accommodation and the more likely that the tax will not be completely shifted, inasmuch as demand may be highly elastic at certain price levels, and thus large groups of buyers may drop out.

For tax and fiscal policy, it seems sensible to keep the level of new taxes or tax changes reasonable, if the consumers are actually supposed to bear them. Extremely high[4] and extremely low rates may in the short run produce highly variable effects on incidence inconsistent with the avowed aims which taxation seeks to achieve. Thus, under favorable conditions, income tax increases with the object of fighting inflation may produce the opposite effect beyond a certain level of total taxation; the tax then becomes inflationary.[5]

II. *Progressive Taxes and the Shifting Process*

With two exceptions the tax rate was in the preceding chapters assumed to be constant. In order to perceive the effects of changing tax rates on the shifting process, we will drop this assumption. In general, progressive taxes on net profit (surplus) do not alter the results of incidence theory under conditions of perfect competition and pure monopoly. If, however, the tax rate is not graduated properly and the progression proceeds extremely steeply, a monopolist may, under particular conditions, obtain equal returns by means of either a price decrease or an increase after deduction of the tax.[6] In a monopolistic position, as Figure VII–1 shows, a progressive tax may leave the

FIGURE VII–1

Average and Marginal Rates of Tax

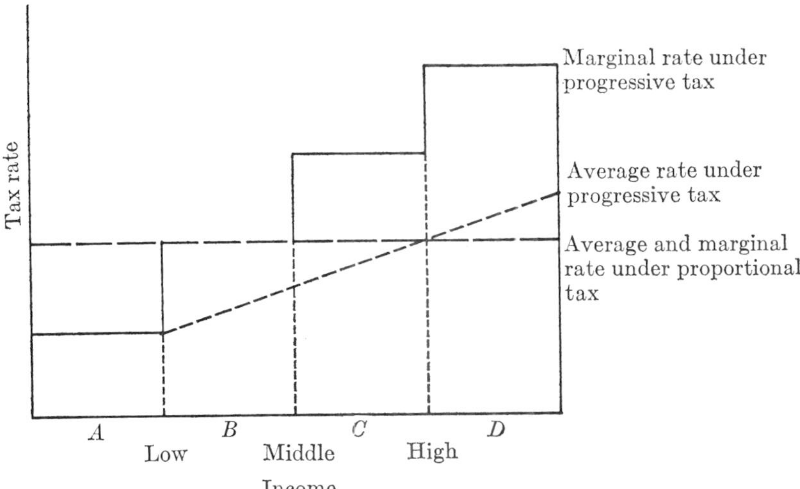

monopoly price unchanged as, for example, Wicksell one-sidedly assumes,[7] or raise or lower it depending on the cost and demand situation. The direction in which the taxpayer will respond is therefore uncertain. This case, is, however, of no practical significance.

Far greater attention should be paid to the effects of progression under monopolistic and oligopolistic competition. When different income (profit) groups are taxed very differently, the actual differences in burden may increase so much that a common price policy, which is the prerequisite for shifting, is prevented at least in the short-run.

A simple graph used by Musgrave to demonstrate the different tax effects on work effort may illustrate this statement.[8] We assume that a progressive tax replaces a proportional income tax of equal yield with public expenditures held constant. As a result both average and marginal tax rates will be increased for the high income group and decreased for all groups with lower incomes. The changes, however, in average rates will be milder than the changes in marginal rates.

It is evident that the progressive tax rate will leave groups A, B, C, and D in very different positions. It is impossible to predict exactly how the groups as a whole will react with regard to forward shifting. Obviously a joint price policy is more difficult than before.

Furthermore, a complete shifting of a progressive tax forces a more than proportional price increase which considerably increases the danger of a fall in demand due to excessive prices and at the same time strengthens latent competition. Therefore, a careful price policy by all market participants, even of the price leader, is essential. Weyermann[9] and more recently Neumark[10] have emphasized this point.

A simplified numerical example will clarify the price increases necessary for a complete shifting:

Let the profit to be obtained before shifting amount to 100,000 DM and the steep tariff show the following steps:

30 per cent from 51,000 to 90,000 DM of taxable profits;
40 per cent from 91,000 to 100,000 DM of taxable profits;
50 per cent from over 101,000 DM of taxable profits.

The tax payer would now have to raise his profit by means of a price increase by 40 per cent of 100,000 DM (= 40,000 DM) to 140,000 DM. At 140,000 DM of taxable profit the amount of tax to be paid rises to 70,000 DM because, as a result of the progression, the rate rises from 40 to 50 percent. Then only 70,000 DM would be left to the taxpayer as profit. To ensure a disposable return of 100,000 DM he would have to raise his price so high that he obtains not 140,000 DM but 200,000 DM. After deducing the tax applicable at this level (namely 50 percent of 200,000 DM = 100,000 DM) he would be left with the desired 100,000 DM profit. In this case, even any loss from declining sales is fully compensated.

Gross profit may be calculated according to the formula:

$$\frac{100 \times \text{net profit}}{100 - \text{tax rate}}$$

Shifting is also made more difficult by the complicated technical lay-out of most modern schedules. It is, on the one hand, not always easy to estimate the necessary price increase and to determine the right level; for example, the marginal tax rates are frequently unknown. On the other hand, the differentiations resulting from adjusting the tax to the personal circumstances of the taxpayers (personal exemptions, allowance for dependents, etc.) strengthen or weaken the progressivity of the tax, and play an important part in the shifting struggle. This applies especially under conditions of imperfect competition, because here the progressive income taxation is far more significant than in typical oligopolistic markets which are mostly subject to a proportionate corporation income tax.

However, under certain conditions such as relatively equal returns and advance tax payments, high tax rates, average cost calculation, a steady demand and an elastic money supply, a (gradual) shifting, even of the higher tax amounts may be possible. This supports Mann's opinion that small firms may receive a tax rent differential.[11]

In summary: in today's prevailing markets, progressive taxes hinder the shifting process, because they tend to differentiate the tax burden more or less strongly and thereby limit an essential pre-requirement of shiftability—joint market behavior. The steeper the progression and the higher the tax rates, the more difficult becomes a complete shifting. In real situations however, other shift-promoting factors may to some extent compensate for the restraining effect of tax progressivity. For example, the customary average advance payments calculated on the income and profits of the preceding year facilitate a partial shifting. In such a case firms are often in a position to manipulate their profit within limits in such a way that a disparity between estimated and real commercial success and hence a higher non-shifted final and supplementary payment is avoided. In addition, the extrepreneur may by means of short-term profit accounting approximately project the results of his activities and with it the probable tax to be paid.

Of course neither even an exact estimate nor complete advance payments nor an individual desire for shifting nor profit calculations through accounting prove anything conclusive about the success of shifting and thus about the actual incidence of a progressive income tax. In the final analysis, in any individual real case all shift promoting and hindering factors must be examined for their effectiveness at the particular time in order to judge the effects of progressivity on incidence.

Notes

1. Cournot's suggestion of dividing a high tax schedule into small parts in order to derive the effects neither solves the practical problem nor elimi-

nates the difficulties of extremely high and low tax rates. See, critically, Schumpeter, *Das Wesen, op. cit.*, p. 478; Fasiani, *Elementi, op. cit.*, p. 202; L. Kullmer, "Zeitwahl und administrativer Vollzug als Probleme einer konjunkturorientierten Finanzpolitik," *FA, NF,* XX (1960), 384.

2. We refer to the Seligman-Edgeworth-Graziani controversy mentioned in chapter V.
3. Schumpeter talks of *Fugen und Risse* in which the burden of the sales tax "nestles," in his often discussed essay "Wen trifft die Umsatzsteuer?," *Der Deutsche Volkswirt,* III (1928), 206.
4. We should mention here another distorting effect of exclusively high taxes: increased tax-free expenditure to save taxes.
5. H. M. Somers in *AER,* XLII (1952), 166; and C. Clark, "The Danger Point in Taxes," *Harper's Magazine,* 1950, reprinted in *Readings in Economics,* ed., P. A. Samuelson, R. L. Bishop and J. R. Coleman (New York, 1952).
6. See chapter 5.
7. Wicksell, *Finanztheoretische Untersuchungen . . . , op. cit.*, p. 11; also Edgeworth, *The Pure Theory of Taxation,* op. cit., p. 97. Seligman's opinion on progression in a short paragraph is very vague (*Die Lehre von der Steuerüberwälzung,* op. cit., pp. 239–240). See more recently K. Schmidt, *Die Steuerprogression* (Basel und Tübingen, 1960).
8. Musgrave, *Theory,* op. cit., p. 244.
9. M. Weyermann, *Kapitalbildung und Steuersystem,* F. List Gesellschaft, Verhandlungen und Gutachten der Konferenz von Eilsen, ed., G. Colm and H. Neisser (Berlin, 1930), I, 283.
10. Fritz Neumark, *Theorie und Praxis der modernen Einkommensbesteuerung* (Bern, 1947), p. 159 and especially p. 160.
11. F. K. Mann, *Gutachten,* op. cit., p. 330.

8

The Influence of Business Cycles and Growth on Shifting

1. General Remarks

Let us drop the assumption of full employment and fixed capacity and consider, first, the effects of the business cycle on shifting. These effects must be separated from the production and employment effects of taxation. It is extremely difficult to isolate quantitatively the effects of pure incidence from those of business cycle and growth. In practice it is almost impossible to say whether a price change is due to taxation or to cyclical movements and in what proportion.[1]

If sales and employment are shrinking in a downswing and if the entrepreneurs try to maintain sales by price reductions, a new tax is far more difficult to shift forward, if it can be shifted at all, than in times of economic expansion and rising prices. On the other hand this phase favors internal and external backward shifting, because the supply of goods, intermediate goods and raw materials as well as labor becomes relatively fixed. As long as prices decrease without a reduction in the quantities offered, shifting to the suppliers will succeed.

Since in such an unstable situation every producer and buyer tries to utilize even the smallest market advantage, even the limited or latent competition in monopolistic markets intensifies, and with it the possibility of shifting.

In the upswing (sellers market) the suppliers are in a much better position with regard to shifting than the consumers. The general optimism, stimulated by even higher nominal profits, encourages simultaneous borrowing and a uniform price policy, because the pressure of competition tends to ease off. This permits forward shifting.

Backward shifting, on the other hand, will be rare during economic expansion because the prices on the supply markets will also normally rise.

The influence of the cyclical trend on incidence is, however, limited to the particular phase of the business cycle. Once the upswing slows down and the market is more balanced, demand "quiets down" and supply "adapts," the influence of the other shifting factors becomes again dominant. The effects of a recession on short-run shifting may be even more differentiated since the reactions of the taxpayers are unpredictable, as the German example in 1967 proved.

Economic and fiscal policy, therefore, should take note of the way in which the shiftability of taxes alters during the business cycle. For example corporate income taxes, intended to be anti-inflationary may have the opposite effect when the intended incidence fails.

2. Shifting and the Trade Cycle in a Circular Flow Approach

Applying a macro-economic circular flow model of the Niehans[2] type to the incidence of profit taxes, Eppler[3] emphasizes the trade cycle as a major factor in the shifting process. Therefore we will deal here with his arguments and results.

If the government introduces a tax on the incomes of entrepreneurs it cuts their disposable income, thereby influencing their propensity to consume and to invest. Government expenditure on goods and services will increase in the same amount as taxes.

The most important parameters in Eppler's model are the propensities to consume and invest of the entrepreneurs (u_1) and the propensity to consume of the workers (u_2). Eppler concludes that the burden on profit decreases the greater u_2. The opportunity to shift the taxes declines, on the other hand, if u_1 is relatively high because in this case the tax falls more heavily on entrepreneurial consumption and investment.

If profit expectations are favorable, "the degree of the functional dependence of the constraining tax effects upon the marginal propensity of entrepreneurial spending is reduced."[4] If the effects of the profits tax are zero, the impact of both parameters u_1 and u_2 have acted in the same direction. Depending on the price elasticity of consumption and investment the rising prices simultaneously support this trend. The wage-price spiral and further increased investments will start a cumulative expansionary process.

Eppler attempts to demonstrate in a numerical example, using "normal values" of $u_1 = 0.9$ and $u_2 = 0.8$ and an increased tax of one percent of GNP, that the entrepreneurs nominally bear nearly half of the tax (0.45 percent). If the rising price level is included, however, their burden becomes higher. In real terms the entrepreneurs can shift only 0.38 percent of the profit tax, while their share of the tax incidence is 0.62 percent.[5] The position of the workers will simultaneously improve since they do not bear any tax burden; on the contrary, their income increases by 0.51 percent. The distribution of income is changed in favor of the wage earners. The expansive effect of government expenditures has nearly fully compensated for the restrictive consequences of the tax.

In the discussion of taxes this type of income redistribution is generally neglected. "Shifting" in this connection does not mean that the workers have to bear the shifted part. Rather, they get only a part of the additional income arising from the expansive development.

Under the extreme assumption that the marginal propensity of entrepreneurial spending (u_1) tends to be zero and that of the workers (u_2) is one, the profits tax does not affect businessmen. While Föhl[6] even concludes that the tax would be entirely shifted in an underemployed economy, Eppler holds that wage earners, too, would be untouched by the tax. "Nobody bears the tax burden and the tax incidence will be zero. This is our tax paradox!"[7]

Blümle[8] attempted to link both modern distribution and neoclassical incidence theory by combining primary distribution and the redistribution of income. The disadvantage of this kind of approach is obvious as we pointed out: in the comprehensive distribution models of Boulding, Kaldor, Preiser, and Bombach, shiftability and incidence of the tax have to be more or less neglected. The results are partly anticipated in the assumptions or parameters. On the other hand, starting from a given income distribution considerably narrows in some cases the implications of macro incidence theory.

Blümle uses a 3-sector-model based on the Kaldor-Bombach framework, to investigate the shifting of a tax on profits, wages, sales and capital return. He concludes that the incidence of the four tax types does not differ. Mostly wage earners bear new tax burdens and the shiftability of a tax depends more on the propensity to save than the tax rate.

In a more general model Blümle proves the conditions which lead to different results in the incidence of a profits and sales tax.

3. Economic Growth and Incidence

If demand and supply change due to technical progress and increasing population, this long-run process may strongly influence incidence just as tax shifting may on its part affect the level and growth rate of income and production.[9] Within the framework of static theory we assume unchanging markets, in which the marginal firms are eliminated by successful tax shifting. Even if we assume that the non-shiftable taxes are partly "absorbed" in surplus capacities, this fact does not explain the striking discrepancy between our experiences and a theory of incidence which explains long-run shifting by an "exodus" of the marginal firms due to taxation.

But, if supply and demand expand, this growth process alters the shifting results considerably.

If producers expect a future increase in sales, they may temporarily forego covering parts of the fixed costs or expanding their credits or dissaving in the hope of shifting the tax when demand increases later on. In this way the market gradually adjusts itself, allowing long-term shifting and (or) paying the tax out of growth profits without a total loss of marginal firms. Yet, whether the shifting has really succeeded or not depends on several conditions. The taxed firm may pay the tax T_t

(1) out of the profit earned in period t. In this case they bear it. Or

(2) out of the net profit increase ΔP of period $t + 1$ or of the following periods $t + 2, \ldots, t + n$.

This may, in turn, be caused by

(a) increased sales at unchanged prices, when, for example, population grows while technical progress remains constant; in this case we are not dealing with a real shifting since the tax T_t plus the raised tax $(T = T_t + T_{t+1})$ are borne by the (enlarged) profit of period $t + 1$.

(b) increased sales at unchanged prices and decreasing unit costs as a result of economies of scale or of technical progress. Here, with reference to incidence, the same applies as under (a) provided the tax has not prevented a passing on of the cost reduction to the buyer through lower prices. If the cost reduction has not been passed on to the consumer, the buyer bears the tax, otherwise the seller does. But compared with the pre-tax status nobody pays. Everything depends on the answer to whom the growth profit "belongs."

(c) increased sales and a higher price, unit costs being constant. As long as the price-determined profit covers the tax, the tax is shifted.

(d) increased sales with an increased price and declining unit costs. In this case, the market adjusts itself most quickly and easily to the tax. Here the tax can be shifted even with growing profit.

(e) as in (d), however, with rising unit costs, when for example population grows faster than productive capacities with unchanged technical progress. Shifting succeeds only to the extent that the price rise more than compensates for the increase in cost.

Under monopolistic and oligopolistic competition, too, a temporary strong tax pressure, because of an absence of a joint price policy or for other reasons, may gradually weaken as the economy expands, so that in the long-run the tax may be shifted.

Thus in the context of economic growth, the conflict between theory and reality disappears. The elimination of the marginal producer is not so important as suggested by the classical theory of incidence. The steady growth of national income, on the other hand, whatever its cause, makes forward shifting of and market adaptation to a tax easy.

Notes

1. On the other hand, the increase in real income resulting from the use of idle capacity can, at stable prices, be clearly separated from the incidence. If the tax is paid out of and borne by the additional incomes from increased sales, then evidently shifting does not occur, because this increase in income is the result of additional entrepreneurial activity and is not a tax shift to other economic groups. If increased sales compensate for the decreased net return per unit the income remains unchanged in spite of the tax; the possible rise in income without tax, however, is taxed away.
2. J. Niehans, "Die Wirkung von Lohnerhöhungen, technischen Fortschritten, Steuern und Spargewohnheiten auf Preise, Produktion und Einkommensverteilung," in E. Schneider, ed., *Schriften des VfS, NF*, Vol. XVII (Berlin, 1959).
3. R. Eppler, *Das Problem der Steuerinzidenz bei den Gewinnsteuern* (Frieburg, Switzerland, 1965).
4. Eppler, *loc. cit.*, p. 128, and "Die Nachfrage als Bestimmungsfaktor der Steuerüberwälzung," *FA*, Vol. XXVI, 3 (1967).
5. Eppler, *Das Problem der Steuerinzidenz*, p. 129.
6. Föhl, "Kritik," *loc. cit.*, pp. 92 and 98, and "Steuerparadoxon," *loc. cit.*, pp. 26–27.
7. Eppler, *Das Problem*, p. 135.
8. G. Blümle, "Verteilungstheorie und makroökonomische Steuerüberwälzungslehre," *JbfS*, XVIII, 3 (1967), 175–214.
9. D. Dosser, "Tax Incidence and Growth," *loc. cit.*, p. 572.

9

Incidence in the Framework of Tax Effects

I. *Substitution Effects and Tax Shifting*

In chapters 2 and 5 we emphasized the importance of substitution effects for the extent of shifting as well as for fiscal revenue. For this reason these relations deserve a more extended treatment.

In Figure V–2 the rectangle KPTL signified the "loss" of tax revenue. Since fiscal policy is mainly interested in short-term gains from a tax, the amount of obtainable revenue plays a more important part in fiscal thinking than the identity of the tax bearer or the tax source. If, for example, the government intends to introduce a consumption tax, it must first get an idea about the current volume of sales. Then it estimates how much the sales will decrease as a result of taxation. The product of sold quantity and tax rate equals the fiscal gain which, when related to the former sales, shows in turn the decline of tax receipts caused by substitution. A tax increase normally does not result in a proportional growth in revenue, except when demand or supply are completely inelastic.

Tax yields increase up to a certain point beyond which revenue may even decrease. This critical turning point is primarily determined by the adaptability of demand. Swift has already proved this simple dependence.

In general, the extent to which there will be an attempt to avoid the tax depends on its level and form, the intensity of demand for the taxed goods and the possibility of buying substitutes. The higher the tax and the less urgent (or more price elastic) the demand, the greater the tendency to avoid taxation and the smaller the fiscal revenues.[1] For, with rising taxes the advantages of substitution grow. At the same time goods and services which so far ranked low in the scale of needs become profitable for the individual so that the structure of the consumption and production plans, and with it the distribution of the productive forces in the economy as a whole, are more or less strongly altered.

Obviously a tax "discrimination" of productive factors may alter the factor combination in the same way as a wage increase. But technical progress, significant for the elasticity of factor substitution, may improve the existing means of production as well as introduce new production processes.[2]

Since Dupuit and Jenkin, numerous eonomists[3] have investigated the loss of social utility through taxation and attempted to determine its size (see Figure V–2). Fasiani and Hotelling[4] start with the proposition that all suppliers whose supply price is below the market price receive a producer rent, and all buyers whose demand price is above the market price receive a consumer rent. If the equilibrium price rises because of the tax, then, depending on the elasticity of supply and demand, the shifted part of the tax will be paid out of the gains from trade of the buyers, the non-shifted part out of the sellers gain. However, as turnover decreases, part of the total surplus is lost[5] (in Figure V–2, EP_p). Depending on the price sensitivity of supply and demand the difference between tax revenue and the reduction of producer and consumer rent is small or large, negative or positive. The total loss of welfare is the smaller the more inelastic the demand. In order to meet the basic criticisms of consumer rent, Joseph deduced the same results by means of indifference curves.[6]

What is the practical value of these welfare theorems? No doubt, the result of each direct and indirect tax avoidance is a reduced turnover which, if viewed in isolation and statically, is to be considered a "loss to society." But once we consider that the means which have been withdrawn from the individual market will again raise the "social gain" when they flow back through public expenditures or the displaced demand, the limited nature of such welfare studies becomes obvious.[7]

II. *Effects of Incidence*

We shall now deal with the psychological and economic effects of incidence which we have identified in the terminological part (Figure II–1). In a kind of *excursus* we will attempt an answer to the question:

How does tax incidence influence work effort and technical progress as well as consumption, investment, and saving?[8]

1. Taxation and Work Incentives

(a) *Effects on Work Incentive and Labor Supply*

In practice, a tax on wages may lessen the incentive to work, strengthen it or leave it unchanged. In theory an income tax lowers the "price" of leisure so that the propensity to offer the same amount of work or more must fall, if the demand for leisure is price elastic. Instead of the Hicksian method which distinguishes between income and substitution effects, we use in Figure IX–1 conventional indifference curves to show the effects of different kinds of taxes.[9]

Assume that the desire for more leisure is price elastic. Then the indifference curves, i, indicate combinations of labor income and leisure which give the individual the same utility. The budget line shows all the combinations of wage and leisure possible at a certain income. Where the indifference curve is tangent to the price line (P_1) the two "goods" are optimally combined before taxation.

Now let a proportional wage (income) tax shift the budget line RM to RM′. Whether the new equilibrium P_2 is to the left or to the right of the previous level at P_1 depends upon the shape and position of the indifference curve. In principle, therefore, a proportional tax may be an incentive or disincentive to work.[10]

If the tax is regressive the budget line will be concave upward (RQ), the tangent point P_3 is above P_2, in other words, the tax regression results in an increased labor supply.

A progressive wage tax has the opposite effect. Here the budget line is concave downward (RN), and is tangent to the indifference curve at P_4, a lower level than P_2. A progressive tax, therefore, leads to a decreased labor supply.

However, as Musgrave rightly states in criticizing Cooper, Scitovsky *et al.*, the results that apply to the individual cannot be automatically transferred to the group. He concentrates on the nature of our problem in a graph we have used in Figure VII–1. The low-income earners in range A have to pay marginal and average tax rates both of which are reduced.

FIGURE IX–1

Effects of Proportional and Progressive Wage Tax

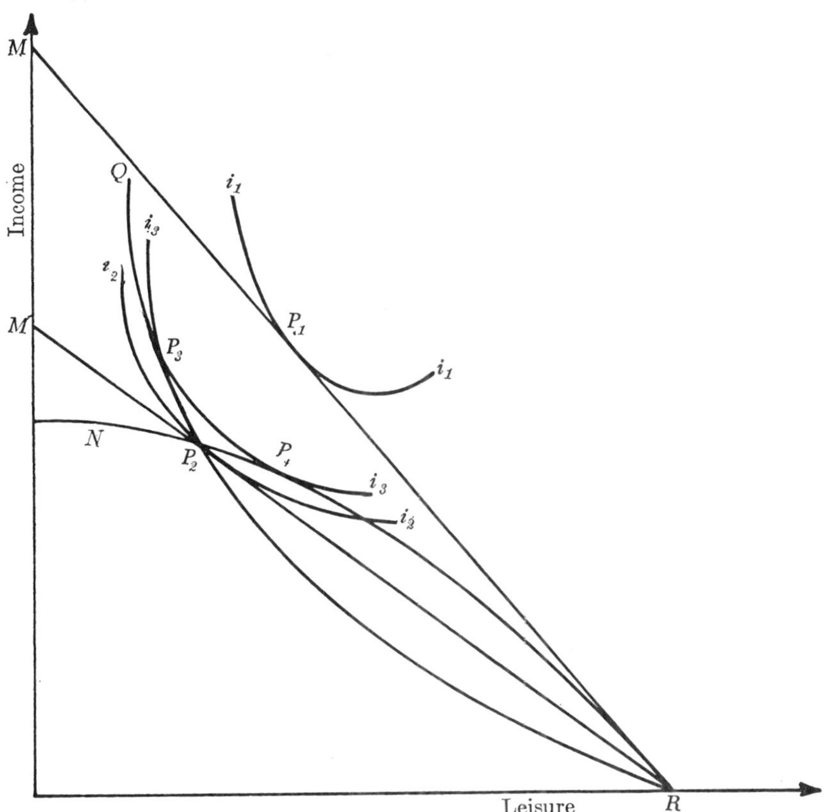

They may either increase or decrease work effort. At the top of the scale are the people in group D, who find both their marginal and average rates of tax increased. As do members of the bottom group, they may either reduce or increase work effort. Workers with low to middle incomes in range B find that their marginal rate of tax is unchanged, while their average rate is reduced. They will reduce work effort. Workers in the middle to high income group, or range C, find their marginal rate increased and their average rate reduced. They will have a twofold reason to reduce work effort.

There is no simple way of predicting what the net result for the groups as a whole will be. Let us suppose that workers in group A raise work effort, while those in group D reduce it. The net result then depends on the amount of increase in group A as against the amount of decrease in groups

B, C and D. These changes in turn depend upon the distribution of income as well as the particular change in the rate structure.[11]

But we should remember that we are dealing here with the effects of intended incidence of the differential type, i.e. the workers fully pay and bear the tax as we *assume*.

As systematic empirical investigations and individual observations show, however (Break, Sanders), labor supply reacts to price changes of leisure, if at all, inversely with an increase rather than a decrease; in other words, the demand for leisure is generally relatively price inelastic.[12]

Especially those important social groups who spend their current income primarily on consumption and who are usually obliged to spend part of their wages on social security and installment payments, do not consider a lowered price of leisure (substitution effect) important compared with the income effect of a tax which affects their consumption immediately. Depending on the situation in the labor market and the stage of economic development, the real effects of a noticeable taxation will be increased effort and/or wage demands. As a rule the second response may predominate when consumption taxes have been shifted forward, the first with wage taxes. In addition, most wage and salary earners can rarely choose freely between work and leisure, because technology determines to a large extent the amount of working hours or because a change of jobs brings with it financial losses. Hence the supply of hours worked is relatively inelastic at least in the downward direction.

However, a sharply progressive income tax may have disincentive effects, particularly in the professions or with additional earnings of family members, part-time jobs or over-time work. Depending on the competitive situation it may lead to a decline of the amount of labor offered or even to a complete withdrawal of labor from the market when for example a professionally active woman becomes a housewife, or it may lead to an early retirement of qualified persons.[13]

A wage tax may arouse anger and a desire to strike back by reducing the work effort. Musgrave calls such a demonstration of the taxpayer to intimidate the government a *spite effect*. But he agrees[14] that the motives or factors behind such a reaction to a wage tax may also operate inversely if the worker considers a special public service financed by the tax revenue a fair equivalent. In war time he even may support the government, in an attitude of public spirit. In this case the disincentive effects of a tax may be overcompensated.

In most social (income) groups the accustomed standard of living has a decisive influence on work effort. It expresses not only the reward for labor and the desire for leisure but also the need for social recognition, power, self-respect, professional success, and a secure occupation, that is, the non-material motives of individual economic activity. The level of the standard of living is generally found acceptable when consumption, saving, leisure, and other non-financial satisfactions are felt to be sensibly balanced. The appearance of new commodities may disturb this long-run equilibrium and lead to an increased work effort. But the opposite may also happen if the new goods are complementary to leisure.

If disposable income exceeds the level necessary for an acceptable standard of living, the material incentives lose importance in favor of the non-pecuniary ones. But it should be remembered that the "normal" standard of living is constantly expected to rise over time under the influence of economic and social conditions. This broader analysis helps to explain why high marginal income tax rates have failed in the last twenty years in many industrial countries to lower either work incentives or the supply of labor.

Our argument is supported by Musgrave's recent interpretation of the American experience:

> Under the present rate structure, about 75 per cent of wage and salary income pays marginal rates of 26 per cent or less. Hardly 10 per cent of such income pays rates of 50 per cent or more. If steep marginal rates give rise to disincentive effects, chances are that these are centered among a relatively small group of high-salary and professional workers. At the same time, these are precisely the groups where non-pecuniary motivations (status, sense of competition, fun of work) are relatively strong. Moreover, to a considerable extent tax rates may have been absorbed in an increased level of top salaries or fees. Shifting of this sort is quite possible since the distinction between demand and supply is blurred in the market for executive talent. Also, pension and other arrangements provide considerable avenues for tax avoidance. Thereby, possible disincentive effects on work effort are dampened, but harm is done by creating immobility of executive talent, similar to that established by seniority and compensation arrangements at the union level.[15]

(*b*) *Effects on Technical Efficiency*

The manufacturer may try to maintain his disposable income by rationalizing his production in order to reduce his cost by the amount of the tax. A direct incentive to improve his production technique or more generally the input-output relationship may be expected primarily when taxes hit hard an important cost factor. The German malt and sugar taxes which led to a better utilization of the taxed raw materials is a frequently quoted if somewhat old-fashioned example. In general a tax may influence technical progress in the same way as a drastic increase in wages or other costs.

2. Tax Impact on Consumption

Whether an increase or decrease in income brought about by taxation will decrease or increase consumption expenditures depends (1) on the ratio of consumption to expected income, (2) on the opportunity to borrow or dissave and (3) on the level, technique and type of tax. Since lower income groups have higher marginal $\left(\frac{\Delta C}{\Delta Y}\right)$ and average $\left(\frac{C}{Y}\right)$ propensities to consume than the higher income groups, a tax induced reduction or increase of those incomes will primarily affect consumption. If the small non-consumed portion of the income of these groups is used to make contractual payments or to save for a particular purpose, an income tax or any tax which is shifted forward will reduce only consumption. At the same time the consumption pattern will shift at the expense of those goods and services whose demand is income or price elastic.[16] This also holds true for the consumption saving ratio. If, for example, a taxpayer in the middle income group does not want to reduce his material standard of living in the short-run, he will reduce his savings quota which is more sensitive to income, or he will dissave or borrow, particularly if he expects his income or prices to rise. Higher income groups with fixed consumption habits will generally maintain their consumption regardless of the type of tax and its incidence.

There exist only a few studies about the tax effects on consumption by income groups and social classes.[17] While a change in inheritance taxation always leaves consumption unchanged, the consumption decreasing or increasing effects of partial expenditure and consumption taxes depend mainly on the price sensitivity of demand for the taxed goods. However, price elasticity may vary within different income groups as well as in an up or downward direction. Thus a decrease of a tax on "standard items" (tobacco, coffee) which is reflected in their prices may raise consumption more than the corresponding lowering of a tax on luxury goods.

The influence of shifted general consumption and sales taxes on consumption cannot be satisfactorily explained and even less predicted without considering the expenditure effects. Viewed in isolation they will, as a rule, reduce or raise aggregate consumption since they affect the lower incomes with higher marginal propensities to consume more than higher incomes. If taxes of this kind lead to noticeable price increases the regressivity of the incidence is likely to lead sooner or later to wage demands.

3. Tax Effects on Propensity and Ability to Save

Since motivations to save differ in nature and intensity, taxation will also affect the incentive to save differently. It seems nearly impossible to determine exactly the effects on saving behavior and to draw general conclusions. It seems therefore best to distinguish several categories of savings motivation.

To the extent to which the amount and kind of saving is determined by voluntary or compulsory insurance or to make an urgent planned purchase, the tax effects on saving are at least in the short-run insignificant. On the other hand, a tax induced change in income may affect more or less strongly that kind of saving undertaken to secure an interest yield from investment, or based on various liquidity considerations (speculation, security turnover).

Most studies are concerned with the tax effects on interest from savings, and mostly with a comparison of the influence of an income and expenditure tax.[18]

> Under an expenditure tax, a person who foregoes a given amount of present consumption and lends or invests his savings, can enjoy a greater increase in future consumption than would be possible under an equal yield income tax. The gain in future consumption may be regarded as a reward for saving or, more accurately, as a reward or incentive for saving-and-lending or saving-and-investing, since the gain is made possible by the interest obtained by lending or investing the savings. The saver is better off under the expenditure tax because postponement of consumption also postpones tax payment, permitting him to earn on the postponed tax.[19]

Moreover: "The rate of return on saving-and-investing will be higher under an expenditure tax than under an equal-yield income tax. Assuming that the propensity to save will respond to some degree to the rate of return, it will be highest under an expenditure tax."[20]

In his general critique of such arguments Johansen[21] believes the reasoning to be correct only for a temporary tax. "The effect of a permanent sales tax, however, would be to reduce the real value of the amount saved up as well as of the sum expended on consumption, that is to say it would reduce the basket of real goods one can procure for the amount saved up, should one subsequently wish to spend the money."[22]

For corporate savings which expanded enormously in the post-war period we have to modify this result, because their motives and objectives differ from those of individuals. "There appears to be a tendency in many countries for company savings to be residually determined after tax has been paid and a more or less traditionally determined dividend is distributed. In such cases a shift between taxation of personal income may influence total saving."[23]

The effect of a tax on the *volume* of saving by income groups depends, as with consumption, first of all on the income elasticity of the different types of saving. Taxation of high incomes tends, as a rule, to absorb what would otherwise be saved. Taxes on small incomes seem to cut down consumption expenditures. An additional tax burden on lower and middle income groups may even lead to dissaving and indebtedness, when consumption is relatively inelastic.

Cyclical movements and mild or strong recessions may alter the priority scale of motives and objectives for saving and thereby the amount of savings. During the mild German recession of 1967, for instance, the desire for security became so strong in the lower and middle income groups that savings rapidly increased despite falling interest rates and stagnating income.

A tax on saved portions of income may influence saving in favor of or at the expense of consumption (e.g. tax-exempt saving, different treatment of distributed profit). Finally, taxing of (interest) returns can discourage the incentive and reduce the ability to save, whereas an inheritance tax has only an indirect effect on the propensity to save.

There is another point of interest. As Musgrave[24] and Johansen[25] argue, even though the average rate of saving for the higher income categories is higher than for the lower income groups, income distribution need not influence total saving. Income distribution and thus tax allocation influence total saving only when the marginal rates of saving vary with income levels. The structure of taxed income actually does not affect total saving as is often assumed.

Since we deal in this chapter with the effects of formal tax incidence, we close with two empirical studies. The first subject for re-

TABLE IX–1

Estimated Effect of Individual Income Tax on Consumption and Saving (in million dollars; data for 1957)

Income before tax by Family unit	*Income before tax*	*Tax*	*Estimated Reduction due to Tax*		*Estimated Reduction in Saving as % of Tax*	*Estimated Level after Tax of*	
			Consumption	*Saving*		*Consumption*	*Saving*
Under $ 2,000	8,440	191	153	38	19.9	10,473	−2,224
2,000– 5,000	68,424	3,891	3,720	171	4.4	65,122	−590
5,000– 7,500	84,058	6,737	5,791	946	14.0	74,070	3,251
7,500– 10,000	56,930	5,079	4,052	1,027	20.2	47,187	4,664
10,000– 15,000	50,566	4,990	3,606	1,384	27.7	39,881	5,695
15,000– 50,000	44,700	7,192	3,539	3,653	50.8	30,160	7,348
50,000 and over	18,700	5,220	1,968	3,252	62.3	7,218	6,262
Total	331,711	33,292	22,764	10,528	31.6	274,111	24,406

search are the effects of the American individual income tax on saving and consumption. We are interested here in the tax-saving relation. Musgrave assumes that the individual income tax which supplies nearly one-half of federal and one-third of total tax receipts stays put with the tax payer. He then estimates actual saving by income brackets as they were after tax as well as what saving would have been in the absence of the tax. He deducts the former from the latter and obtains the estimated decrease in saving due to tax.

An estimated $10.3 billion or 31 per cent of $33.3 billion of individual income tax paid in 1957 was reflected in decreased saving. "This ratio of 31 percent is the *marginal* rate of saving of tax payers (weighted by their respective contributions) over the range of income before and after tax. It is reasonable that this marginal rate should be considered higher than the average post-war rate of 7.2 percent."[26] Since the marginal rates of saving at various points on the income scale differ substantially less than the average rates, even quite considerable changes in the distribution of tax payments between individuals do not affect total saving very much.

In an interesting study, Musgrave also tested the impact of tax structure on the volume of saving.[27] His estimates, based on the same rough assumptions on incidence, are summarized in Table IX–2. As might be expected, estate and corporation taxes are highly savings-intensive. On the other hand, the effects of the individual income tax and sales taxes do not differ much.

Musgrave answers the question on how much larger would private savings have been without taxation as follows:

> We estimate the tax payments of $120 billion reduced saving by $46 billion, the reduction in savings being 36 per cent of total taxes paid. The reduction of $46 billion compares with the previously noted total of private savings after taxes of $74 billion. In other words, the tax structure reduced the hypothetical pre-tax savings total of $121 billion by about 40 per cent. Note also that the ratio for the federal tax structure of 42 per cent lies considerably above the 24 per cent ratio for the state and local structure. The reason for this is to be found very largely in the greater weight of the corporation tax at the federal level.
>
> These totals serve to demonstrate that taxation causes a very substantial reduction in the level of private saving.[28]

4. Taxation, Investment and Risk-Taking

A tax change may influence investment in two ways: (a) it hinders or intensifies the motivations for investment; (b) it curtails or increases the monetary means available for investment.

TABLE IX–2

Estimated Impact of Tax Structure on Saving (in billion dollars)

	Federal	*State and Local*	*All Levels*
Individual Income Tax			
Amount	13.4	0.6	14.0
Percent	31%	28%	31%
Estate, Gift, Inheritance			
Amount	1.3	0.3	1.6
Percent	80%	80%	80%
Corporation Income Tax			
Amount	18.8	1.0	19.8
Percent	80%	66%	79%
Sales Taxes, Excess, Customs			
Amount	2.0	2.2	4.2
Percent	18%	18%	18%
Property Tax			
Amount	—	4.2	
Percent	—	25%	25%
Other Misc. Receipts			
Amount	0.4	1.8	2.2
Percent	18%	18%	18%
Total			
Amount	35.3	10.3	45.6
Percent	42%	24%	36%

(a) If the investment decisions of a firm are entirely determined by the expected return, every direct taxation of profits diminishes the incentive to invest particularly when, in addition, the returns from different real investments are taxed differently or are discriminated against compared with the interest from monetary assets (e.g. government bonds). A steeply progressive income or corporation tax will in addition change the structure of investment at the expense of very risky and therefore very profitable projects. It thus interferes with the market selection of investments and restricts risk-taking, the introduction of technical innovations, and growth.[29] These tax effects in principle harmful to investment and risk-taking are, however, partly compensated for in reality. Intangible values such as the desire for power, business security, social prestige or self-respect play as big a role in the investment decisions of firms as do profit expectations. Even heavy profits taxes may decrease the incentive, though not the financial ability, to invest only to a limited extent. Entrepreneurs may react entirely inversely in a mood of opposition to the government, or they may invest more to demonstrate *Staatsraison* or patriotism in war. In addition it is sometimes impossible for the investor to predict future profits and taxes.

The negative effect on increased risk-taking is also compensated for by the legal possibility of deducting or carrying over part of or all losses. Domar, Musgrave and Rolph[30] even assume quite generally a stimulating effect of a proportional income tax on the propensity and volume of risk-taking. These relations between tax and investment activity explain, along with other reasons (e.g. tax evasion and shifting facilitated in a boom and by expanding consumption as a result of monetary and redistributive policy) why, in recent years even an unprecedented taxation of profits and incomes and a high total tax burden have not prevented in most industrial countries a powerful rise of net investment and technical progress and, as a result, of total output.[31]

Here we have to deal with another paradox in this field. A tax on production or on gross receipts may lead to a lengthening of the average period of investment and thus cause the use of more capital-intensive techniques. This statement of neoclassical theory on general incidence is, however, controversial.

Unlike most critics, Pedone[32] in a recent article argues that it is impossible to work out a general theory of tax incidence on the basis of marginalism, because the marginal productivity theory of distribution (the basis of the neoclassical analysis) is inconsistent.

The traditional theory follows Wicksell's analysis of Böhm-Bawerk's doctrine that "an increase of the average productivity of labor is always possible through the introduction of preparatory work, i.e., a lengthening of the average period of investment of capital."[33] A new tax will lead to a new equilibrium after a reduction of the interest and wage rates and an increase in the length of the investment period. The gross output of the economy will increase via a modification of the technical structure of production.

Pedone's critique may be summarized as follows: It is inconsistent for the marginal productivity theory to let the amount of capital vary with the distribution of income between wages and profits, since it assumes that the amount of all resources (including capital) is given.

Pedone's argument seems obviously weak. As the Stolper-Samuelson article shows, many factor proportions in individual industries are consistent with constant factor proportions in the economy.[34]

(b) Obviously taxation of funds to be invested affects planned investments. A decrease in the volume of investment depends upon the availability and price of bank credit. Taxation that absorbs hoarded money does not directly affect investment financing. If it reduces savings offered through banks and the stock exchange, the costs of credit will rise and investment may decrease, other things being equal, even if, at the current rate of interest, demand for loanable funds remains the same and the supply cannot be otherwise increased at the current rate of interest. If investor and saver are identical, the tax will directly affect the (self-)financing of planned investment. Whether the intended investment will be carried out in this case depends essentially upon sales expectations of the taxed firms or, in general, upon the phase of the business cycle and the trend of growth which in turn are influenced by the effects of public expenditures. If demand tends to increase or investors expect favorable developments even a severe taxation of profits intended for net investment and high credit costs (which however may be written off) may not curtail planned investments. This will be all the more true if, with increasing progression, the incentive grows to avoid tax payment at least partially or temporarily, by additional depreciation and thus to make the state a partner in the financing of the new investments. Under these conditions a profits tax will change the firm's capital composition at rising costs in favor of credits. If the budget is balanced, it has an expansionary effect, and it increases with full employment inflationary forces through credit expansion. In a downswing the effects of such taxation are more or less the opposite.

During a mild or strong recession when growth rates stagnate or decrease, the investors' reaction may be more differentiated. Little empirical material is as yet available.

Since the theories of investment involve, as already mentioned, a complex set of economic and non-economic determinants whose influence changes considerably during the business cycle and growth,[35] various explanations of overall and particular effects of a tax on investment are possible and call for quite different tax policies. A reasonable answer or proposal therefore depends on a realistic assessment of investment behavior in the actual case. Since all determinants in theoretical and empirical analyses have some validity we have to weigh them in each case under the specific economic conditions.

In most empirical and econometric studies of investment behavior we find three of our determinants mentioned above. The investment decisions may depend upon (1) the expected (net) rate of return, (2) changes in consumer demand, and (3) volume and kinds of saving, such as externally and internally available funds and "venture capital."[36]

Musgrave, in a first attempt, has investigated the effects of different tax levels or structures on three types of investment behavior. He has thoroughly analyzed the influence of personal income and corporation taxes on investment, combining theoretical with empirical reasoning.[37] We will not discuss his methods, results and policy conclusions because we are dealing with effects of tax incidence only marginally. And so long as our explanation of *effective* tax incidence is controversial and unsatisfactory and the theory of investment behavior is of restricted use as a policy tool, all empirical and theoretical conclusions concerning tax influence on investment have to remain of dubious value or, at least, unsatisfactory.

Nevertheless, we can conclude the chapter by mentioning a most recent attempt in the empirical field.

In a stimulating study Hall and Jorgenson calculate the effects of a change in tax policy on investment behavior for three major tax revisions in the post-war period using the neoclassical theory of optimal capital accumulation.[38] They consider the effects of: (1) the adoption of accelerated depreciation for tax purposes in 1954, (2) the investment tax credit of 1962, and (3) the depreciation guidelines of 1962. As an illustration, they consider the hypothetical effects of (4) the adoption of the first-year writeoff in 1954 in place of less drastic accelerated depreciation.[39]

Their basic conclusion is

> that tax policy is highly effective in changing the level and timing of investment expenditures. In addition we find that tax policy has important effects on the composition of investment. According to our estimates, the liberalization of depreciation rules in 1954 resulted in a substantial shift from equipment to structures. On the other hand, the investment tax credit and depreciation guidelines of 1962 caused a shift toward equipment.[40]

Concluding Remarks

Since I have usually summarized any conclusions at the end of each section or chapter, I shall not repeat them but shall close with some general remarks on our discussion.

Incidence theory cannot give a simple and definite answer because economic and fiscal phenomena are closely linked in an interdependent and complicated manner. Whoever expects one generally valid simple answer actually overrates theorizing and underrates the objective difficulties and limitations of applicable methods. As modern price theory can no longer be content to develop one universal theory in order to explain all price and competition phenomena, so incidence theory must provide a number of instruments for analyzing concrete tax problems.

The major practical tasks of the theory of incidence are (a) to elucidate how a tax or a subsidy or the whole tax system works from the imposition of a tax to the final distribution of its burden; (b) to specify in particular situations the subjective and objective conditions which affect the course of tax shifting; and (c) to show how controversial tax problems may be solved. Incidence theory, however, cannot make generally valid statements about individual taxes. Even less can theory develop a general schema of shiftability as Seligman and Twerdochleboff[41] have tried to do as part of a systematic treatment of direct and indirect taxation. With only few exceptions and under very special conditions all taxes can be shifted in a market economy. It follows that neither the kind of tax nor the intention of the legislators, by themselves, suffices to guarantee in all cases that the tax payer and tax bearer are identical.

But even where theory shows that on the basis of alternative assumptions there exist a number of possible cases of incidence, this provides an invaluable aid for empirical investigations since it shows how one might go about making such a study, and what are the relevant conditions and variables. A well-founded evalution of any real incidence problems requires then "only" a thorough knowledge of the tax instruments and the effectiveness in each particular case of the factors that make for or prevent shifting. But this makes abundantly clear how difficult it is to solve any real incidence problems by means of econometric and behavioral methods.[42]

Notes

1. If goods are easily substitutable (the cross-price elasticity is high), then demand will move on quickly to the less (or un-) taxed substitute good. For this reason the substitute should be taxed in order to leave the original price relations unaffected.
2. See Pedone, "Una prima analisi dei rapporti tra l'elisione dell' imposta ed il progresso tecnologico," *EcInt,* XVI (1963), 604, and XVII (1964), 17–41, summary in English, p. 43.
3. See among others Marshall, *Principles,* op. cit., p. 468; A. C. Pigou, *The Economics of Welfare* (London, 1932).
4. Fasiani, *Principii di Scienza delle finanze* (Torino, 1941), p. 209; Hotelling, "The General Welfare in Relation to Problems of Taxation," *Econometrica* (1938), pp. 242–269.
5. Marshall (*Principles,* p. 468) discusses the problem of industries to which the law of decreasing and increasing marginal return applies. He concludes that the consumer's loss is greater than tax revenue when marginal returns are increasing. The reverse is true for decreasing marginal returns (increasing costs). But here, too, micro-economic results are one-sided as the losses of manufacturers as well as the effects of government expenditures are ignored.
6. F. M. Joseph, "The Excess Burden of Indirect Taxation," *REST,* VI (1939), 226.
7. See M. Friedman, "The Welfare Effects of an Income Tax and an Excise Tax," *JPE,* LX (1952), 25.
8. See Jürg Niehans, "Die Wirkung von Lohnerhöhungen," *op. cit.,* p. 9.
9. For results which apply to an inferior good see C. Welinder, "Einkommensteuer und Arbeitswilligkeit," *PF,* XX (1965), 238.
10. For details, see Musgrave, *Theory,* op. cit., p. 232.
11. *Ibid.*
12. George F. Break, "Income Taxes and Incentives to Work: An Empirical Study," *AER,* Vol. XLVII (1957), and Thomas H. Sanders, *The Effects of Taxation on Executives* (Boston, 1951). Royal Commission

on the Taxation of Profits and Income, Report 2 (Cmd 9105), (London, 1954). A critical survey of the relevant literature is found in George F. Break's "Income Taxation and Incentives to Work. A Survey of Recent Literature," *Rivista di diretto finanziario e scienza delle Finanze,* XVI (1957), 121.

13. R. Barlow, H. E. Brazer, and J. N. Morgan (*Economic Behavior of the Affluent* [Washington, 1966]) empirically proved that high-income individuals are far from being free agents in deciding how much work to do (p. 150).
14. Musgrave, *Theory,* p. 240.
15. Musgrave in *Fiscal and Debt Management Policies* (Englewood Cliffs, 1963), p. 82.
16. As empirical studies show, income and price elasticities of demand for certain goods do not differ significantly. See Ruth P. Mack, *Economics of Consumption, A Survey of Contemporary Economics,* II (1952), 39–78; also R. Ferber, "How Aware Are Consumers of Excise Tax Changes," *NTJ,* VII (1954), 355; J. F. Due, "Sales Taxation and the Consumer," *AER,* LIII (1963), 1078; Glenn E. Burress, "The Initial Effect of the 1964 Tax Cut on Consumer Spending," *NTJ,* XVII (1964), 265.
17. The results of studies on the effect of disposable income on saving and consumption of different groups are still contradictory (see Mack, *Economics of Consumption*). Therefore, the quantitative impact of the tax effect can generally not be determined, but only its direction. See also R. Goode, "Taxation of Saving and Consumption in Underdeveloped Countries," *NTJ,* XIV (1961), 305.
18. B. Hansen, *The Economic Theory of Fiscal Policy* (London, 1955), chapter 8; M. A. Willemsen, "The Effect upon the Rate of Private Savings of a Change from a Personal Income Tax to a Personal Expenditure Tax," *NTJ,* XIV (1961), 101; A. C. Harberger, "Taxation, Resource Allocation, and Welfare," in *The Role of Direct and Indirect Taxes in the Federal Revenue System.* A Conference Report of the NBER and the Brookings Institution (Princeton, 1964), p. 58; J. A. Pechman, *Federal Tax Policy* (Washington, 1966), p. 62.
19. Richard Goode, *The Individual Income Tax* (Washington, 1964), p. 40. "A wealth tax of course falls directly on accumulated savings. It will more sharply restrict opportunities to add to future consumption power by saving than will a general income tax of equal yield or an expenditure tax." (p. 42). Under a wealth tax, therefore, the propensity to save will be lowest.
20. Goode, *loc. cit.,* p. 42.
21. L. Johansen, *Public Economics* (Amsterdam, 1965), p. 302.
22. *Ibid.*

23. *Ibid.* For critical reasoning see also Harberger, *op. cit.*, p. 61.
24. Musgrave, "Effects of Tax Policy on Private Capital Formation," *Fiscal and Debt Management Policies,* p. 60.
25. Johansen, *op. cit.*, p. 301.
26. Musgrave, in *Fiscal and Debt Management Policies,* p. 61. The author himself mentions the weak points in the estimating procedure.
27. Musgrave, p. 65.
28. *Ibid.*, p. 66.
29. Werner Ehrlicher, "Die Wirkungen der Unternehmungsteuern auf Investitionen, Gewinn und Löhne," *FA, NF,* XVIII (1957–58), 373; Helmut Schneider, *Der Einfluss der Steuern auf die unternehmerischen Entscheidungen* (Tübingen, 1964).
30. E. D. Domar and R. A. Musgrave, "Proportional Income Taxation and Risk-Taking," *QJ,* LVIII (1944), 404; Rolph, *Theory of Fiscal Economics, op. cit.*, p. 285.
31. For special problems in underdeveloped countries see J. Heller and K. M. Kauffmann, *Tax Incentives in Less Developed Countries* (Cambridge, Massachusetts, 1963).
32. A. Pedone, "Taxes on Production and the Average Period of Investment—A Critique of the Neoclassical Analysis of General Incidence," *PF,* XXI (1966), 488–502.
33. K. Wicksell, *Finanztheoretische Untersuchungen, op. cit.*, p. 32.
34. W. F. Stolper and P. A. Samuelson, "Protection and Real Wages," *RES,* IX (1941), 58–73.
35. The other tax effects change too.
36. See J. K. Butters, L. E. Thompson, and L. S. Bollinger, *Effects of Taxation on Investments by Individuals* (Cambridge, 1953); J. R. Meyer and E. Kuh, *The Investment Decisions: An Empirical Study* (Cambridge, 1957); R. Solow, "Technical Progress, Capital Formation, and Growth," *AER, P and P,* LII (1962), 76–87; R. Eisner and R. H. Strotz, "Determinants of Business Investment," in *Impacts of Monetary Policy,* Commission on Money and Credit (New York, 1963).
37. Musgrave in *The Role of Direct and Indirect Taxes in the Federal Revenue System,* p. 83.
38. R. E. Hall and D. W. Jorgenson, "Tax Policy and Investment Behavior," *AER, LVII* (1967), 391–414; furthermore E. C. Brown, "Tax Incentives for Investment," *AER, P and P,* LII (1962), 335–345; and O. Eckstein, "Comparison of European and United States Tax Structures and Growth Implications," in *The Role of Direct and Indirect Taxes in the Federal Revenues System,* pp. 217–285.
39. Hall and Jorgenson, pp. 412–413.
40. *Ibid.*
41. Seligman, *op. cit.*, p. 387; and W. Twerdochleboff, "Die Theorie der

Steuerüberwälzung in der neuesten Literatur," *ZgSt,* LXXXVI (1929), 537.

42. H. C. Recktenwald, ed., *Finanztheorie,* 2nd. ed. (Köln, 1970), and *Nutzen-Kosten-Analyse und Programmbudget* (Tübingen, 1970) and *Die Nutzen-Kosten-Analyse* (Tübingen, 1971).

Selected Bibliography

Adelman, M. A. "The Corporate Income Tax in the Long Run." *JPE,* XLV (1957), 151–157.

Adler, John H. "The Fiscal System, the Distribution of Income and Public Welfare." In *Fiscal Policies and the American Economy.* Edited by Kenyon E. Poole. New York, 1951. 359–400.

Albers, Willi. "Preisliche Wirkungen der Besteuerung," *FA, NS,* XVI (1955/56), 227–257.

Arndt, Helmut. "Zur mikroökonomischen Analyse der Überwälzbarkeit der Einkommensteuer und zur Frage der Übertragung von Modellergebnissen auf historische Tabestände." *FA, NS,* XXI (1961), 47–59.

Arnold, Sam. "Forward Shifting of a Payroll Tax under Monopolistic Competition." *QJ,* LXI (1947), 267–284.

Bain, A. D. "Tax Incidence and Growth: A Comment," *EJ,* LXXIII (1963), 533–535.

Bannink, R. "The Incidence of Taxes and Premiums for Social Insurance on Family Budgets." *PF,* XV (1960), 72–93.

Barna, Tibor. *Redistribution of Incomes through the Fiscal System in 1937.* Oxford, 1945.

Barrère, A. "L'analyse de la répercussion et de l'incidence de l'impôt par la méthode de flux." *RSLF,* XXVII (1965), 21–40.

Bauer, Russell. "The Probable Incidence of Social Security Taxes." *AER,* XXVI (1936), 463–465.

Beard, T. R. " Progressive Income Taxation, Income Redistribution and the Consumption Function." *NTJ,* XIII (1960), 168–177.

von Beckerath, Erwin. "Die Theorie der Steuerverteilung," In *Economia politica contemporanea, saggi die economia e finanza in onore del Prof. Camillo Supino.* II (Padova, 1930), 369–385.

Behrmann, J. N. "Distributive Effects of an Excise Tax on a Monopolist." *JPE,* LVIII (1950), 546–548.

Bhargave, R. N. "Incidence of Taxation." *IEJ,* II (1954–55), 37–45.

Bibliography on Taxation in Underdeveloped Countries. Cambridge, Massachusetts, 1962.

Bishop, George A. "The Tax Burden by Income Classes, 1958." *NTJ*, XIV (1961), 1–40.

Black, Duncan. *The Incidence of Income Taxes.* London, 1939.

Blümle, G. "Verteilungstheorie und makroökonomische Steuerüberwälzungslehre." *JbfS*, XVIII (1967), 175–214.

Bodenhorn, D. "The Shifting of the Corporation Income Tax in a Growing Economy." *QJ*, LXX (1956), 563–580.

Braess, P. *Steuersystem und Preisniveau.* Leipzig, 1933.

Break, George F. "Income Taxes, Wage Rates, and the Incentive to Supply Labor Services." *NTJ*, VI (1953), 333–352.

———. "Excise Tax Burdens and Benefits." *AER*, XLIV (1954), 577–594.

———. "Income Taxation and Incentives to Work. A Survey of Recent Literature." *Rivista di diritto finanziaro e scienza delle Finanze*, XVI (1957), 191.

———. "Income Taxes and Incentives to Work." *AER*, XLVII (1957), 529–549.

Brown, E. Cary. "The Corporate Income Tax in the Short-Run." *NTJ*, VII (1954), 240–241.

Bruck, J. "Die Körperschaftsteuer als Kostenfaktor." In *Finanzwissenschaftliche Forschungsarbeiten.* Köln, 1950.

Buchanan, James M. "La Metodolgia della Teoria dell'Incidenza: Una Rassegna Critica di Recenti Contributi Americani." *Studi Economici*, X (1955), 377–399.

———. "The Economics of Earmarked Taxes." *JPE*, LXXI (1963), 457–469.

Buchanan, James M., and Forte, Francesco. "Fiscal Choice Through Time: A Case for Indirect Taxation?" *NTJ*, XVII (1964), 144.

Bureau of Internal Revenue of the U.S. Treasury Department. *An Analysis of the Processing Taxes Levied under the Agricultural Adjustment Act.* Washington, 1937.

Burress, Glenn E. The Initial Effect of the 1964 Tax Cut on Consumer Spending." *NTJ*, XVII (1964), 265–273.

Christian, V. L. Jr. "The Incidence of Compacts, Gasoline Consumption and Tax Revenue." *NTJ*, XIV (1961), 375–381.

Clark, C., and Stuvel, G., eds., *Income and Wealth:* Series X. "Income Redistribution and the Statistical Foundations of Economic Policy." Oxford, 1964.

Coates, W. H. "Incidence of the Income Tax." In *Appendices to the Report of the Commission on National Debt and Taxation.* London, 1927. Pp. 65–113.

Colm, Gerhard, and Tarasov, H. *Who Pays the Taxes?* TNEC-*Monograph* No. 3 (1941). 76th Congress, 3rd Session, Washington, D.C.

Colm, Gerhard and Wald, Haskell P. "Some Comments on Tax Burden Comparisons." *NTJ,* V (1952), 1–14.

Conrad, A. H. "On the Calculation of Tax Burdens." *Econ.,* XXII (1955), 342–348.

Cosciani, Cesare. "Zur Frage der Überwälzbarkeit einer Körperschaftsteuer." *FA, NS,* XIX (1959), 240–269.

Cragg, John G., Harberger, Arnold C., and Mieszkowski, Peter. "Empirical Evidence on the Incidence of the Corporation Income Tax." *JPE,* LXXV (1967), 811–891.

Crum, W. L. "The Taxation of Stockholders." *QJ,* LXIV (1950), 15–56.

David, M. "Economic Effects of the Capital Gains Tax." *AER, P. and P.,* LIV (1964), 288–298.

Davidson, Paul. "Wells on Excise Tax Incidence in an Imperfectly Competitive Economy." *PF,* XVI (1961), 201–209.

Davis, D. G. "Relative Burden of Sales Taxation in California." *AJE,* XIX (1960), 289–296.

Davis, David, G. "The Sensitivity of Consumption Taxes to Fluctuations in Income." *NTJ,* XV (1962), 281–290.

Doeblin, E. *Monopole und Besteuerung.* Berlin, 1933.

Domar, E. D., and Musgrave, R. A. "Proportional Income Taxation and Risk-Taking." *QJ,* LVIII (1944), 387–422.

Dosser, Douglas. "Linear Programming and Public Finance." *PF,* XV (1960), 51–61.

———. "Tax Incidence and Growth." *EJ,* LXXI (1961), 572–591.

———. "Tax Incidence and Growth Further Considered." *EJ,* LXXIII (1963), 547–556.

———. "Allocating the Burden of International Aid for Underdeveloped Countries." *RESt,* VL (1963).

Due, John F. *The Theory of Incidence of Sales Taxation.* New York, 1942.

———. "The Incidence of a General Sales Tax." *PF,* V (1950), 222–239.

———. "Towards a General Theory of Sales Tax Incidence." *QJ,* LXVII (1953), 253–266.

———. "Studies of State-Local Tax Influences on Location of Industry." *NTJ,* XIV (1961), 163–173.

———. "Sales Taxation and the Consumer." *AER,* LIII (1963), 1078–1084.

———. "The New State Sales Taxes." *NTJ,* XXI (1967), 266–287.

Edgeworth, F. Y. "The Pure Theory of Taxation." In *Papers Relating to Political Economy.* II (London, 1925), 63–125.

Ehrlicher, Werner. "Die Wirkungen der Unternehmungsteuern auf Investitionen, Gewinne und Löhne." *FA, NS,* XVIII (1957/58), 373–412.

Empoli, Attilo da. *Teoria del'incidenza delle imposte.* Reggio-Calabria, 1926.

Eppler, R. *Das Problem der Steuerinzidenz bei den Gewinnsteuern.* Freiburg, Switzerland, 1965.

Fagan, Elmer D. "Tax Shifting and Laws of Cost." *QJ,* XLVIII (1933), 680–710.

———. "Tax Shifting in the Market Period." *AER,* XXVII (1942), 72–86.

———. "The Shifting of Sales Taxes under Joint Costs." *PF,* VIII (1953), 338–354.

———., and Jastram, R. W. "Tax Shifting in the Short-Run." *QJ,* LIII (1939), 562–589.

Falck, G. von. *Kritische Rückblicke auf die Lehre von der Steuerüberwälzung seit Adam Smith.* Dorpat, 1882.

Fasiani, Mario. "Elementi per una teoria della duravata del processo traslativa dell'imposta in una societa statica." *GE,* 1929.

———. *Principii di scienza delle finanze.* Torino, 1941.

Fecher, Hans. "Einige Bemerkungen über 'Incentive-Wirkungen' der Einkommensbesteuerung." *PF,* XX (1965), 76–111.

Ferber, R. "How Aware Are Consumers of Excise Tax Changes." *NTJ,* VII (1954), 355–358.

Fieser, Max E., and Ranlett, John G. "In-Lieu Taxation: A Methodological Comment." *NTJ,* XVIII (1965), 97–103.

Foehl, Carl. "Kritik der progressiven Einkommenbesteuerung." *FA, NS,* XIV, 1 (1953), 88–109.

———. "Das Steuerparadoxon." *F.A.,* NS, XVII (1956), 1–37.

Friedlaender, Ann F. "Indirect Taxes and Relative Prices." *QJE,* LXXXI (1967), 125.

Friedman, M. "The Welfare Effects of an Income Tax and an Excise Tax." *JPE,* LX (1952), 25–33.

Frisch, Ragnar. "The Dupuit Taxation Theorem." *Econ.,* VII (1939), 145–150.

———. "A Further Note on the Dupuit Taxation Theorem." *Econ.,* VII (1939), 156–157.

Goedhart, C. "Some Reflections on the Scope and Methods of a Macro-Economic Theory of Tax-Shifting." *PF,* XIII (1958), 7–12.

Goeseke, G. "The Effects of Redistribution on Size Distribution of Personal Income and Household Net Income in Germany in 1955 and 1959." In *Income and Wealth,* Series X. Edited by Colin Clark and G. Stuvel. London, 1964, pp. 220–247.

Goffman, Irving J. *The Burden of Canadian Taxation.* Canadian Tax Foundation. Toronto, 1962.

———. "Incidence of Taxation in Canada." *PF,* XIX (1964), 44–67.

Goode, Richard. "The Corporate Income Tax and the Price Level." *AER,* XXXV (1945), 40–58.

———. "Some Considerations on the Incidence of the Corporation Income Tax." *JF,* VI (1951), 197–199.

———. "Taxation of Saving and Consumption in Underdeveloped Countries." *NTJ*, XIV (1961), 305–322.

———. "Rates of Return, Income Shares, and Corporate Tax Incidence." In *The Corporation Income Tax: Papers Presented at the Symposium on Business Taxation*. Edited by M. Krzyzaniak. Detroit, 1966.

Gordon, R. J. "Incidence of Corporation Income Tax." *AER*, LVII (1967), 102–105.

Hady, T. F. "The Incidence of the Personal Property Tax." *NTJ*, XV (1962), 368–384.

Häuser, Karl. "Die Unüberwälzbarkeit der Einkommen- und Körperschaftsteuer bei Gewinnmaximierung." *FA, NS*, XX (1960), 422–435.

———. "Einiges über die Wirklichkeit und über die Unüberwälzbarkeit der Einkommensteuer, Eine Replik." *FA, NS*, XXI (1962/63), 429–440.

Häuser, Karl, and Richter, Rudolf. "Zum Problem der Einkommensteuerüberwälzung." *FA*, NS, XVI (1955/56), 258–273.

———. "Eine Duplik zum 'Steuerparadoxon.'" *FA, NS*, XVII (1956/57), 38–40.

Hall, C. A., Jr. "Direct Shifting of the Corporation Income Tax in Manufacturing." *AER*, LIV, *P. and P.* (1964), 258–271.

Hall, R. E. and Jorgenson, D. W. "Tax Policy and Investment Behavior." *AER*, LVII (1967), 391–414.

Haller, Heinz. "Netto-Umsatzsteuer versus Gewinnsteuer." *FA, NS*, XVI (1955), 201–266.

———*Die Steuern*, Tübingen, 1964.

Harberger, Arnold C. "The Incidence of the Corporation Tax." *JPE*, LXX (1962), 215–240.

Head, J. G. "The Case For A Capital Gains Tax." *PF*, XVIII (1963), 220–249.

Hicks, Ursula K. "The Terminology of Tax Analysis." *EJ*, LVI (1946), 38.

Higgins, B. "The Incidence of Sales Taxes." *QJ*, LIII (1939), 275.

——— "The Incidence of Sales Taxes, A Note on Methodology." *QJ*, LIV (1940), 665–672.

Hinrichs, Harley H. *Dynamic-Regressive Effects of the Treatment of Capital Gains on the American Tax System During 1957–59*. Washington, 1963 and *PF*, XIX (1964), 73–83.

Holden, Grenville. "Incidence of Taxation as an Analytical Concept." *AER*, XXX (1940), 774–786.

Holzman, F. D. "The Burden of Soviet Taxation." *AER*, XLIII (1953), 548–571.

Jackson, F. H. *Tax Burden and the Hawaiian Tax System*. Honolulu, 1960.

Jaskari, Osmo V. *A Study in the Theory of Incidence of Taxation*. Helsinki, 1960.

Jenkins, H. P. B. "Excise-Tax Shifting and Incidence. A Money-Flows Approach." *JPE*, LXIII (1955), 125–149.

Joseph, F. M. "The Excess Burden of Indirect Taxation." *RESt,* VI (1939), 226–231.

Kaizl, J. *Die Lehre von der Überwälzung der Steuern.* Wien, 1882.

Kalecki, Michael. "A Theory of Commodity, Income and Capital Taxation." *EJ,* XLV (1937), 444–450.

Kendrick, M. S. "The Incidence and Effects of Taxation: Some Theoretical Aspects." *AER,* XXVII (1937), 725–734.

——— "The Processing Taxes and Some Problems Raised by Them." *JPE,* XVII (1935), 307–317.

Kendrick, M. S., and Jackson, F. H. *Economic Impact of Tax Reduction. Honolulu,* 1960.

Keynes, John M. "The Colwyn Report on National Debt and Taxation." *EJ,* XXXVII (1927), 198–212.

Kilpatrick, Robert. "The Forward Shifting of the Corporate Tax." *Yale Economic Essays,* V (1965), p. 355–422.

Kimmel, Lewis H. *Taxes and Economic Incentives.* Washington, 1950.

Kisker, K. P. "A Note on the Negative Income Tax." *NTJ,* XX (1967), 102–105.

Krelle, Wilhelm. "Zur Wirkung der progressiven Einkommensbesteuerung." *FA, NS,* XVI (1955/56), 22–30.

Krzyzaniak, Marian and Musgrave, Richard A. *The Shifting of the Corporation Income Tax.* Baltimore, 1963.

Krzyzaniak, Marian, ed. *Effects of the Corporation Income Tax: Papers Presented at the Symposium on Business Taxation.* Detroit, 1966.

Laspeyres, E. "Statistische Untersuchungen zur Frage der Steuerüberwälzung, geführt an der Geschichte der preußischen Mahl- und Schlachtsteuer." *FA* (1901), 46–242.

Lintner, John. "Effect of Corporate Taxation on Real Investment." *AER,* XLIV (1954), 520.

Little, J. M. D. "Direct Versus Indirect Taxes." *EJ,* LXI (1951), 577–584.

Littmann, Konrad. "Finanzpolitik, räumliche Gleichgewichte und Optima, kreislauftheoretische Betrachtungen über die Wirkungen der staatlichen Aktivität auf die räumliche Faktorverteilung." *Schriften des VfS, NS,* XXXII (Berlin, 1964), 61–119.

Mann, Fritz Karl. "Überwälzung der Steuern." *HdSt,* VIII, 336–362.

Marchal, J. "L'incidence des impôts cédulaires sur la revenue." *PF,* IV (1949), 323–342.

McLure, C. "Commodity tax incidence in open economies." *NTJ,* XVII (1964), 187–204.

———. "The Interstate Exporting of State and Local Taxes: Estimating for 1962." *NTJ,* XX (1967), 49–77.

von Mering, Otto. *Die Steuerüberwälzung.* Jena, 1928.

Mieszkowski, Peter M. "On the Theory of Tax Incidence." *JPE,* LXXVII (1967), 250–262.

Mombert, F. "Contribution à une étude théoretique des incidences de l'impôt sur les sociétés." *RSLF,* XXIV (1962), 437–460.

Morgan, D. C. Jr. "Reappraisal of Sales Taxation: Some Recent Argument." *NTJ,* XVI (1963), 98–117.

———. *Retail sales tax—An Appraisal of New Issues.* Madison and Milwaukee, 1964.

Musgrave, R. A. "General Equilibrium Aspects of Incidence Theory." *AER, P. and P.,* XLIII, 2 (1953), 504–517.

———. "On Incidence." *JPE,* XXXII (1953), 306–323.

———. "The Incidence of the Tax Structure and Its Effects on Consumption." In *Federal Tax Policy for Economic Growth and Stability.* Joint Economic Committee (1955).

———. *The Theory of Public Finance: A Study in Public Economy.* New York–Toronto–London, 1959.

———. "Growth with Equity." *AER, P. and P.,* LIII (1963), 323–333.

———. "On Measuring Fiscal Performance." *RESt,* XLVI (1964), 213–220.

Musgrave, Carroll, Cook and Frane. "Distribution of Tax Payments by Income Groups: A Case Study for 1948." *NTJ,* IV (1951), 1–54.

Musgrave, Richard A. and Daicoff, Darwin W. "Who Pays the Michigan Taxes?" In *Michigan Study Staff Papers.* Lansing, Michigan, 1958, pp. 131–183.

Musgrave, R. A. and Richman, P. D. "Allocation Aspects, Domestic and International." In *The Role of Direct and Indirect Taxes in the Federal Revenue System.* Princeton, 1964.

National Tax Foundation. *Tax Burdens and Benefits of Government Expenditures by Income Class, 1961–1965.* New York, 1967.

Netzer, Dick. *Economics of the Property Tax.* Washington, 1966.

Neumark, Fritz. *Theorie und Praxis der modernen Einkommensbesteuerung,* Bern, 1947.

———. "Alte und neue Probleme der Finanzwissenschaft." *FA, NF,* XVI (1955/1956), 1–15.

Niehans, Jürg. "Die Wirkung von Lohnerhöhungen, technischen Fortschritten, Steuern und Spargewohnheiten auf Preise, Produktion und Einkommensverteilung." *Schriften des Vfs, NS,* XVII (Berlin 1959), 9–94.

Nöll von der Nahmer, Robert. *Lehrbuch der Finanzwissenschaft,* 2 vols., Köln and Opladen, 1964.

Oakland, W. M. "The Theory of the Value-Added Tax: II—Incidence Effects." *NTJ,* XX (1967), 270–281.

Orr, Larry L. "The Incidence of Differential Property Taxes on Urban Housing." *NTJ,* XXI (1968), 253–262.

Paish, F. W. "The Real Incidence of Personal Taxation." *Lloyds Bank Review,* NS, no. 43 (1957), pp. 1–16.

Pantaleoni, M. *Teoria della traslazione dei tributi.* Roma, 1882.

Parks, Robert H. "Theory of Tax Incidence: International Aspects." *NTJ*, XIV (1961), 190–197.

Peacock, Alan T. "Théorie moderne de l'Incidence de l'impôt et Sécurite sociale." *RSLF*, XLVII (1955), 347–360.

Pechman, J. A. *Federal Tax Policy*. Washington, 1966.

Pedone, Antonio. "Taxes on Production and the Average Period of Investment: A Critique of the Neo-Classical Analysis of General Incidence." *PF*, XXI (1966), 488–506.

———. *The Budget and the Intersectoral Income Distribution*. Institut International de Finances Publiques, Congrès de Prague, 1967.

Penner, R. G. "Uncertainty and the Short-Run Shifting of the Corporation Tax." *Oxford Economic Papers*, NS, XIX (1967), 99–110.

Pfaff, M. and Pfaff, A. Distributive Effects of the Grants Economy. Unpublished paper for the VXXXII annual meeting of the AEA in New York, 1969.

Prest, A. R. "Statistical Calculations of Tax Burdens." *Econ.*, XXII (1955), 234–245.

———. "Observations on Dynamic Incidence." *EJ*, LXXIII (1963), 535–547.

———. "The Budget and the Distribution of National Income." In *Institut International de Finances Publiques*. York, 1968, pp. 80–98.

Ratchford, B. U. and Han, P. B., "The Burden of the Corporate Income Tax." *NTJ*, X (1957), 310–324.

Recktenwald, Horst Claus, "Bedeutung, Grenzen und neuere Entwicklung der Steuerüberwälzungslehre." *FA, NS*, XVI (1955), 274–295.

———. *Die Finanzwissenschaft unserer Zeit*. Stuttgart, 1965.

———. *Finanztheorie*. Köln, 1969. And *Finanzpolitik*, Köln, 1970.

———. *Nutzen-Kosten-Analyse und Programmbudget*. Tubingen, 1970.

———. "Steuerwirkungen." *HdS*, X, (1959), 182–191.

———. "Zur Lehre von den Marktformen." *WWA*, LXVI (1951). Reprinted in: A. Ott, *Preistheorie*, Köln, 1965.

Report of the Committee on National Debt and Taxation, No. 290. London, 1927.

Richmond, R. L. "The Incidence of Urban Real Estate Taxes." *Land Economics*, LXIII (1967), 172–80.

Robertson, D. H. "The Colwyn Committee, the Income Tax and the Price Level." *EJ*, XXXVII (1927), 566–581.

Robertson, J. E. "Comparative Tax Burdens for a Midwestern City." *NTJ*, XV (1962), 260–267.

Rolph, Earl R. "A Proposed Revision of Excise Tax Theory." *JPE*, LX, 2 (1957), 102–117.

———. *The Theory of Fiscal Economics*. Berkeley and Los Angeles, 1954.

———., and Break, George F. "The Welfare Aspects of Excise Taxes." *JPE*, LVII (1949), 46–54.

———. "The Economic Effects of a Federal Value Added Tax." In Committee on Ways and Means. *Excise Tax Compendium—Compendium of Papers on Excise Tax Structure.* Washington, 1964.

Roskamp, Karl W. "The Distribution of Tax Burden in a Rapidly Growing Economy: West Germany in 1950." *NTJ,* XVI (1963), 20–35.

———. "The Shifting of Taxes on Business Income: The Case of West German Corporations." *NTJ,* XVIII (1965), 247–257.

Rostvold, G. N. "The Shifting, Incidence and Effects of the Corporate Net Income Tax in a Macroeconomic Setting." *PF,* XIV (1959), 164–187.

———. "Distribution of Property, Retail Sales, and Personal Income Tax Burdens in California." *NTJ,* XIX (1966), 38–47.

Schlesinger, Eugene R. "Corporate-Income Tax Shifting and Fiscal Policy." *NTJ,* XIII (1960), 17–28.

Schmidt, K. D., Schwarz, U., and Thiebach, G. *Die Umverteilung des Volkseinkommens in der Bundesrepublik Deutschland—1955 und 1960.* Tübingen, 1965.

Schmoelders, Günter. "Monetäre Theorie der Steuerüberwälzung?" *FA,* IV (1937), 280–290.

Schneider, Helmut. *Der Einfluß der Steuern auf die unternehmerischen Entscheidungen.* Tübingen, 1964.

Seligman, E. R. A. *The Shifting and Incidence of Taxation,* fifth revised edition, New York, 1969.

———. *Studies in Public Finance.* New York, 1969.

Shibata, H. "The Theory of Economic Union: A Comparative Analysis of Customs Unions, Free Trade Areas, and Tax Unions." In *Fiscal Harmonization in Common Markets,* vol. I, *Theory,* edited by C. S. Shoup. New York and London, 1967.

Shoup, Carl S. *Shifting and Incidence Theory: Taxes on Monopoly.* New York, 1950.

———. "Some Problems in the Incidence of the Corporation Income Tax." *AER, P. and P.,* L (1960), 457–469.

Solitor, Richard E. "The Enigma of Corporate Tax Incidence." *PF,* XVIII (1963), 328–352.

"State Income Taxation of Mercantile and Manufacturing Corporations." Hearings before the Special Subcommittee on State Taxation of Interstate Commerce of the House Committee on the Judiciary. 87th Cong., 1st sess., Dec. 4–13, 1961. Washington, 1962.

Stockfish, J. A. "Investment Incentive, Taxation, and the Accelerated Depreciation." *SEJ,* XIII (1957/58), 28–40.

———. "On the Obsolescence of Incidence." *PF,* XIV (1959), 125–148.

Stucken, R., and Ehrlicher, W. "Zur Frage der Überwälzung der Unternehmersteuer." *FA, NS,* XIV, 2 (1953), 367–377.

Tabatoni, P. "Concept et méthode dans la théorie de l'incidence de l'impôt." *RSLF,* No. 4 (1952), 24–36.

Tarasov, Helen. "Who Does Pay the Taxes?" *Social Research,* Supplement IV (1942).

Timm, H. "Finanzpolitische Autonomie untergeordneter Gebietskörperschaften (Gemeinden) und Standortverteilung. Ein Beitrag zur ökonomischen Beurteilung des Finanzausgleichs." *Schriften des VfS, NS* XXXII, (Berlin, 1964), 9–60.

University of Wisconsin Tax Study Committee. *Wisconsin's State and Local Tax Burden.* Madison, Wisconsin, September, 1959.

Wagner, Adolph. *Lehrbuch der politischen Ökonomie,* 5, Vol. III, Leipzig and Heidelberg, 1883.

Walker, David. "The Direct-Indirect Tax Problem: Fifteen Years of Controversy." *PF,* X (1955), 153–177.

Welinder, Carsten. "Grundzüge einer dynamischen Inzidenztheorie." *WWA,* LI (1940), 83–126.

Wells, Paul. "General Equilibrium, Analysis of Excise Taxes." *AER,* XLV (1955), 250–262.

———. "Einkommensteuer und Arbeitswilligkeit—Einige steuerpolitische Gesichtspunkte." *PF,* XX (1965), 233–250.

———. "Excise Tax Incidence in an Imperfectly Competitive Economy." *PF,* XIV (1959), 203–216.

Wertheimer, Robert G. "Tax Incentives in Germany." *NTJ,* X (1957), 325–338.

Weston, F. J. "Incidence and Effects of the Corporate Income Tax." *NTJ,* II (1949), 300–315.

Wicksell, Knut. *Zur Lehre von der Steuerincidenz, Akademisk Afhandling.* Upsala, 1895.

Williams, A. "Review: *The Shifting of the Corporation Income Tax,* by Krzyzaniak, M. and Musgrave, R. A." *Econ,* XXXII (1965), 97.

Wise, J. "The Effect of Specific Excise Taxes on the Output of the Individual Multiproduct." *RESt,* XXIX (1962), 324–326.

von Wysocki, K. "Der Einfluß von Steuern auf Produktions- und Kostenfunktion," *ZfB,* XXXIV (1964), 15–36.

Zeitel, Gerhard. *Die Steuerlastverteilung in der BRD.* Tübingen, 1959.

Zubrow, C. A. "The Erosion of the State Income Tax." *NTJ,* XIII (1960), 59–68.

Name Index

Subject Index

Professor Recktenwald is professor and Prorektor at the Friedrich-Alexander University, Erlangen-Nürnberg, Germany. He has written extensively in the fields of economics and public finance.

The manuscript was prepared for publication by Sandra Shapiro. This book was designed by Mary Jowski. The text type used is Caledonia, designed by W. A. Dwiggins in 1937. The display face is Helvetica. The book is printed on Warren's Olde Style Antique paper and bound in Columbia Mills Atlantic vellum cloth over binder's boards. Manufactured in the United States of America.